THE
MARSHALL
PLAN
SUMMER

THE
MARSHALL
PLAN
SUMMER

An Eyewitness Report
on Europe and the Russians in 1947

Thomas A. Bailey

HOOVER INSTITUTION PRESS
Stanford University • Stanford, California

©1977 by the Board of Trustees of the
  Leland Stanford Junior University
All rights reserved
International Standard Book Number: 0-8179-4201-7
Library of Congress Catalog Card Number: 77-2433
Printed in the United States of America

Contents

Foreword

This book is not a scholarly monograph on the Marshall Plan. It is primarily a journal that describes in intimate detail conditions in the sick countries of Europe at the time the Marshall Plan was struggling to be born. The emphasis is on the patients, not the doctor.

In the troubled summer of 1947 I was commissioned by the National War College in Washington to undertake an inspection tour of Europe, preparatory to teaching in that institution during the fall semester. I ranged widely, from England to Austria, from Italy to Sweden, but my principal concern was the four-power occupation of Germany and Austria. Everywhere I kept full notes on what I saw and heard, particularly on the scores of interviews with prominent officials and others.

I had no intention at the time of publishing these findings, but now feel a scholarly obligation to do so. My original plan was to leave such materials in my collected papers, but who would know they were there? Besides, some of my pencilled jottings are so cryptic, cramped, and smudged that I am the only one who can decipher them all. They are now available to scholars in the archives of the Hoover Institution at Stanford, under the designation "The Thomas A. Bailey Collection on Europe in 1947." Included are the recorded recollections of my ninety-seven students who had recently served in the armed forces, as well as much information gathered at the National War College.

Basically, this book is a diary—a primary source—and as such, an historical document of some value. In the nature of things it is in part a personalized memoir and a travelogue, with the fate of the Marshall Plan the underlying theme and connecting tissue. I have recorded a number of incidents that may seem trifling, but a small anecdote can be worth a thousand words. I have also included details about food and types of transportation, largely because they are a part of quickly forgotten social history that will become increasingly valuable with each passing decade.

The Marshall Plan, so-called, has often been hailed as the greatest act of statesmanship in the nation's history. What I observed in Europe abundantly confirmed the need for America's helping hand. Marshall's original suggestion at Harvard in June 1947 was the major defensive response to what appeared in Washington to be Soviet aggression in the early stages of the Cold War. This far-sighted proposal, which resulted in the recovery of sixteen beneficiary nations, may well have saved democratic Europe from Communism and the United States from another great depression. Much of what I here record relates to the urgent need for some such plan, especially in view of what appeared to be the alarming posture and tactics of the Soviet Union.

Before reaching Europe I was not told at the National College that I must look for bad things about the awful Russians. I arrived with what I think was an open mind, but I observed and heard little to support the view that the Soviets were friendly, cooperative, and trustworthy allies from whom America and the Western democracies had nothing whatever to fear. Some of my other findings, especially those relating to ethnic groups and various nationalities, may also seem harsh. But I would ask the reader not to blame the messenger for his message; I am trying to tell it "like it was."

For critical comments on individual chapters or groups of chapters I am indebted to the following scholars who have been or are connected with the Hoover Institution and Stanford University: Dennis L. Bark, Paul M. Cocks, Alexander DeConde, Paul B. Ryan, Stanley L. Sharp, Peter Stansky, Wayne S. Vucinich, and Gordon Wright. Jessie Applegarth contributed her usual superb typing.

All three maps in this book are adapted from Thomas A. Bailey, *A Diplomatic History of the American People,* 9th edition, copyrighted 1974, pp. 780, 782, and 791, and are reprinted by permission of Prentice-Hall, Inc., Englewood Cliffs, New Jersey.

THOMAS A. BAILEY
Professor Emeritus, History
Stanford University

The Onset of the Cold War

*The patient [Europe] is sinking while the doctors
deliberate.*

Secretary of State Marshall
Radio address, April 28, 1947

Early in February, 1947, Vice Admiral Harry W. Hill, Commandant of
the National War College in Washington, ascended three flights of
stairs and dropped into my office in the old sandstone History Building at Stanford University. He was then recruiting a staff of five civilian instructors for the autumn semester of 1947, and I suspected that
before he made his sales pitch he wanted to make sure that his prospect looked reasonably normal. Evidently reassured when I spoke
without a speech impediment, he presented in glowing terms the
objectives and achievements of his institution, now in its first year,
and indicated that he would like to have me join the staff for the
autumn semester of 1947.

Up to this point I had known virtually nothing about the National
War College, and in fact was slightly disturbed by the choice of a
name. The opposite number in England was called The Imperial Defence College. The United States had recently fought in the greatest
war of all, and people were sick of the very thought of more bloodshed. In addition, the charter of the new United Nations, with its
emphasis on preserving peace, had been threshed out with appropriate ceremony in an historic conference at nearby San Francisco in the
spring of 1945. I was privileged to attend one public session in the
spacious Opera House, where one could sense not only the feeling of
optimism but also the birth pangs of the new world organization.

To quiet my qualms, Admiral Hill carefully explained that the War

College was basically a peace college, at least as far as the first semester was concerned. As then operating, the student body consisted of a group of about 115 specially chosen officers from the Army, Navy, Marine Corps, and Air Force. Interspersed with them were ten foreign-service officers, whose presence provided a desirable leavening. Diplomats should be well informed about the military soundness of diplomatic positions that they assume in their dealings with foreign powers. At the same time, military men should be aware of the commitments, actual or potential, that the diplomats are making or are about to make for them to sustain. Without such knowledge, any planning of high quality is difficult to achieve. Military men should learn that wars are usually fought for political ends, and that if final victory can be achieved without unnecessary bloodshed or complete chaos, so much the better for all concerned, except perhaps for martial reputations. This is a generalization that many American generals have never fully appreciated, from Douglas MacArthur in Korea to William C. Westmoreland in Vietnam.

My special interest as an historian happened to be American diplomatic history, and I suppose for that reason Admiral Hill had me on his list of possible recruits. I had been teaching a course on the subject at Stanford for about fifteen years, and in 1940 had published a basic textbook entitled A *Diplomatic History of the American People.* (An elderly lady once picked it up in a bookstore and was heard to remark, "We have to be careful what we write these days about American history; we have to be very diplomatic.")

Emphasis in this title on the role of people was deliberately designed to highlight the central theme of the book. The United States is a republic with a democratic form of government, and hence in the long run and on basic issues, the American people themselves determine the broad lines of foreign policy. Secretly and in the short run, the politicians in Washington can make decisions contrary to the will of a majority or a vocal minority of the voters, but they do so at the risk of ultimate repudiation by the voters. Some critics still argue that public opinion has nothing whatever to do with the formulation and conduct of American foreign policy, and for them I would point to several impressive examples. Without adequate regard for ultimate public reactions, five Presidents—Truman, Eisenhower, Kennedy, Johnson, and Nixon—got the nation ever deeper into the jungles of Vietnam. An aroused electorate finally forced the United States out of Vietnam. Congress, responding to such pressures, not only compelled President Nixon to end his defiant bombing of Cambodia, but also passed legislation designed to limit severely the president's war-making powers.

The visiting Admiral Hill had probably heard of me because of my association with the Naval Academy at Annapolis, of which he later became superintendent. Shortly after the *Diplomatic History* was published in 1940, it was adopted by the Naval Academy for a basic course enrolling about one thousand midshipmen. It was so used for about twenty years, when the big required class was dropped in favor of a much smaller elective one.

On a half-dozen or so occasions, one of them when I was later teaching at the National War College, I have addressed the assembled midshipmen at Annapolis. They made a splendid audience of clean-cut young men. I can still recall the stirring sight as they swung briskly up the path in formation and filed into the assembly hall. My lectures usually stressed the theme that because public opinion in America determines the broad outlines of foreign policy, the individual American citizen has a heavy obligation to inform himself as best he can so that he can direct American foreign policy—his foreign policy—along farsighted and prudent lines.

Against this background, Admiral Hill's offer to teach in Washington had much appeal. My interests had long included military history, partly because shooting usually takes over when diplomacy stops. Undoubtedly my knowledge would be broadened by seeing the military brass, the navy braid, and the scholarly diplomats working together at the top-level National War College—"the school for Admirals." The so-called military mind held no horrors for me, even though it suggested to some narrowness, rigidity, and stupidity. My belief, fully confirmed at the War College, was that there were and are many keen minds in the military. I also believed that brains of brass could be found in all walks of life, from the business world to diplomacy.

Historians of social and intellectual history are unduly snobbish when they look down their scholarly noses on the lowbrows who study war. Military affairs are often sufficiently complex to challenge the best intellects; they are also frequently more important in the overall picture than the social and intellectual history that has been cynically labeled "sociable and ineffectual history." For example, the results of General Burgoyne's surrender at Saratoga in 1777 are just as worthy of scholarly study as the impact of Mrs. Amelia Bloomer's bifurcated bloomers on morals and mores in the nineteenth century.

In touting the National War College to me, Admiral Hill presented a seductive bill of goods. The salary was in excess of my stipend at Stanford, and besides I could learn much in Washington, about substance and point of view, as indeed turned out to be the case. As frosting on the cake, Admiral Hill offered to send me to Europe under the auspices of the National War College. My tour of inspection would include England, France, Italy, and the zones and sectors occupied by American troops in Germany and Austria. The armed services would fly me across the continent at their expense, and transport me around American-occupied Germany and Austria. As a civilian I would have to pay transportation and other costs across the Atlantic and in those parts of Europe not occupied by American forces.

Admiral Hill's bait of a trip to and through Europe had powerful attractions, especially at this critical point in postwar history and under circumstances that no ordinary academician could hope to duplicate. I had not yet visited the mother continent, and this gap in my education was somewhat embarrassing to one who was studying and teaching American diplomatic history. Admiral Hill believed, and correctly so, that my usefulness to the War College would be greater if I went abroad for several months to become better acquainted with current happenings before assuming my teaching duties.

Despite the enticements that Admiral Hill dangled before my eyes, I hesitated before accepting his proposition, largely because I was being asked to leave my wife and fourteen-year-old son in California for seven months. My spouse was not well, for she had not fully recovered from a fractured skull and other injuries resulting from an accident with her horse in 1942. We talked this invitation over at length in the family circle. My wife said that she was not proud of my nonexistent military record and that I ought to do something for my country, even though the shooting had stopped. Fortunately, the nation had never been in such desperate shape that it needed a soft-handed academician, then in his forties, for front-line duty. Of course I had done my bit by teaching a large group of aspiring officers at Stanford and Harvard. But after the war, partly because of my wife's accident, I had declined an opportunity to teach history to American soldiers in England and France who were awaiting transportation home. In the end, my wife agreed that we should both make the sacrifice and that I should go to Europe and then to the War College.

Departure day finally arrived, and in the late afternoon of June 5 we flew out of Moffett Field, a Navy base located about a dozen miles southeast of Stanford. The plane was a reliable C-54, a Navy version of the civilian DC-4, which had proved to be a thoroughly reliable four-motor propeller craft. An attactive young WAVE announced as we took off, "Next stop, Washington D.C.," and fortunately her terse announcement proved correct. She also served dinner and breakfast, at a cost of $1.25 for each. The expense of transporting me with a high-priority listing was borne by the government, but it could not have cost much because the plane was scheduled for departure whether I went along or not.

This was my first long-distance flight, and my lively imagination caused me some disquietude. My first experience with an airplane had been nearly twenty years earlier, when, as a young instructor at the University of Hawaii, I flew from Oahu to the island of Maui to give the word on current events to two ladies' clubs. I still remember that sinking feeling when the ground dropped away beneath me and I could almost see the sharks below in the blue, white-crested water.

Flying across the continent, I spent a restless night in a semi-reclining position. In one stretch over the Mississippi Valley we passed through a severe thunderstorm, with lightning flashing threateningly on both sides. The cabin was not pressurized as it would be today, and the rapid descent caused acute pain in my ears as I attempted to apply counterpressure with a handkerchief pinched to my nose. As was not uncommon for me in those days, my eardrums remained thousands of feet in the air for a half-day or so after we had thumped down.

On arriving at the Washington airport, I was met by Colonel David H. Baker of the War College faculty, accompanied by a black chauffeur driving the Army automobile. Both my baggage and I were deposited at the B.O.Q. (Bachelor Officers' Quarters), located within a stone's throw of the imposing brick structure that housed the National War College. The B.O.Q. was a temporary wooden structure in the nature of Army barracks, totally without the air conditioning that Washingtonians now need to survive in the summer months. My quarters consisted of two small rooms containing a sturdy bed; the shower room was located down the hall. The furniture and furnishings were definitely keyed to plain living and high strategic thinking, but I had no complaints. Such accommodations were quite adequate for bachelors or otherwise footloose males; unattached military men can usually make do without lace curtains.

I promptly paid my respects to Admiral Hill, who had done such a persuasive selling job and who greeted me most cordially. I was also introduced to my office, which consisted of a desk and some closely guarded filing cases in a large room, mercifully air-conditioned. A fellow civilian instructor was assigned to another desk in the opposite corner. From my window I had an excellent view of the spacious outside grounds, much of which was given over to a golf course for the officers. Many a time, when the five-o'clock bugle blew and the Stars and Stripes were lowered, I saw the players drop their clubs and assume the proper stance until the ceremony was completed. I never ceased to be moved by this pledge of dedication to country and flag.

Within the ivy walls of academe, I had been accustomed to meet my classes and keep office hours for conferences with students and others. At other times I would be in committee meetings, preparing lectures, or engaging in research in response to the pressures of the "publish or perish" requirement. I quickly discovered that Admiral Hill expected me to put in my seven- or eight-hour stint either in the classroom or in my office. I complied with his wishes, although on weekends I sneaked off to the Library of Congress and foresightedly gathered some of the materials for a book published thirty years later on the slogans, sayings, and songs of American history.

Another problem that presented itself was the presence of the School of Advanced International Studies (S.A.I.S.), under the guidance of Dr. Halford L. Hoskins. He had recently moved his operation from Tufts College in Massachusetts to Washington, D.C., and had invited me to leave Stanford and join his faculty. For various reasons my response had been negative, one of them being the uncertain financial future of the institution, which then existed on a hand-to-mouth basis but was ultimately taken over by the Johns Hopkins University. Dr. Hoskins still wanted me to lecture there in the evenings or on some other part-time basis. My enthusiasm for this kind of service was restrained, as was that of Admiral Hill, whose evident displeasure caused me to drop further negotiations. His greatest worry seemed to be that a slip of my lip might betray some of the highly confidential information that was being disclosed at the War College. But perhaps a more compelling motive for him was the fear that my moonlighting in this fashion might drain some of the energy that he quite properly expected me to pour into my duties at the War College.

Admiral Hill was an engaging personality; Professor John D. Hicks of the University of California (Berkeley) once told me that this naval officer was just about the best salesman he had ever met. The Commandant was undeniably a top-ranking naval officer, for he had commanded the battleships that had bombarded the Japanese-held island of Tarawa ("bloody Tarawa") in 1943. His barrage had not succeeded in knocking enough of the defenders out of their caves, but probably no fire by big guns would have done so in the relatively short time allotted the task. I presume that Admiral Hill suffered some criticism for the severity of the losses, but I do know that he would become hotly defensive of Admiral William F. ("Bull") Halsey, who had been lured almost fatally out of position in the epochal battle of Leyte Gulf late in 1944.

On one occasion at the College, Admiral Hill scolded the assembled student body with considerable heat. He was disturbed by their alleged defeatism in discussing a particularly knotty strategic problem involving military operations in the teeth of insuperable obstacles. His precise words, as I recall them, were: "If it's impossible, do it anyhow." He seemed to be paraphrasing the motto adopted during the war by the U.S. Army Corps of Engineers and other branches of the armed services: "The difficult we do immediately. The impossible takes a little longer." On hearing such talk, the group of officer-students at the College began to exchange sidelong glances, as though they could not quite believe their ears.

Himself a man of action, Admiral Hill entertained an exaggerated opinion of the capacity and versatility of the academic intellect. Perhaps he had developed an inferiority complex after having heard too many sneers about the "military mind." To me he expressed the opinion that the great academic intellects whom he had attracted to the College as civilian instructors could develop a mastery of any given subject in a few days of intensive study. He even believed that a one-track historian like me could learn enough about nuclear physics in a few days to discuss the atomic bomb in its technical details with the students entrusted to his instruction. At the allotted time during the forthcoming semester I did my inadequate best.

Most of my preliminary briefing before I left Washington was conducted by Major General Alfred M. Gruenther. He also had the largest hand in arranging my itinerary and in cabling ahead instructions regarding my coming to the proper authorities in Germany and Austria. As deputy to Admiral Hill, he had been brought back from the Military Government in occupied Austria, where he had seen at first hand vivid exhibitions of Russian suspicion and hostility toward the United States. My notebooks still contain the names of a number of people with whom he suggested that I might have fruitful interviews, and although I did not manage to see them all, he did supply me with some excellent leads. My recollection is that either he or Admiral Hill provided me with an imposing letter of introduction on War College stationery, and it never failed to open the necessary doors at the American military establishments and even the embassies. The word was out that foreign-service officers helped to make up ten or so members of the student body in Washington.

General Gruenther, with his brilliant record as a staff officer, impressed me as having one of the sharpest minds I have ever encountered in any walk of life. He was reputed to be one of the crack bridge players who consorted with General Eisenhower. He kept his body well tuned by playing tennis on the courts between the Bachelor Officers' Quarters and the Officers' Club. I was not surprised when he was chosen to serve, from 1953 to 1956, as the Supreme Allied Commander of the NATO forces in Europe.

Before taking off for Europe, I attended two lectures at the War College in an auditorium that was ideally air-conditioned and lighted. As the lecturer came onto the platform with Admiral Hill, the student body rose as one man and remained standing until the Commandant came down from the platform and took his seat in the front row. This mark of respect, which I later saw accorded to him scores of times, never failed to impress me.

Because the second semester concentrated on military affairs, the speakers on these two occasions were both generals. General Ira C. Eaker, a prominent figure who had been in charge of the bombing of Germany, lectured on air power. The other officer, whose name I did not record, spoke interestingly on chemical warfare, which is now in disrepute. Both presentations were clear and informative; they provided further refutation of the common jeer about the alleged impenetrability of the military mind.

During informal discussions with Admiral Hill and others associated with the College, I was privileged to have a few words with one of the most highly respected diplomatic minds of his generation, George Frost Kennan. I had met him for the first time some months earlier at Stanford. He had been sent out from Washington on a tour of the Middle West and West to enlighten the people in the provinces about the direction and conduct of American foreign policy. One of his major themes was that Soviet actions since the end of the war had dispelled Roosevelt's dream of friendly cooperation with the USSR to achieve One World. Kennan remarked to me that at Stanford particularly, his views had fallen on stony ground. I assured him that this had not been my reaction.

Kennan impressed me as a brilliant and highly articulate architect of American foreign policy. This judgment was further confirmed by the half-dozen or so penetrating and beautifully written books he subsequently published. On February 22, 1946, he had sent to the State Department his famous "Long Telegram" from Moscow, where he was then serving as minister-counselor. This costly message of eight thousand words, which detailed the alarming nature of "antagonistic" Soviet pressures, hit official Washington with bombshell impact. It had much to do with his being brought home and made Director of the Policy Planning Staff of the Department of State, a position he held when the Marshall Plan was struggling to be born.

Kennan's Long Telegram probably helped to inspire Truman's enunciation of the Truman Doctrine before Congress less than a year later, on March 12, 1947. In this special hard-line message the President announced his determination to take the ideological counteroffensive against Soviet aggression, and he asked the Congress to appropriate $400 million for military aid to Greece and Turkey to save them from a threatened Communist or Soviet takeover. This was an early invocation of the so-called policy of "containment," which proved to be the major opening defensive-offensive shot in the Cold War against a steadily encroaching Communist power. The Communists at home and abroad naturally burst into a condemnation of U.S. "dollar imperialism" and imminent "world domination."

As we now know, George Kennan was the mysterious Mr. X who later created a sensation by his article in *Foreign Affairs,* July, 1947, advocating the principle of "containment." He had chosen anonymity because of his delicate position in the State Department, but his authorship could not be concealed for long. When I once asked a brigadier general at the College if Kennan was really Mr. X, his reply was that when one occupies the same office with a man who dictates his correspondence to his publisher, one begins to put two and two together.

The irony is that Kennan strongly opposed the sweeping stance that Truman took in implementing the policy of "containment." The President's memorable message committed the United States to resist dangerous Communist pressures not only in Greece and Turkey, but also on behalf of "free peoples" in any part of the world. Kennan believed, as his writings have shown, that the role for Uncle Sam of self-appointed world policeman was unrealistic and dangerous. Yet he was disturbed unduly, because Truman did not actually interpret his doctrine in that extreme light. But his presidential successors, perhaps without thinking of the Truman Doctrine, did extend the global application to Korea and Vietnam, with humiliating consequences that are still coming home to roost. The concept of containment was not easy to contain. Indochina proved that there are limits to the police power of the United States, or at least limits to the willingness of the American people to make the sacrifices necessary to support such an overextended policy.

During the course of these early informal discussions with Kennan at the War College, someone mentioned the Truman Doctrine. His response was that before long we would all be hearing things that would make the Truman Doctrine look like small potatoes indeed.

Our conversation occurred about the time that Secretary of State Marshall supposedly unveiled the Marshall Plan at the Harvard commencement exercises. Incorporated in his address were a few lines to the effect that if the war-blighted and near-bankrupt nations of Europe would get together and prepare a shopping list of their essential economic needs for recovery, the United States would give serious consideration to providing the necessary dollars, "so far as may be practical. . . ."

This was not a "Marshall Plan" or any other kind of plan. There never was a "Marshall Plan," only a "Marshall Proposal." Presented in this rather vague and offhand way, it initially made little splash in America, and even in Europe the proposed beneficiaries did not respond by tossing their hats in the air with joy. The European Recovery Program—the real Marshall Plan—was not put together by the concerned European nations until about fifteen weeks after the hint at Harvard. Some eight weeks after Marshall's speech, an official in the State Department wrote in a confidential memorandum, "The 'Marshall Plan' has been compared to a flying saucer—nobody knows what it looks like, how big it is, in what direction it is moving, or whether it really exists."

The near-bankrupt British, whose postwar balance of trade was suffering from a "dollar hemorrhage," had already sought a gift, or at least an interest-free loan, from their American cousins. They finally had to settle for a fifty-year loan of $3.75 billion at an interest rate of 2 percent, plus some disagreeable trade restrictions. There was much opposition in the United States to a further "bailing out" of Britain, especially among Irish-Americans, who voiced the slogan, "There'll always be an England—with her hand out." Congress grudgingly passed the appropriation in July, 1946, after a delay of more than six months during which inflated prices reduced the purchasing power of the loan by millions of dollars. I was to encounter considerable bitterness in London over this whole huckstering business. Many Britons felt that they were entitled to speedier and more generous treatment after having endured Hitler's fury, much of the time alone, since September, 1939, more than two years before America was plunged into the conflict by Pearl Harbor.

As I boarded the train in Washington on June 11, 1947, to go to New York and then overseas, my impressions of the War College, its personnel and facilities, were highly favorable. But I was somewhat bothered by the extremely hard line that everyone there seemed to be taking toward the Soviet Union. The USSR was now regarded as a potential adversary rather than as a one-time ally that could be counted on for some degree of postwar cooperation. This distrustful attitude reflected the President's new "get tough with Russia" policy, as proclaimed in the Truman Doctrine during March of 1947. Soviet distrust of the United States had bred mistrust in the United States in an ever-widening and ever-deepening vicious circle.

The wartime alliance with Moscow had obviously been a marriage of convenience, for war and politics still make strange bedfellows. The hard-beset Soviets, out of deference to the United States, had temporarily shoved their priority of Communist world domination onto the back burner. But I could still nurse a faint hope, in line with the late President Roosevelt's policy, that something might be gained if the Western powers treated the once-outcast USSR with sympathy and generosity. The Russians might conceivably be weaned away from their nasty ideas of world revolution and cooperate in bringing about One World through the newborn United Nations. Such a course was a long-shot gamble, but the certain alternative was Two Worlds and a probable nuclear holocaust.

Given Moscow's Marxist-Leninist ideals and aims, there was something to be said for the Soviet case in analyzing most of America's misunderstandings and clashes with the Communist system. There are always two or more sides to every complex international dispute, usually because the contestants are arguing from different premises, both physical and ideological. One could even put in a good word for Benedict Arnold and Adolf Hitler. This view had crept into my lectures at Stanford, in what some of the students appreciated as a "balanced" interpretation. I even followed this approach to a limited extent in my writings of the period. When a third edition of my *Diplomatic History* came out in 1946, I sent a reprint of the newest chapter to Professor Raymond J. Sontag, the distinguished authority on European diplomatic history at the University of California (Berkeley). He graciously responded by writing that what I had to say was all right but he wondered why I had to lean over "so far backward" to be fair to "Uncle Joe" Stalin.

Actually, I had explained earlier in my book that when the Communists had seized power in Russia in 1917, they had openly declared ideological war on the non-Communist world. They had made clear that they would use all necessary means, including force, to achieve their goal of Communist world revolution. They had sustained and were sustaining an elaborate and expensive propaganda campaign that, among other provocations, had caused the United States to deny them recognition for sixteen long years. Even after the recognition agreement was signed in Washington in 1933, Moscow openly flouted this solemn pledge not to promote Communist propaganda in America.

Then came the fateful summer of 1939. Stalin was fearful of an assault by Hitler, for Communism and Naziism were in the highest degree antipathetic. During these years, conservative voices in the West were openly hoping that Hitler would attack the Soviet Union, and that the two great menaces would bleed each other to death on the icy steppes of Russia. Then the Free World could feel free. The British and French envoys made halfhearted attempts in Moscow during the summer of 1939 to negotiate a defensive pact with Stalin, but the dictator's patience gave way when satisfactory guarantees were not forthcoming. Behind their backs he cynically signed a nonaggression pact with Nazi Germany in August, and thus gave Hitler the go-ahead signal for World War II. Stalin evidently reasoned that the Germans, after crushing Poland, would presumably bleed themselves white in attacking the "impregnable" Maginot Line of France, and that the USSR would thus remove the menace in the West while emerging as the supreme colossus of Europe.

By one way of calculating, Stalin's nonaggression pact with Hitler triggered World War II. In a secret protocol at the same time, Stalin was promised a huge slice of eastern Poland, which he proceeded to seize, jackal-like, with his invading army. But Stalin's fine schemes backfired, for the defenses of France speedily collapsed and Hitler emerged victorious in June, 1940, without having exhausted himself. A panicky Stalin, hoping to put more real estate between himself and a victorious Hitler, speedily seized the three Baltic republics of Latvia, Lithuania, and Esthonia, all of which had formerly been under tsarist rule. A few days later he invaded and grabbed Romania's Bessarabia and Northern Bukovina. A year later, in June, 1941, Hitler launched his long-expected assault on Russia, and the democracies of the West now had on their hands not a genuine ally but a distrusted dictatorship fighting a common foe.

Apologists for Stalin argue that the outbreak of World War II was the fault of Britain and France because they had not come forward soon enough or convincingly enough with adequate defensive guarantees for the USSR against Hitler. This is roughly equivalent to saying that the bank teller is to blame for his own murder because he did not hand over the cash fast enough to an armed bandit.

Japan's attack on Pearl Harbor in December, 1941, plunged the United States into the war as a formal ally of the Soviet Union. During subsequent months the bitterest and most prolonged source of friction between the USSR and the other Allies was the slowness of the Western Powers in mounting a genuine second front before 1944. In desperate shape defensively, Stalin was frantically eager to have the British and Americans launch a massive attack on French soil in 1942 to

THE THREE MUSKETEERS . . .
Roosevelt, Churchill, and a distrustful Stalin
(by Reg Manning in the *Arizona Republic*, 1943 by permission.)

divert invading German divisions from his vitals.

The Western Allies rather vaguely promised such a second front in 1942, and then in 1943, but they did not deliver it until 1944. On the basis of what we now know, the democracies did not have the strength to launch a successful assault in 1942, and the odds were not too favorable in 1943. The British remembered keenly their enormous losses of manpower in France during World War I. Besides, the Russians had done nothing for them in the way of a second front when Britain so desperately needed one during the blitzing in 1940–1941. Stalin was not only a partner in crime with Hitler, but he had been a chief supplier. By virtue of a trade agreement that preceded the fatal nonaggression pact by five days, he had provided Germany with food, oil, and other supplies through the back door.

Stalin bitterly accused the Allies of now deliberately doing what some unfriendly spokesmen had been suggesting before the war came: Let the two menaces destroy each other. Communists and other pro-Soviet spokesmen in America were saying that the Allies should launch a second front anyhow, even though success was impossible. Even a failure would encourage the Russians to hold on longer, the argument ran, because they would know that the hearts of the democracies were in the right place. But, as the bloodily repulsed Allied raid on the French coast at Dieppe revealed in August, 1942, a catastrophic failure would only delay and make more difficult a later invasion—one that had some real prospects of success. Besides, if the situation had been reversed, Stalin probably would have been even less willing to come to the rescue of the West than were his Western allies in 1942–1944.

Stalin's frustrations were so deep, prolonged, and bitter that the democracies feared the worst. He might even patch up some kind of separate peace with Germany, as the Bolsheviks had done in 1918. At the same time, Stalin was fearful that the West might sell him out by some kind of stab-in-the-back deal with Hitler. One of the main reasons for Roosevelt's enunciation of the controversial doctrine of unconditional surrender at Casablanca early in 1943 was a desire to quiet Stalin's fears of a separate deal with Hitler. Such a sop seemed all the more necessary because the proposed second front of 1943 was again being postponed in favor of the diversionary North African invasion.

On June 6, 1944, the Allied D-Day invasion of France finally came, and it teetered between success and failure during the early days. When the news was announced in Moscow by radio, a general feeling of relief swept through Russia. General John R. Deane, the head of the American military mission, put on his cap and went for a walk through the busiest streets of Moscow. He expected to be cheered by the men and embraced by the women, but no one paid the slightest attention to him. The news had already been broadcast by radio, and, besides, the general feeling was "It's about time," especially after all those disappointing postponements.

Stalin's abscess of suspicion burst in April, 1945, when the Americans were negotiating for the surrender of the German forces in northern Italy. Suspecting incorrectly that these troops were about to be released by the Western Allies for service against Russia, Stalin fired off an abusive telegram to President Roosevelt in language that was difficult to pardon. Roosevelt died knowing, or strongly suspecting, that his gamble on Stalin's future good behavior, which had been immensely costly in lend-lease and other support, had failed or was doomed to failure.

The ugly truth is that the Soviets, unlike the British, had never been on genuinely friendly terms with the Washington government, although much of the latent hostility was papered over during the war. Early in 1947 the veil of secrecy was partly lifted when General John R. Deane published his book *The Strange Alliance*, which might better have been entitled *The Strained Alliance*. This exposé did not come to my attention until after my return from Europe. If I had read it sooner, it would have enabled me to understand better what was brewing in the cauldrons known as the four-power occupations of Germany and Austria. One should add that the "capitalistic" British, led by Communist-hating Churchill, also experienced much suspicious and unfriendly treatment from their Russian ally. Some of it was outrageous, especially in connection with the costly British sacrifices in trying to get lend-lease shipments through Hitler's submarine packs to frozen northern Russia.

General Deane had served as head of the American military mission in Moscow beginning in 1943. Later one of the major generals at the National War College confided to me some revealing information about the background of the sensational book. Deane, he said, had waited until early 1947 to break into print, for by that time he had retired from the Army. He had not asked the War Department for permission to publish for fear of a refusal; he had wisely preferred to present the Pentagon with an accomplished fact. Even so, he barely escaped a court martial for having broadcast top-secret data.

General Deane's sensational exposé, which was subsequently bolstered by his dispatches published in *Foreign Relations of the United States*, makes clear the essentially one-way nature of Russo-American "friendship" during the war. The two giant powers had been unfriendly ideological rivals long before Pearl Harbor; beneath the surface, and often on the surface, they remained such during the war. The Russians repeatedly revealed pathological suspicions of their American and British allies, just as the Russians had been traditionally distrustful of foreigners during the long centuries of tsarist misrule. The Soviets denied visas or delayed issuing them for periods of four to eight weeks to important American visitors, including those who had no purpose but to help the Soviets defeat the common enemy. The Russians freely accepted military secrets from the United States while not volunteering their own, and this was one valid reason for not giving them the secrets of the atomic bomb. They were annoyingly reluctant to reveal the details of their own shortages so that the United States could fill the gaps with enormous shipments. They requested lend-lease materials that they did not then need, presumably to stockpile them for future use against capitalistic foes, possibly through client nations.

This list of grievances could be greatly lengthened, but a few more examples will suffice. After long delays, and with great reluctance, the Russians finally permitted the Americans to land their bombers on Soviet soil so that the crews could increase their effectiveness by bombing German cities on the way back to England or Italy. The shuttle base at Poltava in the Ukraine was reluctantly and belatedly granted and then prematurely closed. When Germany surrendered, the Soviets released the sickly and debilitated American prisoners of war in remote places, despite the agreement at Yalta and the hardships involved, including great distances from medical care. Presumably these GIs were regarded as possible spies. General Deane concluded that the Russians were keeping their secrets and reducing the American presence to a minimum so as to prepare better for a future war against the capitalists, including the help-giving United States.

General Deane's disturbing views, only partially summarized here, were confirmed for me by scores of American officials, military and diplomatic, whom I met in Europe. This was especially true in Germany and Austria, where the Russian occupiers were physically present. Everywhere I saw and sensed evidence of unfriendliness, even hostility. My "balanced view" of Soviet-American relations gradually gave way to a conviction that as long as the Kremlin was determined that the world must be Communist, and as long as the United States was resolved to preserve its democratic freedoms, there would always be fear and consequent friction.

2

Battered Britain

Mr. Marshall's speech at Harvard was the first sign of American statesmanship since the death of Roosevelt.

New Statesman and Nation
(London), June 14, 1947

Slightly apprehensive of ditching in the Atlantic, I flew out of New York on the afternoon of June 12 in one of the new four-engine, propeller-driven Constellations of the American Line. It was about the last word in luxurious transatlantic transportation. Unfortunately we developed some engine trouble before landing at bleak Gander, Newfoundland, and we laid over in this God-forsaken Army-Navy airport for about five hours while awaiting repairs.

At about 1:00 the next morning we took off for Ireland. I slept fitfully in a semireclining position, and when I awoke about 5:00 A.M., I sensed that something was wrong. The rising sun seemed to be at our backs instead of ahead in the east. The word passed rapidly that the captain, after flying nearly half the distance across the Atlantic, had decided that two of the engines were misbehaving and that he had better turn back. Some of the passengers felt that he should have taken a chance and pressed on. But the day was Friday the thirteenth, and superstition may have helped to persuade him not to pass the point of no return with two rough engines. I am no mechanic, but I could see oil gurgling up on one of the wings from one motor, and although this may have been a normal outlet, it did not look reassuring.

After we limped back into Gander, the American Overseas Airlines paid for our meals, defrayed the costs of cablegrams regarding hotel reservations and other commitments, and put us up at a barracks hotel. During the long wait I whiled away the time by writing some letters home and conversing with fellow passengers, including a young English nobleman, Lord Derwent, who evidently had been lecturing in the United States. His lordship had discovered Kentucky bourbon whiskey on his travels, and it so fascinated him that he carried a bagged bottle that he occasionally sampled.

After we had taken off for a second time, the engines behaved themselves and we touched down at the Shannon airport in Ireland without incident. I saw a good deal of Ireland ten years later, but on this occasion only glimpsed its emerald hues and grassy meadows. The country was obviously underdeveloped, that is, unblanketed by slums, sludge, and smog. What struck me most forcibly at Shannon was the presence of bilingual signs at the airport in English and Gaelic. Lord Derwent remarked to me that all this double talk was utter nonsense, for an Irish brogue was the language of Ireland, and Gaelic was a difficult tongue known only to a few antiquarians. The Irish have hated the insides of their British conquerors for something like three centuries, yet they are saddled with the language of their conquerors, like the people of India, and they were struggling vainly against it as best they could.

The fight-loving Irish had remained officially neutral in World War II, thus depriving the British of former naval bases on the south Irish coast that were desperately needed for combatting U-boats. Winston Churchill revealed in his memoirs that the London government seriously contemplated seizing the bases, but in the end shied away from the consequences of heavy-handed actions. Thousands of British lives were lost and hundreds of thousands of tons of shipping were sunk as a result of Irish neutrality and obduracy. Yet many stout Irish lads volunteered to fight against Hitler under the British Union Jack.

After reaching London, I engaged a room in the Kensington area at the Princes Court Hotel, a name that gives a false aura of royalty and grandeur. I had expected to stay for about a week at one of the more modest establishments, but was unable to secure a reservation in time. The best alternatives seemed to be to turn to the advertising columns of the London *Times*, and there I found what seemed to be attractive accommodations at the Princes Court. This proved to be a run-down lodging house that had seen many better days. My room boasted one swaybacked bed, as well as an all-purpose bathtub and a chain-pull toilet—somewhere down the hall. Although the destruction of this hotel would not have been catastrophic, it evidently had survived the German bombs and rockets unscathed. The same could not be said of some of the neighboring buildings or those just across the street.

The Princes Court functioned on a B-and-B basis, which presumably meant bed and breakfast. The morning repasts ran heavily to hot tea and porridge (oatmeal mush in the United States) and kippered herring, neither of which was an item of my diet at home. But I happen to like fish, even for breakfast, and can tolerate porridge, so I was content to do as the Britons did while in Britain. After all, as the saying went, England was a large lump of coal surrounded by fish. At one of the London restaurants I even sampled whale steak, which had been touted during the recent food-short war. To me it was neither tasteful nor distasteful.

The dozen or so other breakfasters at the Princes Court viewed me with un-British curiosity, perhaps even suspicion. My light-colored and lightweight summer suit betrayed my American connection, and on one occasion I suspected that a couple of strong-voiced Britishers, evidently business men, were speaking for my benefit when they described in unflattering terms a wretched American movie that they had seen the night before. On the other hand, I must say that most of the British whom I encountered, from cab drivers to townsfolk, were courteous and helpful. I recall particularly how one middle-aged woman, having overheard my inquiries, ran after me to point out a good place at which to dine. I gathered that most of the British felt some gratitude for what the Americans had contributed during the recent conflict to help stamp out the menace of Hitlerism.

During the war, relations between the Yanks and the British, especially the soldiers, had been bittersweet. The "Limeys" had especially resented GI boastfulness, disagreeable allusions to the Britishers' lack of guts in not fighting their last two wars, and particularly the "swiping" of their girls by the newcomers. The American "invaders" had hit it off unusually well with the children, to whom they had dispensed gum and other goodies. Yet the local populace had been especially shocked by the discriminatory treatment meted out by the white soldiers to the black ones, especially the ban on eating or drinking together that was the practice in the American South during these years. The white GIs had been greatly displeased by the intimate relations between the black Americans and the English girls, who often became pregnant and gave birth to dark-skinned babies.

The British had been especially impressed with the dignity of the blacks, compared with the boisterousness of the whites. A current barb had run, "I don't mind the Yanks, but I can't say I care for those white chaps they've brought with them." As for the GIs in general, a cutting complaint had been that they were "overpaid, overfed, oversexed, and over here." This gibe had prompted the GI retort that the British servicemen were "underpaid, underfed, undersexed, and under Eisenhower."

Long before leaving America, I had learned that an impoverished Europe was desperately short of cigarettes. Although not a smoker, I undertook to improve my status as an ambassador of good will by bringing along a couple of cartons of Lucky Strikes. I finally succeeded in getting rid of them all. Yet this largesse may have been something of a mistake, because I found it embarrassing to offer people cigarettes without joining them myself. One rather awkward incident occurred at the Imperial Defence College in London. But I did manage to give away whole packages here and there, including one to the heavy-smoking, hard-bitten manageress of my lodgings. A young woman employed by the U.S. Army told me that she was able to purchase Lucky Strikes for sixty cents a carton, whereas the British had to pay sixty-five cents a pack. She said she felt "like a dog" in these circumstances, yet, like Maria Theresa of Austria in the first partition of Poland, "she wept but she kept on taking."

My first impressions of London's public servants were on the whole most favorable. British customs officials proved unfailingly efficient and courteous, in marked contrast to some of the brusque uncivil civil servants whom I have encountered on reentering the United States. London's two-decker bus system, which was surprisingly inexpensive, impressed me as highly satisfactory, especially in the frequency and punctuality of its operation. A hurry-up American could never cease to be amazed by the patience and discipline that the British passengers showed in queuing up at the bus stops. Standing in line was an old British custom ingrained by shortages of various kinds during and after the recent war.

London's famous black cabs—awkward, unpretentious, inexpensive, and ubiquitous—were readily available, except during rush hours. The solemn cabbies, unlike those of New York, were usually imperturbable and uncommunicative. But there were a few exceptions. One of them seemed annoyed by the characteristic American haste with which I tried to extricate myself and my luggage from his cab in front of my so-called hotel. Another reprovingly shouted to an absent-minded women pedestrian, "Watch the lights, lady" (pronounced lie-dee). Still another roundly cursed, in Shakespearean idiom, a group of U.S. servicemen who were thoughtlessly wandering into the street in his path.

British travelers in America during the nineteenth century had repeatedly observed that the energetic Americans always seemed to be in a terrible hurry. The British, as I had expected, seemed not to be. Even the ambulances responded to emergency calls with less breakneck speed and screeching than their American counterparts. The British must have had even less tendency to rush about after the war than before it. Battered and exhausted, they were not going anywhere. They seemed to laugh less and with more restraint than Americans, no doubt partly because they had less to laugh about. Winston Churchill had proclaimed that he had not become prime minister to preside over the "liquidation of the British Empire." And he did not, for that process, including the loss of India, was being carried forward by the Labour government of Clement Attlee.

Like other American visitors in London, I was impressed by the large number of small, low-powered automobiles that were built for transportation rather than ostentation. Only one American-made car caught my eye the first day, although I spotted a few more later. At Oxford, a new Ford-Mercury was enough of a novelty to attract a small knot of the curious.

Bicycles were much more in evidence in London than in the cities of America, though much less so than in Denmark and Holland. Some of them were designed with sidecars or pull-carts, which made progress more difficult. Yet the persistent use of this cheap form of transportation by both sexes did something to refute the charge that the British, some of whom pedaled furiously, were notoriously deficient in energy.

The frightful damage inflicted by Hitler's blitz in 1940, followed by the V-1 and V-2 rocket-bombs, had been considerably patched up. But live bombs were to be discovered for many years to come. I did not visit the areas where the worst damage had occurred, but elsewhere wooden screens of various kinds had been erected between buildings to conceal the wreckage. Everywhere one could observe bomb-pocked structures, including the heavily damaged tower of the Houses of Parliament building and the slightly damaged but soot-blackened St. Paul's Cathedral, which had miraculously escaped destruction. In one place, innocuous wild flowers were blooming in the ruins.

After witnessing the bomb-flattened cities of Germany a few weeks later, I concluded that the British had providentially come off considerably better than their enemy. Churchill in fact had made the "rubble bounce." The war-weary but victorious Britons certainly showed more energy, enterprise, and optimism than their fallen foes in picking up the pieces and restoring a semblance of normality. An appreciable amount of new construction was actually going forward.

Englishmen have a reputation for minding their own business, and in this regard they lived up to expectations. After failing to purchase a satisfactory cap in New York before departing, I arrived in London in a rainstorm with a Panama hat and a thin summer suit. Nobody in the crowds seemed to be staring at me as some kind of odd-ball, although I probably was the only visitor to Europe that season so attired. On another occasion, a fire truck clanged by and the people around me hardly looked up, quite unlike their curious American cousins. I suppose they had seen and heard so much fire-fighting equipment during the blitz and later that the novelty had almost completely disappeared.

After the buffeting the British had endured, I had expected to find the people weary, strained, and underfed. On the contrary, they seemed reasonably energetic, relaxed, and well nourished, quite in contrast to the half-starved Germans I was soon to observe. The small children looked especially robust and pink-cheeked, and I learned that special efforts were being made to supply them with milk and meat. In the restaurants one had no trouble securing butter, although my understanding was that both it and bread were rationed for home consumption. There were food shortages, however, but few visible signs of extreme deprivation. I did see an old woman pawing through a garbage can near Piccadilly Circus, but such a sight was not altogether uncommon in America, especially during the depression years.

Clothing, which showed the effects of rationing, was obviously not up to prewar standards. Lord Derwent, whom I had met crossing the Atlantic, had been wearing a somewhat threadbare suit. I later lunched with a member of Parliament who casually remarked, in reference to straitened British finances, that he was wearing a suit left by a brother killed in the war. On the other hand, some of the more prosperous gentlemen on the streets were smartly attired in the traditional garb, complete with bowler (derby hat), gloves, and cane. On the whole the British seemed better dressed than one might have expected in view of their recent and continuing ordeal.

The war had proved to be an especially grievous burden to the women, as was suggested by the spectacle of a one-legged mother on crutches wheeling a baby carriage. Yet there seemed to be an unusual number of pretty girls. Obviously because of financial distress, most of them were not so luxuriously attired as their overdressed American counterparts. A visitor saw few silk or nylon stockings, but plenty of black cotton substitutes. Some of the shabby clothing would not have done credit to a rummage sale in the more fortunate United States.

Prostitutes who had accommodated the visiting American servicemen during the war were out on the streets in force, especially in the Piccadilly area, where they were known vulgarly as "Piccadilly Lilies" or "Piccadilly Commandos." As far as I could observe, the bobbies left them alone if they kept moving and did not make themselves conspicuously offensive.

I walked countless miles through the streets of London, soaking up the atmosphere and learning as much as I could about the English in their own habitat. Late one afternoon I noticed an attractive young woman, well dressed but overdressed, standing near the edge of the sidewalk. As I came abreast of her, she suddenly said, "Hello," and smiled, showing exceptionally white teeth. I was thinking about other things than she was, and instinctively answered with a "hello," perhaps subconsciously thinking that she was a friendly former student of mine. Then she added, "Wouldn't you like to come with me?" By this time a great light had dawned and I hurried on ahead, leaving her standing there in her purple shoes.

After walking a minute or two, I looked back and saw this predatory female in conversation with a young man who had the appearance of being an American college boy seeing the town. Perhaps he was pricing her services or, as a student of sociology, was inquiring why a nice girl like this one was engaged in an ancient but disreputable profession. I subsequently learned from an American who had made direct inquiries that there was one price for a solo experience and a considerably higher one for an all-night rendezvous. The figures relayed to me did much to explain why these good-time girls could afford such expensive, if gaudy, trappings.

Three years earlier, so an ex-GI had recently informed me, the going price had been two to four pounds, but it had dropped somewhat after the D-Day invasion of France had drained off most of the soldiers. In such circumstances venereal disease is always a problem, but I was a little surprised to see contraceptive devices prominently on display in the drugstore windows of London.

Indoor dens of sin that had catered to lonesome GIs and others were not hard to find. One of them, alluringly named the New Orleans Club, had stationed a pimp on a chair outside the front door with instructions to hand out cards and say to passersby, "Don't you want to come upstairs for drink and girls?" I shook my head and quickly passed on, wondering how many GIs had been drugged and robbed in such dives.

A vaudeville house (music hall), known as The Old Windmill, stood in a conspicuous spot in London and advertised that it had never missed a show during the war, even during the worst days of Hitler's bombing. There were chorus girls, in addition to vaudeville acts featuring coarse jokes about current peeves. Among them were barbs directed at Emanuel Shinwell, the Labourite Minister of Fuel and Power, who had not managed to provide enough fuel during the preceding bitter winter and spring. The entertainers also made snide references to the woman-hungry American GIs who drove their jeeps recklessly through the streets and whistled wolfishly at the English girls. The high point of the show was the sight of a completely immobile nude female in the distance, posed as a classical Greek statue. The British censors of that day evidently worked on the principle that nudity with mobility is iniquity. They reasoned, no doubt correctly, that more arousal was achieved in American burlesque houses by the bump-and-grind gyrations of the striptease artists.

While speaking of sin, I must refer again to the London bobbies, who at that time carried no firearms. In my experience they were invariably courteous and helpful. I asked several of these chin-strapped guardians of the law if it was true that the American GIs had behaved badly while on leave in London, and was informed that such tales were greatly exaggerated. The police seemed to realize that these lads, who were far from home and often facing imminent death in Europe, were just letting off a little steam. If things got too rough, the bobbies simply called in the American Military Police (MPs), who could be counted on to do their duty—sometimes to overdo it by cracking a few heads.

On Sunday, June 15, with nothing better to do, I boarded a train for Oxford with the intention of visiting the university. My deep interest in this hallowed institution went back to my undergraduate days at Stanford, when I had applied for a Rhodes Scholarship and had been one of the dozen or so unsuccessful finalists from the state of California. There was a possibility that one day I might be asked to teach there for a year, but although the opportunity finally came some twenty years later, personal reasons kept me from accepting.

As an unheralded visitor at Oxford on Sunday, I could do little more than examine the exterior of the physical plant, although ten years later I made a more extended visit in the company of my wife. I carried away a lasting impression of the narrow streets, the flagstone sidewalks, the cobblestone walls, and the ancient but not too comfortable buildings. Above all I was impressed with the antiquity of the institution. Some of the stone steps were worn down about six inches, and the official list of the Vicars of St. Giles' Church went back to the year A.D. 1226, eleven years after King John issued the Magna Carta at Runnymede.

A visit to Cambridge University a few days later was of unusual interest to me, primarily because I had been forced, for personal reasons, to decline an invitation to teach there during the preceding academic year, 1946–1947. This decision turned out to be most fortunate, because that winter happened to be the most severe in more than half a century. Much of the sparse plumbing at Cambridge froze, and my wife, recovering from a near-fatal horseback accident, probably could not have survived the ordeal. At all events, it seemed proper to express my regrets in person, and by letter I made known my presence in London to George Macaulay Trevelyan, the eminent British historian and the Master of Trinity College. I expected that he would make an appointment, but instead he promptly sent me a telegram inviting me to lunch.

Trevelyan turned out to be a crisp, elderly gentleman of seventy-one, who received me most cordially. The lunch was excellent, consisting of some kind of stewed lamb, but I was reluctant to eat heartily because meat was still being rationed. (I afterward learned that we must have consumed nearly his entire week's supply.) At the luncheon table my host remarked casually that his *English Social History* (1942) had earned royalties of £42,000 (about $170,000 in 1947), but that the near-confiscatory income tax had taken £39,500. Not until then did I fully realize how deeply the "soak the rich" philosophy of the government was taking its bite. But my host, quickly quieting any fears about his solvency, added that he had other means that were not so heavily taxed, and that his situation was only further evidence of Britain's serious financial straits.

A discussion of economic problems led naturally to Trevelyan's mentioning the housing crunch. He observed that the shortage of dwellings was critical, especially after the German blitzing and bombing, and that there was no ceiling on inflated prices. He remarked that England had once been rich but that after two world wars she was poor; the wealthy class was being leveled down. When I offered him one of my embarrassing Lucky Strike cigarettes, he declined, saying that he preferred Turkish cigarettes to American brands because there were no problems with Turkey of an adverse balance of trade and dollar exchange. Many Britons were giving up smoking, I learned, because of the heavy tax on cigarettes.

After lunch, Trevelyan took me on a personal tour of several of the most famous colleges, including his own Trinity. He explained that the priceless stained-glass windows had been removed from the King's College chapel following the launching of Hitler's blitz. At one point in our conversation, he remarked that the ancient buildings, for all their grandeur, were inordinately expensive to keep in repair.

Petrol (gasoline) was still being rationed in England, and I was somewhat surprised and slightly embarassed when Trevelyan asked his chauffeur to take the limousine out of the garage to show me the American Military Cemetery located a short distance outside the town. About seven thousand white crosses marked the graves of American men who had lost their lives in England, most of them in the suicidal air war against Hitler. The Stars and Stripes was kept permanently at half-staff on this impressive spot, which provided a magnificent view of the rolling green countryside. Trevelyan was especially proud of this cemetery, and he asked me to tell the people back in America how deeply he and the British people appreciated the sacrifice of these young lives in defense of freedoms that the two peoples mutually cherished.

My gracious host was clearly pro-American in his sympathies; at one point in the conversation he declared that Britain, in providing the South with commerce destroyers like the *Alabama,* had behaved badly toward the North during the Civil War of 1861–1865. He was true to the liberal Whiggish principles of his father, the historian-politician George Otto Trevelyan, and to those of the father's uncle, the famed historian-essayist Thomas Babington Macaulay, who evidently was responsible for my guide's middle name. Macaulay had attended Trinity College, Cambridge, of which his grandnephew was now Master. My host particularly directed attention to the statue of his granduncle in the Trinity chapel. He remarked that his father had told him that it was a good likeness of the face, but that Thomas Babington Macaulay had never crossed his legs that way. He added that the poet Lord Byron, who had also been a student at Trinity, had rebelliously kept a bear because dogs were not allowed.

A focal point during my stay in London was the American Embassy, which faced on Grosvenor Square and brightened the landscape with three or four American flags. In the Square itself, workmen were busily clearing a place for a monument to Franklin D. Roosevelt, which the appreciative British themselves were erecting. The necessary funds had been raised, even oversubscribed, by a public appeal.

The Embassy building itself was a rather pretentious brick structure, quite in contrast with the humiliating quarters that many previous representatives of a niggardly Uncle Sam had been forced to occupy. But in reality the structure was not quite what it appeared to be, for at that time a large section of it was serving as residential apartments. On one occasion, I glanced across the inner court and glimpsed a woman, presumably a tenant, in the process of rearranging some of her clothing.

Subsequently the Washington government acquired the entire building and then, in an appalling display of bad taste, spread across the front a sixty-foot replica of an American eagle, painted in gold, of all colors. When I saw it ten years later I felt that either a more modest decoration or none at all would have served the purpose better and would have seemed less like rubbing in America's superior influence and affluence.

Numerous contacts with the Embassy during my two visits to London in 1947 impressed me with the large amount of space given over to military and naval affairs. The military attaché, Major General Clayton L. Bissell, impressed me as energetic, efficient, highly intelligent, and slightly suspicious. Despite my credentials from the National War College, he was reluctant to give out any information of a specific military nature. His reason was that it had all been reported to the War Department, which, he seemed to suggest, was where one could more properly ask for it. He probably was right. But I did learn that the British and American Combined Chiefs of Staff were still operating, and to this degree the war was not over yet. General Bissell did say that there was no naval competition between Britain and America, because a nation could not have rivalry unless it could envision the possibility of war with a rival. He stated categorically that he could conceive of no critical situation in which the navies of Britain and the United States would not be on the same side. The only potential enemy of both was the Soviet Union, which at that time was in a position to conduct serious naval operations against Britain and the United States only with submarines.

Arrangements were also made in London for me to visit the Imperial Defence College, the opposite number of the institution I was representing. (The British name was less likely to disturb pacifists.) In response to questions directed to me by the staff, I explained to the best of my ability what I thought the College in Washington was trying to do. The two institutions seemed to be aiming at the same general objectives, including the exchange of several officer-students. There were three or four Americans in the London institution, to counterbalance the three Britons who were about to enter the National War College.

During the lunch and a partial tour of the Imperial Defence College, I noted the antique accommodations, including an old-fashioned washbowl in the washroom. The heating facilities could not have been adequate during the past dreadful winter, for I was told that the professors had lectured in overcoats to shivering students. The small library evoked some complaints about the difficulty of securing American books because of the critical shortage of dollar exchange.

Before leaving the Imperial Defence College, I sat in on a lecture by a Professor Coupland on India, at a time when Britain was within two months of divesting herself of the richest and most troublesome jewel in her colonial diadem. He impressed me as being unusually well informed, so much so that I began scribbling notes in my pocket notebook. This operation was promptly abandoned when one of the few American students in the College whispered to me that note-taking was a violation of the rules, although it was not at the National War College in Washington. Professor Coupland's judgment that the achievement of India's independence would be Britain's proudest moment was called into question by subsequent events. The compromise division of India into India and Pakistan, which was followed that same year by the frightful disorders involving Hindus and Muslims, supplied a red-letter date for the world—blood red, that is. About a half-million people died.

My most vivid recollection of the Imperial Defence College involves General William J. Slim (later Field Marshal and Viscount). He arrived a little late for lunch, swinging up the path with erect military bearing. In a crisp voice, the kind that one associates with a man born to command, he apologized for being late by referring to the pressure of other engagements. To my shame, I did not know then but learned later that he had established a brilliant military record. His crowning achievement was to drive the Japanese out of Burma with the Fourteenth British Army in some of the bitterest and most prolonged fighting of the war. He referred more or less in passing to those Jap "bahstards," but spoke with compassion of the British women and the tragic ordeal that they had recently endured. "It's a jolly shame," he observed laconically.

While exploring the many byways of London, I managed to secure a special diplomatic pass from the Embassy that permitted me to see the mother of parliaments in action. First came the House of Lords, which was temporarily holding forth in the King's Robing Room, or so I was informed. The House of Commons had suffered such serious bomb damage that its members were now meeting temporarily in the usual quarters of the House of Lords.

My visit to the Lords lasted five and one-half hours, and so entrancing was the exhibition that I did not once move from my upholstered seat. One of the guards, whatever his official name was, complimented me on my staying power, which was superior to that of most of the noble Lords. Forty-nine of them were present when the golden mace was brought in with appropriate pageantry, but only nine remained at 7:40 P.M. when it was removed. My sources told me that there were more than eight hundred peers, but that only about three hundred of them ever bothered to attend the sessions. A few were young, but many of them were elderly and decrepit.

An atmosphere of futility hung over the debates, for the House of Lords, ever since the bloodless revolution of 1911, had been shorn of most of its power and reduced to little more than a venerable figurehead. About all the Lords could do was to propose amendments to bills passed by the House of Commons, and even in this area they had to be careful not to be too assertive. The threat was ever present, even in June, 1947, that the government in power, in this case that of the Labour party, would create enough new peers to override a rebellious House of Lords.

The level of debate, with respectful allusions to "my noble friend," compared favorably with that of the United States Senate, the self-styled "greatest deliberative body in the world." Their lordships, with varying local accents, drew upon wide experience in government and business, and my feeling was that much wisdom and talent were being wasted in the House of Lords. Members tended to speak without shouting, unlike their American counterparts in Congress, but at times they could not be heard distinctly above the noise of the workmen outside who were removing the rubble left by Hitler's bombs.

Debate ranged from the imminent elevation of Ceylon to Dominion status (1948), which one speaker approved, to the shortcomings of the incumbent socialist (Labour) government. Alluding no doubt to the past paralyzing winter, one member provoked laughter when he hoped that if the Socialists went to hell, as he evidently thought they would, the Labourite fuel minister, Emanuel Shinwell, would mercifully have charge of the heating. On the other hand, one member remarked that "keep to the left" was perhaps the safest rule of the road.

The next day a debate on foreign affairs was due in the House of Commons, and I was fortunate enough to secure a special diplomatic pass from the American Embassy to enter the tiny gallery of the temporary quarters of the House of Commons. There I spent seven consecutive hours, but was not permitted to scribble down my notes until after I had left.

The session opened, like that of the Lords, with colorful pageantry; liveried bearers brought in the traditional mace. The question hour passed with evident evasiveness on the part of those interrogated, and then the regular debate began. There was considerable confusion, punctuated by much interruption and some jocularity, as well as by the traditional approving cries of "Hear! Hear!" and admonitory shouts of "Order! Order!" A spectator sensed considerable tension between the Conservatives and the ruling Labourites, who had gained power less than two years earlier.

At one point in the proceedings, a Conservative member rose and

repeatedly shouted, "Is there a doctor in the House?" Among mur-
murs of concern, an affirmative response was forthcoming, and one
member, evidently a doctor, stood. The speaker who had shouted then
said something to the effect that the physician ought to examine the
heads of the Labourites. On this occasion the House was more dis-
orderly than I have ever seen its American counterpart. I have recently checked the official reporting of this interchange (June 19), and
find that it has been softened somewhat, just as the members of Congress manage to "doctor" their language as it is reported in the *Con-
gressional Record*.

"A QUESTION OF GEOGRAPHY"

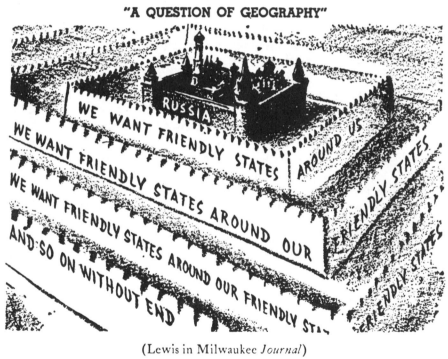

(Lewis in Milwaukee *Journal*)

Anthony Eden, tall and handsome but then without a portfolio in
the Cabinet, spoke eloquently for the Conservatives and displayed
considerable polish, although at other times he put his feet on a desk,
as was sometimes done, and displayed socks that had slipped down

his shanks. On the whole there seemed to be less standing on dignity in the House of Commons than in the House of Lords. Foreign Secretary Ernest Bevin, a burly man who had fought his way up in the ranks of organized labor, spoke vigorously for the Labourites, and the House seemed to be more tense than usual when he had the floor.

A visitor could sense the concern of the House of Commons over the recent outward reachings of the Soviet Union. Premier Ferenč Nagy of Hungary had recently been overthrown by the local Communists while he was vacationing in Switzerland. Several members of Commons who had just returned from visiting ill-starred Hungary expressed their grave disquietude. One could sense in this body an awareness of the overshadowing presence of Europe, especially the Soviet Union, and a general feeling that the Russians had now gone too far. No more appeasement was wanted. As could be expected, the Labour speakers tended much more to stand up for the USSR, and several Communist or pro-Communist speakers defended actual or prospective Communist designs on eastern Europe.

As a valued ally, the United States was treated with considerable respect, partly no doubt because of the looming Red cloud of Soviet Communism. But the recent American loan—belated, restrictive, and allegedly ungenerous—still rankled. Critics lashed out against Yankee "dollar imperialism," attacked Uncle Sam's regionalism in Latin America, and deplored America's recent increase of the tariff on wool. Although one speaker insisted that the United States had prospered from World War II, others argued that America had been openhanded. With reference to gold, of which Uncle Sam had an abundance locked up, one member remarked pointedly that it was like manure: to be useful it had to be spread around.

Returning to the Embassy, I encountered several old friends, including Professor Allan Nevins, the eminent historian from Columbia University, who was then serving as a public-affairs officer. He had earlier taught for a total of about two years in England, one of them at Oxford University, and he firmly believed that the British were a "truly civilized people," more so, I gathered, than the Americans. He first arranged for me to attend a reception at the house of Ambassador Lewis W. Douglas, whose honored guests were a dozen or so visiting female teachers from the United States. They were participants in an exchange program involving a comparable number of British pedagogues, who presumably had already left for America. The young ladies were intelligent, personable, and much excited about their great adventure. But they did complain about the critical shortage of textbooks and other supplies, owing to the war and its aftermath. The exchange of teachers no doubt would prove reciprocally advantageous, but we had a feeling that this effort was but a small drop in an enormous bucket.

When I was not elsewhere engaged, I was briefed in depth by the officials at the American Embassy, principally attaché Samuel D. Berger. During our discussion of the terrible ordeal of the war, he cautioned me not to count the British out, for they had great resilience, as indeed proved to be the case. Berger regarded the Labour victory in 1945, followed by the nationalization of the coal industry in January, 1947, as a scrambling of socialistic eggs that could never be unscrambled. Even some Conservatives had favored the takeover of the mines, which were currently suffering from a slowdown of labor and a breakdown in transportation from the mine shafts.

The battered British, I also learned at the Embassy, lived in fear of another great depression in the United States that would pull them under, just as the Soviets were hoping for one that would land them on top. Concerned Britons had deeply resented American interference in their Palestine mandate, with its rebellious and terroristic Jews, but the feeling was now less bitter because the problem had been dumped into the lap of the United Nations during the preceding April. Other sources of Anglo-American friction were the increased tariff on British wool, and the reluctantly advanced loan to Britain which, though amounting to a whopping $3.75 billion, was proving to be an inadequate finger in the dike.

By now it was as plain as the London Bridge that the American loan to Britain was only a stopgap. As a consequence, the British had welcomed the glimmer of hope in Secretary Marshall's Harvard speech delivered earlier in the month—a suggestion so general that it was being referred to in England as the "Marshall Idea" rather than the "Marshall Plan." The British had been greatly relieved by the Truman Doctrine, enunciated some two months earlier, for it had enabled them with some grace to transfer the burden of saving Greece to the broad back of the rich and unexhausted Uncle Sam. Mr. Berger further stated that Britain and America were already drawn together in a de facto alliance, and that the British, traditionally inimical to one-nation domination of the Continent, were struggling to establish a new balance of power. (It came in less than two years, with the historic North Atlantic Treaty Organization—NATO.)

As for the specter of a westward-encroaching Soviet Union, Mr. Berger reported that the British had long memories of Stalin's unpredictability, and they feared for the future. Foreign Secretary Ernest Bevin, as well as other leading Labourites, had expected the

Russians to act up after the war, but not so menacingly. The recent Communist coup in Hungary had given Labour a severe jolt. Bevin was now taking the line that the "appeasement" of Russia had ended and that Great Britain would work for European reconstruction with or without the Soviet Union. Communists in the labor unions would have to be watched, my informant said, but pro-Russian Labour spokesmen did not carry much weight. The British Labour Party was Christian Socialist rather than Marxist Socialist—a fact that American conservatives did not fully appreciate when they had criticized the recent loan to Britain as supporting "too damned much socialism, too damned much Communism."

Much of what I learned from official sources was confirmed by the daily press, notably *The Times* of London. On the day of my arrival, June 14, a "leader" appeared regarding the groping steps that were being taken toward the concept of a Marshall Plan and the task of easing the widening gap in the dollar balance of payments. Foreign Secretary Bevin, on hearing of Marshall's Harvard speech of June 5 while at home, had promptly established contact with the Foreign Office. He later declared in public that he had "grabbed the Marshall offer with both hands" and that the brief remarks of the American Secretary constituted "one of the greatest speeches made in world history."

On June 13, the French Foreign Minister, Georges Bidault, invited Bevin to Paris for a discussion of the epochal proposal. On June 19, *The Times* reported the Anglo-French invitation to the Soviet Foreign Minister, V. M. Molotov, to join them in conference. He soon arrived with a small army of eighty-nine experts and clerks. On June 22, Bidault spoke optimistically to the French National Assembly to the accompaniment of applause, except by the Communists, who remained silent and sullen. The same day I departed for France, confidently expecting to hear more about the uncertain fate of the "Marshall Idea."

In leaving England's "tight little isle," I carried with me considerable faith in the ability of what Churchill called "this English race" to bounce back after taking full advantage of America's outstretched hand. My optimism would have been dampened if I had realized how near financial collapse the British were from the financial burdens and dislocations of two world wars. The worst problems of Britain were not readily visible to a visitor's eye. They embraced the low production of labor; the lost overseas markets, including those in prostrate Europe; the adverse dollar balance; and the rapidly vanishing American loan. Official Washington and Prime Minister Attlee were then estimating that the fund would all be gone by the end of the year, for the rapid rise in wholesale prices (about 40 percent) had reduced the purchasing power of the original figure by about one billion dollars.

The stout-hearted Britons, who were obviously not suffering nutritionally, looked better outwardly than they felt inwardly. One could detect their doggedness, self-reliance, and inner discipline, as well as their instinct for unity and survival. But the human spirit, like an old and hardened rubber band, can be stretched to the point where a complete bounceback is impossible. The boarding up of the bombed-out buildings might conceal much physical damage, but the four-year effusion of "blood, toil, tears, and sweat" had left a deep inner malaise.

3

The French Connection

*Meanwhile the economic situation of two of the
leading countries, namely England and France, is
deteriorating with terrifying rapidity. If nothing is
done for them within two to three months, they both
face genuine hunger by winter, and other compli-
cations of unpredictable dimensions, with un-
foreseeable effects in other areas of the world.*

George F. Kennan
Director of Policy Planning Staff
Department of State, September 4, 1947

My trip by train from London to the English Channel on June 22 was
swift, smooth, and uneventful. I took particular note of the lush green
countryside, for only a day earlier spring had officially surrendered to
summer. The historic white cliffs of Dover loomed in the background
as we pulled away on a cross-Channel ferry for the French port of
Calais, some twenty miles distant. Happily the often turbulent waters
of the Straits of Dover were on their good behavior, and the crossing
proved to be millpond-smooth and in complete harmony with the
glorious sunshine. No one appeared to be in the throes of seasickness
—a malaise that had tortured countless thousands of travelers over the
centuries.

During the brief crossing, I struck up a conversation with a middle-
aged Englishman who evidently was bound for the continent on a
vacation. During our brief interchange he spoke with bitterness of
Hitler's blitz and, waving his hand in the general direction of Germany, he said that in two world wars "Jerry" had managed to blight
the lives of the English people. Among varied grievances he mentioned the machine-gunning of children at play by German aviators.
This conversation sticks in my memory because it was so un-
characteristic of what I heard while in England. The British people,

with their traditional stiff upper lip, were going about the business of picking up the pieces without undue whining. They doubtless were partially comforted by the knowledge that British bombers had returned Hitler's lethal visitations with more than compound interest.

Paris, which had surrendered in 1940 without a struggle, was to exhibit few visible scars of war, but the same could not be said of the tight little harbor of Calais. Its waters were littered with wreckage, its shores were dotted with destruction. Yet some reconstruction was in progress. Upon boarding a fast train for Paris, we followed the coastline for about an hour, and en route passed many shattered buildings. The French, in fact, had lost twice as many structures in the recent limited war with the Germans as they had lost in the four-year war of 1914–1918. As we passed through the beautiful grain-growing countryside, we reached Amiens, where Napoleon had concluded an abortive peace with Great Britain in 1801. Leaving this railroad center, we rolled on into Paris, which came on us rather suddenly owing to the absence of extensive suburbs.

The French, more than the English, had resisted mechanization, and a visitor could spot quite a few horse-drawn cabs in Paris in addition to the numerous motorized taxis. Upon discovering that the automobiles were all taken, I boarded one of the ancient vehicles and clattered through the streets of Paris on a high perch to my hotel. I felt highly conspicuous but soon comforted myself with the realization that nobody was paying the slightest attention to me. My immediate destination was Le Grand Hotel, which may have been grand before World War I but by now was distinctly down at the heel.

Before and between my interviews with various officials and nonofficials, I tramped so many miles over the sidewalks of Paris that I developed blisters on my feet. Adding to my discomfort, the temperature during one warm spell rose to ninety-nine degrees; that was reported to be the hottest June day in forty-seven years and no doubt added to the severe summer drought that then afflicted much of western Europe. The French policemen, unlike the London bobbies, were armed with clubs and also revolvers. They were unfailingly helpful in redirecting me when I became lost. Fortunately my hotel was near the Place de l'Opéra, and my standard procedure was to point in the direction where I thought it was located and laboriously pronounce its name in my fractured French. The police would then eagerly straighten me out with appropriate Gallic gesticulation.

Locating the American Embassy was one of my first tasks. I not only had business there, but I also wanted to see how well Uncle Sam, notoriously niggardly in earlier days, had provided for his overseas servants. The Americans had no reason to hang their heads in shame.

The Embassy was a handsome stone structure facing the Place de la Concorde, close to the spot where Marie Antoinette had lost her head to the guillotine in 1793. Even so, some of the war-spawned functions of the Embassy had spilled over into supplementary quarters. The official list of personnel, which contained more than one hundred names, was almost as long as that of the huge American staff in London.

In Paris the physical scars of war, contrasted with the deep-seated psychological ones, were conspicuous in the sprinkling of cripples. Aside from the usual amputees, this unfortunate group included a few people with missing hands, presumably lost during the recent conflict. The casualty lists were doubtless being augmented by the taxi drivers who raced through the streets with reckless abandon. Their habit on nearing an intersection was to put a heavy hand on the horn and a leaden foot on the accelerator. The noise was unnerving, especially when one was trying to rest in the hotel. When I returned to Paris ten years later, the blasting of horns had been outlawed, at least for taxi drivers, and the new regulations were being so rigidly enforced that an eerie silence prevailed at night.

Food presented no real problem during my week in Paris, June 22 to June 29, 1947. Evidently the standard ticket for bread rations was not needed when I ate at my once-glamorous hotel, but in outside restaurants the story was different. Near the end of my first day I entered an eating establishment and placed my order. Midway during the meal my waitress approached me and demanded my "tee-kay." Not knowing that the word ticket had been Frenchified, I responded with a blank look. She repeated the word several times, each time raising her voice until she was fairly screaming. Some nearby diners, aware of my confusion, explained to me in English that what she wanted was a ration ticket, which had not been issued to me. This international crisis ended when the waitress shrugged her shoulders and departed in disgust, perhaps muttering something about those "stupid Americans."

Shortly after this incident I was told that the standard loaf of bread had become somewhat yellower, owing to the shortage of wheat and the infusion of 20-percent American corn. Clever Communist propaganda was harping on the groundless accusation that corn from the United States produced pellagra and other hazards to one's health, especially impotence. The moral seemed to be that self-respecting Frenchmen, who traditionally believed "l'amour the merrier," should spurn imports from capitalistic Uncle Sam.

Parisian food was relatively costly in the summer of 1947 because of war-spawned inflation. A skimpy breakfast cost me about $1.30, and a

lunch that consisted of a mushroom omelette with bread accounted for
$1.70. The bright blue California skies of France produced California-
like delicacies, including blood-red strawberries and golden apricots,
a generous supply of which I bought from a handcart peddler across
from Notre Dame Cathedral. Not thinking of the various kinds of
communicable diseases that were then cursing Europe, I ate these
unwashed delicacies on the spot with great relish.

French women added grace and color to the streets and shops. They
seemed unusually well dressed, especially for this period of postwar
scarcity, and I learned that they had exceptional talent for making
much out of little stylistically. They not only wore attractive clothes
but carried them off with a flair, even in the stilt shoes then in vogue.
Probably the rationing of food, imposed during the war and continuing rigorously, had resulted in trimmer figures.

In mentioning the women walking the streets I am not referring to
streetwalkers. Only one rather repulsive prostitute on a busy corner
gave me a suggestive wink and nod, although a few others were obviously going about their ancient business. Pimps seemed much more
in evidence; several of them fruitlessly asked me if I did not want
something "exceptionally nice." Related to these gentry were the mo-
bile hawkers of conventional postal cards, who would mutter furtively
under their breath and in English, "You like dirty pictures?" I did not
favor these gentry with my patronage, although I could see that they
were making some sales to curious younger men.

Other shady characters abounded, especially near the American Express headquarters, a tourist center. My summer attire, including my
shoes, proclaimed me to be a gullible American tourist, and I was
repeatedly approached by sleazy individuals who asked in good English, "Something to sell?" One quickly learned that these gentlemen
were black marketeers engaged in purchasing cigarettes or American
currency with devalued francs, as they had earlier done from visiting
U.S. troops. Both of these operations were illegal, and I invariably
hurried on with a shake of my straw-hatted head and what I thought
was a French negative. I had no desire, especially given my official
responsibilities, to be lodged in a local bastille.

In the area of legitimate entertainment, a newcomer noted numerous movie houses, most of them apparently exhibiting Hollywood
films. To some degree the French were gradually becoming Ameri-
canized, partly as a result of the semifriendly invasions by the so-
called "new barbarians"—the GIs. As a part of my cultural research, I
did what many American tourists were wont to do and bought tickets
for both the Folies-Bergère and the rival Casino de Paris. Some of the
voluptuous young women appeared in what Eve in the Garden of

Eden would have regarded as a small fig leaf. (The rumor was that during the recent bitter winter they had come onto the stage slightly blue from the cold.) Yet the heaviest applause from the predominately French audience was elicited by acts involving singers and strong men. One of the female performers was a black woman, who provided further proof that the French, as veteran colonialists in Africa, were much more color-blind than the Americans. The vaudeville acts were punctuated by sharp digs at the uncouth and vulgar tourists and servicemen from the United States. Especially emphasized were the noisy chewing of gum and the condescension in passing out valuable cigarettes to poor-relation French allies.

The GIs had turned out to be a serious problem, and the French as a whole had evidently been glad to see most of them go home. After the D-Day invasion of 1944, the Americans had helped mightily to liberate France, but in some instances they had so far forgotten their manners as to mistreat the French females in a way that was traditionally reserved for the wives and daughters of the enemy. When the GIs reached Paris, they had received hysterical acclaim, and their efforts had been further applauded when they drove eastward to crush Germany. The American troops, for their part, felt that they had "bailed out" the French "quitters" and "collaborators," and that these "ungrateful frogs" did not adequately appreciate their deliverers.

Then had come long weeks of inaction while the GIs were awaiting home-bound transports, and the morale of the American troops had sagged badly. The mutinous "I wanna go home" movement had brought action in the long run, but not enough ships in the short run. The impatient soldiers had been further depressed by the knowledge that many of them were scheduled for further service in smashing Japan. Given the combination of inaction and lowered morale, many of these boorish GI Joes, once greeted as deliverers sent from heaven, had managed to make themselves increasingly offensive to the cultured Parisians. Disapproving Frenchmen had regarded these involuntary guests as looters and rapists, who were boastful, ignorant, intolerant wife-stealers. The American veterans themselves had viewed the "lazy" French "frogs" as money-grubbers who were arrogant, backward, decadent, unsanitary, and ungrateful.

One interesting detail I learned at the American Embassy helped to explain the growing unpopularity of the boastfully victorious American soldiers. Under the Geneva Convention the United States Army supplied its German prisoners with the same rations that it provided for its own men. Hungry Frenchmen were angered when they discovered that the hated foeman was being much better fed than they were. They had not so much as seen oranges for about four years, and now the Yankees were feeding them to the German despoilers. When a Paris newspaper published a photograph of a scantily-clad Florida Orange Queen, it added the query, "When was the last time *you* ate an orange?"

The atmosphere finally became so tense late in 1945 that Leo C. Rosten, a popular writer of political science, was called upon by the Army to produce a remarkable illustrated booklet, evidently issued early in 1946 and entitled *112 Gripes about the French*. Each complaint was listed in the form of a question, after which came a paragraph or so of refutation.

Among the many gripes of the GIs, Rosten found charges of French cowardice or "lack of guts" in yielding to the Germans and then collaborating with them, even to the extent of "shacking up." (Many French citizens regarded the disciplined German soldiers as better occupiers than the GIs.) The Yankees also resented French ingratitude after Uncle Sam had rescued France in two successive wars, and they had much to say about French decadence and untrustworthiness. The GIs likewise complained about such deficiencies as primitive plumbing, the smelly outdoor urinals lining the streets of Paris, the manure piles in the front yards of farmers, the general war-spawned shabbiness, and the material backwardness.

Various French practices also came in for heavy criticism, especially gouging by French shopkeepers burdened with inflation—a complaint that homesick American doughboys had voiced in 1917–1918. Also resented were the flourishing black market, once a patriotic child of the German occupation, and French "mooching" of candy, cigarettes, and food. Desperate hunger knows little pride.

The GIs, as unwilling tourists, had likewise griped about the French females. At the theaters the girls demanded tips as usherettes and served as attendants in the men's washrooms—both old French customs that I personally witnessed. Another charge was that the women were "easy pickups"—a strange complaint from red-blooded men who were on the prowl for pickups. A current French barb was that the Americans had "the morals of a tomcat and the finesse of an Army tank." Many of the Yankee "invaders" regarded France as a "giant brothel." A cultured professor of music in Paris reported that GIs had repeatedly knocked on his door and gaily inquired. "Is this the whorehouse?"

Many of Uncle Sam's soldier boys actually liked the German girls better, as had been true after World War I in the occuped Rhineland area. The blonde *Fräuleins* were more like the girl left behind in Peoria. Hitler's *Herrenvolk* had escaped the prolonged ordeal of occupied France, and in May, 1945, the German people seemed cleaner, less shabby, more efficient, more industrious, better disciplined, and better able to run an orderly government, especially a dictatorship. But, as Rosten pointed out, the Germans had followed the Hitlerian Pied Piper like sheep and were now reaping the fruits of their blind orderliness.

Rosten's little primer of gripes probably had a quieting influence on the homesick GIs, most of whom had already departed. But officials at the American Embassy were fearful that this publication by the Army would have a bad effect if it should fall into the hands of the French, as it inevitably did. They quickly translated and published it. I asked one of the officials at the Embassy what the reaction was to this lengthy defense of alleged Gallic shortcomings, and he responded that the French were delighted with aspects of it. They were pleased that at least one American could understand that most of their so-called faults had grown largely out of their having been crushed, humiliated, occupied, robbed, enslaved, and divided by Hitler's military might—a nightmare that had lasted for four long years. Many Frenchmen, confirming the proverb that absence (also absinthe) makes the heart grow fonder, were now saying that the departed GIs had not been so bad after all. Some of the French were unhappy because the Americans had not left sooner; others, especially the Communists, were apprehensive of their possible return with the Marshall-Plan dollars deplored by Moscow.

A common complaint of some of the French people, although by no means all, was that the Americans butchered the beautiful French language while trying to speak it with a Yankee accent. At the time Paris was liberated in 1944, President Roosevelt, for whom the French had a high regard, addressed a radio message to the liberated nation in what was supposed to be their own tongue. Evidently it made a deep impression. I asked one of the French-speaking specialists at the Embassy how good the President's pronunciation had been. "So bad as to be moving," he replied.

Between official appointments, I visited the gallery of the National Assembly. The acoustics were excellent, and the interior of the chamber seemed more beautiful than that of the American Congress or of the British Parliament. Only about 70 of the 618 members were present, 186 of them Communists, the largest single bloc. Much of the oratory was impassioned, with the result that the session was generally in an uproar. Speakers shouted for order or interrupted one another as they fought to gain the floor. The presiding officer would first try to calm the offending member or members; then he would pound with his ruler (not an Anglo-Saxon gavel); then he would seize the bell clapper and add to the clatter. While all this uproar was going on, some of those present were reading newspapers or other material, and I assumed that the session was a rather quiet one as such affairs went. It was temperamentally Latin rather than Anglo-Saxon.

Much of the dissension, I gathered, was caused by the Communists. In the first general election after the war, they had polled about five million votes, a slight plurality over the closest rival. Yet they had been unable to form a ministry, and in May, 1947, the month before my arrival, Premier Paul Ramadier had dismissed the Communist ministers from the government. Ugly demonstrations by protestors were still to be feared, and I noted some neatly piled wooden barriers stacked outside the quarters of the National Assembly for use by the police to repulse possible attacks.

A totally different experience was my visit to the French counterpart of the National War College, an "Institut" for advanced military studies. My recollection is that the building was both antiquated and dilapidated, and that the school had not yet fully begun operations. General Charles Mast was the *Directeur,* a position that he was to hold from 1947 to 1950. He was himself a distinguished army commander who had been stationed in Algeria in 1942, at a time when the Allies had made their risky landings, and he had contributed to the success of the invasion by a secret meeting with General Mark W. Clark and Robert Murphy.

My principal objective in interviewing General Mast was to explain to him what the Americans were doing at the National War College and to elicit from him any information that would be useful in Washington. The driver who took me to my appointment was a young army major who spoke fluent French and who did any interpreting that was needed. My notes, which I recorded shortly after the meeting, are so skimpy that I probably told the General more than he told me. But he did express a desire for better coordination between the military and the other branches of the French government. Highly interesting was his observation that in a few years France and America would have no military secrets from one another—a prophesy that turned out to be wide of the mark, particularly regarding nuclear armaments. Haughty and independent-minded General Charles de Gaulle, after serving as the provisional head of government following the liberation, was waiting in the wings, but he did not return to power until 1959, at the time of the Algerian crisis.

Some rather dirty Moroccan soldiers in French uniforms had been in evidence at the military institute, and as we left I made some relevant remark to the major who was my interpreter-guide. He assured me with refreshing frankness that he had high respect for the French army, navy, and foreign office, but little indeed for other departments of the government.

As an historian rather than a part-time tourist, I found the monuments and memorials of France of absorbing interest. In Paris the impressive tomb of Napoleon Bonaparte caused me to wonder why the French people should so honor a man whose grandiose ambitions had bathed Europe in blood for nearly two decades and snuffed out the lives of hundreds of thousands of able-bodied men. When the paths of *gloire* lead to a humiliating collapse, such as France had just suffered at the hands of Hitler, the shame burns all the deeper.

The ornate cluster of imposing buildings at Versailles, some twenty miles from Paris, reminded me of the long-lived "Sun King," Louis XIV, who had established his court there in 1682. In 1947 France was still a leading colonial power, stretching from Algeria and Morocco to Madagascar and Indo-China, to say nothing of numerous other outposts. One learned in Paris that the French Communists, though reared under traditional colonialism, were reluctantly following the bidding of Moscow in cheering the rebels in Morocco and Madagascar. As for Indo-China, the frightful drain on troops and finances was already being felt, and the French peasants in particular were beginning to cry out against supporting with blood and money an Asiatic colony that profited only a relatively few big bankers and rubber barons.

During this busy week in Paris my primary task was to tap the brains of eleven experts who were in a good position to know something about what was then going on in France. Six of them were officials connected in some way with the American Embassy, and five were associated with the media. Included was the man in charge of the French version of the Gallup poll, whose pollsters, he said, aroused considerable suspicion among the shell-shocked pollees of France.

Among the newspaper or radio men consulted were Harold Callender of the *New York Times*, a journalist who had recently talked with Premier Ramadier, and David Schoenbrun of the National Broadcasting Company, whose headquarters were located in the building of the New York *Herald-Tribune*, Paris edition. Incidentally, the *Herald-Tribune*, an excellent journal that was printed in English, was widely read by tourists in Europe, where it was judged by some to be the best American newspaper published anywhere.

Much of what these experts had to say was pure speculation, though generally well-informed speculation, but most of it was factual. My informants were in general agreement that France—beaten, occupied,

and humiliated—was a nation that could be neither ignored nor regarded as a major force. Her navy was decimated and her army was
inadequate, scattered as it was to the far corners of the globe. The
trouble spots included Vietnam, where the new thirty-years war under Ho Chi Minh had erupted after the big one ended. In a sense,
debilitated France was a world in microcosm, where the forces of
Communism, reaction, and liberalism were contending violently with
one another at close quarters and with few holds barred.

My sources agreed that France, with all the fight taken out of her,
had sunk into a despairing mood that combined fear, insecurity, envy,
and pessimism. Many thoughtful Frenchmen had concluded that another war was probable, perhaps inevitable, with the French masses
doomed to bear the brunt. The most likely foes at the moment were
the Soviets, nominal allies of France since 1944. The French did not
want to provoke them, yet the Russians had moved menacingly westward by taking over much of eastern Europe and about half of Germany. As had happened after World War I, many Frenchmen feared
that a resurgent German Reich would soon be plotting a war of
revanche.

If a conflict should come, the French feared Uncle Sam could not be
counted on to rush to the rescue for a third time within thirty years.
The recently unveiled atomic bomb was a source of considerable
worry to Frenchmen. In the event of war, the Soviet juggernaut probably would lunge toward Paris, and the United States might have to
drop atomic bombs on the French cities to drive out the Russians.
France was caught in the middle between two powerful antago-
nists, and was bound to suffer in the crunch. The Americans, who
were far removed from the potential battleground, could afford to take
chances; the French, who were under the gun, could not. A strong
feeling prevailed that the 125,000 or so American troops still stationed
in Europe were not going to remain much longer. If I had suggested
that about 300,000 Yankee soldiers would still be there some thirty
years later, my listeners would have branded me a lunatic.

Soviet Russia, most of the American experts agreed, would need
considerable time in which to recuperate and consolidate its gains.
Meanwhile the crucial question was whether the numerous and noisy
French Communists would win control of the government and invite
in the Moscow Communists. At the very least, the local leftists could
be counted on to agitate for policies that dovetailed dangerously with
those of the Kremlin. This strategy they had conspicuously followed
from 1939 to 1941, during the life of the fateful Hitler-Stalin pact. At
all events, the French Communists could be expected to weaken the
republic so seriously that it could not be relied on as a useful member

of an Anglo-American bloc designed to halt the westward push of the Soviets.

The burgeoning strength of the French Communists was unquestionably disquieting. Aside from their ineffective plurality in the National Assembly, they controlled about 80 percent of the labor unions. Their agents were fomenting or supporting rebellion in such far-flung French colonial outposts as Morocco, Algiers, Indo-China, and Madagascar. Whatever their personal feelings, the French Communists were anti-American insofar as they pursued the party line emanating from Moscow. The ugly alternatives for France seemed to be a triumph of the Communist left or a dictatorship of the right under the retired but not retiring General Charles de Gaulle.

Further insights into America's propaganda war came from an official of the United States Information Service. A part of his job was to mail out to the French provinces printed material designed to combat Communist gains. On a wall of his office he had hung a huge map of France, and on it he had stuck little flags showing the exact locations of the places to which his propaganda literature was going. The heavy response through letters assured him that his seeds were falling on fertile soil, although he complained that the United States was not bestirring itself nearly enough. He surprised me by saying that the Russians were spending more money for Communist propaganda in France than the United States was providing for its worldwide informational program. Even the financially prostrate British were outspending the American propagandists in France, for they were more keenly aware than the United States of the importance of this ideological battlefield.

Yet some of my sources believed that the Communist threat in France was being somewhat overplayed in America. Even if the Communists did gain control, so the argument ran, they would be first of all French nationalists and only secondarily responsive to the will of the Kremlin. But relying on the good behavior of the French Communists was, from the American point of view, a desperate gamble. If the West guessed wrong, how could it ever regain the lost ground?

Somewhat reassuring was additional information gleaned about the French Communists. Their leaders in the labor unions had clawed their way up to power, not so much because they were Communists as because they were young, vigorous, clever, and tough. Their Socialist rivals had proved to be too old and lethargic. Further, the six million votes cast for the Communists in 1945 were misleading. Perhaps only one million of the ballots came from card-carrying party members; the others had voted for Communist candidates as a protest against existing conditions for the working class rather than as an endorsement of

Marxist-Leninist ideology. A young woman who represented *Newsweek* in Paris told me that she had made a practice of asking taxi drivers why they voted Communist. A common answer was that they could obtain potatoes on their ration card if they were able to show that they had cast their ballot for Communist candidates. Voters of this realistic persuasion were then known as "stomach Communists."

Greatly to my surprise, I heard little comment on the historic Marshall Proposal during my inquiries in Paris. My sources reported that about a week passed before the implications of the Secretary's hint at Harvard really penetrated the public consciousness, and even then it had the effect of offering only a ray of hope, not a sunburst of reality. Yet one result was that the French were somewhat more disposed than earlier to try to pull themselves out of the mire—with a strong assist with the dollar-dripping hand of Uncle Sam.

As fate would have it, the heralded Big Three conference of foreign ministers met secretly in Paris on June 27, five days after my arrival. It adjourned in disageement on July 2, three days after my departure for the American zone of Germany. Naturally I was not privy to what was going on behind closed doors, but the press was full of rumor, speculation, and fact about the embryonic Marshall Plan, with its emphasis on self-help.

The three convening foreign ministers were Bevin of Britain, Bidault of France, and Molotov of Russia, who came with a small army of specialists, some of whom were suspected of being spies. The Soviets had a splendid opportunity to snarl up the Marshall scheme merely by joining the participating nations, throwing monkey wrenches into the machinery, and rendering unpalatable to Congress the voting of the necessary billions for Communists. Instead they chose to slap aside the helping hand of Uncle Sam and walk out. They offered many excuses, but the compelling reason for their withdrawal seems to have been that if their subservient satellites came into the Marshall camp, Soviet control over the governments and economies of these "captive nations" would be irreparably weakened. One of the favorite Soviet arguments was that the Marshall Plan would interfere with the sovereignty of independent states by requiring information about their economic status. This was a strange line to be taken by a regime that since 1940 had wiped out the sovereign nations of Latvia, Lithuania, and Esthonia, and in other ways had encroached upon or destroyed the independence of a half-dozen or so other nearby sovereign states. The Soviet newspaper *Pravda* had hypocritically responded to the Marshall speech by condemning "doctrines invented by American imperialists for enslavement of European peoples. . . ." In American eyes, the Russians were the enslavers.

Undaunted by Molotov's walkout, Bevin and Bidault issued an invitation on July 4 for a general conference at Paris, to which twenty-two nations were invited—all Europe west of Russia with the exception of fascist Spain. Eight nations that were under the thumb or shadow of Moscow declined voluntarily or were forced to decline, notably Poland and Czechoslovakia.

Meanwhile French fingers were crossed. The people of France harbored memories of 1919, when President Wilson had persuaded the French to give up the German Rhineland in return for a treaty of guarantee sponsored by the United States—a treaty that was never even acted upon by the Senate. The French had learned the bitter lesson that whatever schemes the American president proposes in the way of treaties or appropriations must be implemented by action of the legislative branch. French skeptics would believe that there really was a Marshall Plan when Congress appropriated the necessary billions of dollars. Even then, many Frenchmen feared that Uncle Sam was not in the game to stay and that problems could not be solved simply by throwing Yankee gold at them. As for the newly born United Nations, it inspired little confidence. The French, remembering well the defunct League of Nations, were fed up with schemes that netted nothing but more trouble.

To put it bluntly, my inquiries led me to realize more clearly that the French did not like Americans. This unpleasant fact should not be especially disturbing, because one authority on French history, himself an American who had lived in France, once remarked to me that the French do not even like one another. In the summer of 1947 they were nursing many grievances against the Yankees. These complaints grew largely out of the belated coming of the Americans, their having overstayed their welcome, and their reluctance to do more for a people that had already abased themselves before the conquering Germans. Some Frenchmen, notably the Communists, professed to feel that Uncle Sam was now trying to do too much with Marshall dollars.

Students of the European scene told me that the French people secretly admired—or rather envied—American material wonders. These ranged from the New York skyscrapers to the Panama Canal, which, incidentally, the Frenchman Ferdinand de Lesseps had attempted without success to build. One oddity was that while the Communists openly assailed capitalistic America for its overgrown corporations, the rightists secretly admired the efficiency of its huge industrial complex. The French intelligentsia, then as now, were smug in the belief that the crude Americans were materialistic barbarians and that the only truly civilized nation was France, with its rich cultural traditions. During America's quarrel with the French in the

1920s over repaying France's World War I debts, a French spokesman had acidly remarked that the United States was the only nation that had ever passed from barbarism to decadence without undergoing civilization. The problem was largely the result of ignorance and indifference. A well-informed official at the U.S. Embassy told me that the French knew less about the United States than they did about the Balkans.

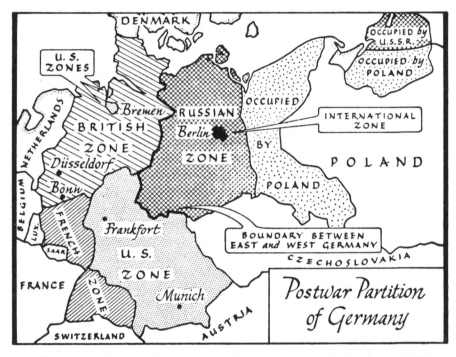

(Thomas A. Bailey, *A Diplomatic History Of The American People*, 9th edition, © 1974, p. 780. Reprinted by permission of Prentice-Hall, Inc., Englewood Cliffs, New Jersey.)

As my train pulled away from Paris toward the American zone of Germany, I carried with me the impression that the French, despite their deep pessimism and fear of the future, had shown considerable resilience since the war. My feeling was that they were somewhat better off than they were willing to admit, although still not in good shape. One heard that Paris, where inflation was rampant, had become the most expensive city in the world. National bankruptcy was freely predicted. Yet I had to remind myself that Paris is not France, and that the provinces were making a substantial recovery. Food production was up, despite the black market and the blighting effect on crops of the late frost and early drought. Damages were estimated at half a billion dollars.

The true picture, as I learned many years later from then-secret official reports, was considerably worse, for the national government was nearing insolvency. The gold reserve was melting away, to the accompaniment of an increasingly adverse balance of trade. Food had to be purchased from abroad in large quantities by a France that was ordinarily self-sufficient; adequate coal production and improved transportation were still gigantic problems. Overseas markets had vanished as former customers sank into poverty, and the industrial plants were badly in need of modernization at a time when strikes were crippling them. The army was a costly burden to maintain, and the overseas colonies, once a gold mine, were now draining away the economic and physical lifeblood of the nation, notably in rebellious Vietnam.

To top it all off, the citizens of France were resorting to their traditional game of evading taxes. "The Frenchman will die for his country," the proverb runs, "but he won't pay for it." When I was still in Paris, Premier Ramadier told Ambassador Caffery that "France's economic reconstruction is more advanced than its moral reconstruction." France was desperately in need of Marshall dollars, and, to anticipate, she ultimately became the second largest beneficiary with $3.19 billion, ranking below Great Britain, which received $3.834 billion.

The inclusion of France in the Marshall Plan, together with the self-exclusion of the Soviet Union, did not mean that during these postwar years there was an absence of friction between the United States and France at the highest levels. On the contrary, as pro-Moscow revisionist historians should note, there were periods when Washington encountered more difficulty with the French than with the Soviets. In the four-power military government of Germany, the French, as well as the Russians, repeatedly resorted to the veto in the Allied Control Council in Berlin.

Briefly the background is this. General Charles de Gaulle, then the leading French spokesman, had journeyed to Moscow in December, 1944, while the war was still being waged, to conclude a twenty-year treaty of alliance with the Soviet Union. At the Yalta Conference, in February, 1945, Stalin agreed to permit France to have a German zone of its own, but it was to be carved out of the larger zone already allocated to the Americans. At the four-power Potsdam Conference in 1945, the French were not represented, for they had been vanquished by Hitler and had contributed relatively little to the defeat of Germany. Accordingly, France was not bound by the restrictions set forth in the Potsdam Protocol for the reconstruction of Germany. This fact alone accounts for some of the subsequent French vetoes in the Allied Control Council in Berlin.

French policy regarding beaten and neighboring Germany ran remarkably parallel to that of the Soviet Union in important respects. Neither wanted a powerful, menacing, prosperous, and completely reunited Germany to rise from the rubble. Both had suffered frightful devastation in repeated wars with Germanic invaders. Neither wished to see an adjacent Germany become the dangerous economic colossus it had been before the war. Both wanted to prevent Germany from becoming completely unified economically, especially around a revived Ruhr industrial complex, with magnates like the Krupps of Essen in firm control. Both hoped to slice off from Germany territorial annexations, a large one for the Soviet Union in the east, and one about as spacious for the French in the west, specifically the Rhineland, that is, Germany west of the Rhine River. The French also coveted a large hand in the Ruhr industrial complex (east of the Rhine) and at least the annexation of the coal-rich Saar basin in the Rhineland. In the end, the Russians obtained much of East Prussia. The French failed in the Ruhr, as did the Soviets, and retained only temporary control of the Saarland, which joined the Federal German Republic in 1957. France lost out altogether in the Rhineland.

In seeking to dismember Germany, many French Communists parted company with the Russian Communists, who were scheming for a united Germany under the control of Moscow. This quarreling among the victors helped to save West Germany from dismemberment, while demonstrating that French Communists sometimes could put the interests of their own country above the objectives of the Kremlin.

My odyssey did not take me to the French zone of Germany, although I passed through it on the train en route to Frankfurt and must have skirted the northern edge of it when later leaving Cologne. My journal records encountering the party of Averell Harriman as it entered this area. But I learned from other sources that the French zone, although the smallest and poorest of the four, sustained the largest occupation staff. The area bordered on France and the French occupiers tended to add even distant relatives to their immediate families. In addition to extracting legitimate reparations for damage done by the German invaders, the new overlords in this zone engaged in considerable black marketeering and other forms of exploitation. Yet because of centuries of proximity and consequent friction, the French understood better the psychological problems of the Germans than did the more distant British, Americans, and Russians.

— 4 —

The American Zone of Germany

*I had understood that the United States had a firm
policy to increase the industrial level in Germany
and to expedite its economic recovery to reduce the
cost to the American taxpayer, to help European
recovery, and to resist Communist penetration of
western Europe by providing a better atmosphere
for democracy to grow.*

General Lucius D. Clay
U.S. Military Governor of Germany
July 16, 1947

My journey from Paris to Frankfurt, headquarters of the military establishment in the American zone of Germany, covered about three hundred miles. Most of the trip must have occurred at night because my
diary notes begin with observations on the Saar Basin—that coal-rich
and controversial area in the French zone bordering France. One
could see the French flag on display and French army officers going
about their business.

This border area had suffered some destruction during the war, but
evidently the damage was not severe and some repairing was going
forward. Farming vehicles were being drawn by horses, and occasionally slow-moving oxen were straining at the yoke. As elsewhere
in Europe, a considerable number of women were laboring in the
fields. One American officer later remarked to me that such heavy
work, he believed, had resulted in the unusually high number of
hunchbacked children. The German laborers in evidence, many of
them with hard and downcast faces, seemed unusually thin, as might
have been expected in view of the critical shortages of food. On the
other hand, the children in this area did not appear to me to be in

exceptionally bad shape. Many had generous patches on their clothes, and one lad was shuffling about in a worn pair of oversized men's shoes.

At the huge and battered Frankfurt railway station, in which many homeless people still slept at night, I was greeted by two American Army officers who had been sent from the military headquarters. My bags were carried to our automobile by a gaunt and middle-aged German civilian who had possibly fought for Hitler. I asked my two-man reception committee about the propriety of tipping him, but was advised that this gesture of goodwill was unnecessary. Whether he was being paid by the Army or whether one was supposed to show only contempt for the fallen foe I never learned. In any event a tip in American money would have been of no use to him, although I did not know this at the time, but a few cigarettes would certainly have been welcomed.

While I was operating in or near Frankfurt, the Army put me up in style at the Victory Guest House on the outskirts of Frankfurt, at a charming village called Koenigstein, where the Very Important People (VIPs) stayed, including, I supposed, visiting Congressmen. This hostelry, small but elite, was a villa whose prewar ownership was unknown to me. It was equipped with modern conveniences, including a French-style douche bowl (bidet), and must have been expropriated by the Army from a wealthy German owner. One of my few fellow guests proved to be none other than Rita Hayworth, the beautiful and talented movie star. I assumed that she was there to entertain the troops, as other entertainers, including Bob Hope, were being scheduled to do. Miss Hayworth and I both ate some of our excellent meals in the small, Army-provisioned dining room, but I resisted the temptation to speak to her. My hosts told me that she was eminently agreeable, but she no doubt was being pestered enough by autograph hunters and name droppers.

When not on official business, I roamed about the tiny but picturesque village of Koenigstein, absorbing the atmosphere. The most conspicuous landmark was a thick-walled medieval castle, somewhat dilapidated but strategically located on a nearby hill, which commanded a stunning view of the red-roofed hamlet below. One evening, at about sunset, I was walking through the seemingly deserted village when a sudden burst of beautiful choral singing by young male voices arose from one of the buildings. Precisely where it came from remains a mystery, because it died away before I could investigate. It must have originated from thirty-or-so boys attending some kind of school located here. They served as a reminder that the prewar Germans loved singing, especially group singing with beer, and that they had a great musical tradition. But I wondered why, in the midst of all this hunger, destruction, and humiliation, anyone would want to sing, especially so harmoniously.

I had spent my own funds since leaving Washington, but upon arriving in Frankfurt "I never had it so good," as the current saying went. My excellent food and superb lodging cost me only ninety cents a day. I had at my disposal while on land a Chevrolet or other car, complete with driver, and while in the air I travelled in regulation Army aircraft.

Other necessities required only trifling sums. Haircuts in Frankfurt under Army auspices cost only twenty cents, and my shaggy locks needed attention at a local barber shop. American currency was not used in the American zone, presumably to combat the black market, and regulations required newcomers to exchange their dollars for scrip. (One resourceful major showed me a fifty-dollar bill that he had secretly stashed away in his wallet as "mad money.") As was then unknown to me, American cigarettes passed for small change, and I created something of a scene when I attempted to tip my German barber with scrip. He spurned it with various negative gestures and futile attempts at English, but I stupidly hastened away and left it on the counter. Subsequent inquiry revealed that it was illegal for him to use American scrip but that he would have appreciated a few cigarettes. Much of Germany was then on a cigarette-based economy.

An initial task at Frankfurt was to pay my respects to General Clarence R. Huebner, the commanding U.S. officer in the American zone of occupation and the former commander of the First Infantry Division invading France in 1944. At that time his distinguished military career was a blank to me, but I later heard him spoken of with admiration at the National War College.

At Huebner's headquarters I was ushered into a large room, at the far end of which the General sat at his desk, beside which, if memory serves me, stood a large American flag on a stand. I walked rather self-consciously across the room and shook hands with him, and he then motioned to a chair. He had been apprised of my coming, probably by General Gruenther in Washington, and he volunteered assurances of the VIP treatment I was already receiving. More than eighty members of Congress were to come through the American zone of Germany in the summer and fall of 1947, and my ego swelled slightly when I found myself bracketed with such exalted company.

My host was frank to say that the main purpose in occupying the non-Russian zones of Germany was to keep the Russians out, although

he attached much importance to continuing the process of denazification, which affected about one-third of the population. He was
confident that as long as one American soldier remained on German
soil the Soviets would refrain from committing a deliberately provocative overt act. American and British occupying troops, he felt, were
the best guarantees of peace, and hence American officers were not
suffering from a not-wanted complex, whatever the Germans might
think. General Huebner was not delighted with the naive lads being
sent over from the States as soldiers, but they were doing all right. At
all events, he would not keep one American soldier one day longer in
Germany than needed. I later learned from his officers that he had
greatly improved morale and discipline in the Army by heavy emphasis on drilling. He believed that there was no substitute for "combat
readiness."

General Huebner urged me to insert a paragraph in one of my forthcoming lectures at the National War College to the effect that every
officer in this complex new world should be a diplomatist. He found
the situation in Germany especially difficult to handle because of its
abnormality. Everyone seemed to be abnormal, from the DPs (displaced persons), to the demoralized Jewish survivors, to the defiant
ex-Nazis, to those drab and patched civilians who had tolerated or
actively favored the presence of the Nazis. He warned me that if I
interviewed Germans, the result would be as many different views as
there were interviewees. In his opinion the German civilians did not
look starved, but their caloric intake was so low that they seemed
listless. On full rations, he said, they could do a full day's work; on half
rations, one-tenth of a day's work.

In front of this huge headquarters building I witnessed an inspiring
sight near sundown. First there was an impressive parade of the
skirted WACs, and then the tiny force of several hundred soldiers and
their officers stood at proper attention as a gun was fired and the Stars
and Stripes was lowered against the backdrop of a gutted building. A
Negro band then struck up an appropriate air. My thoughts turned to
the hundreds of thousands of crack American troops who had fought
their way across France and Germany, and then had clamored with
success to come home at war's end. I marveled that this tiny force,
serving as a kind of tripping device, could be counted on to maintain
the peace at this spot in a humiliated and resentful Germany. Of
course, about 125,000 American troops were still stationed elsewhere
in the American zone and the American sector of Berlin.

Frankfurt did not seem so badly battered by Allied bombing as
anticipated or as I later witnessed in places like Berlin and Munich.

Smoldering Frankfurt station, March 30, 1945

(U. S. Army photograph)

But the damage was appalling enough: of about 177,000 houses, only 44,000 still stood. The imposing American headquarters were located in the huge I. G. Farben building, which had come through the war intact and which, according to rumor, had been deliberately spared by American bombers so that it could be used during the forthcoming occupation. I personally doubted that American strategists had looked this far ahead, but was later assured by an Air Force colonel at the National War College that they had done so. There were also disturbing tales in Frankfurt of selective immunity for buildings in which American dollars had been invested.

Most of the information I picked up in Frankfurt came from two majors and a colonel attached to general headquarters. One of the civilian officials invited me and the colonel to have lunch with him at his residence, and the shipped-in food was exceptionally tasty, even by the standards of the better eating places in the United States. Thinking to please my host, I remarked that the luncheon was "indecently good." I meant this in a complimentary spirit, but afterwards regretted having said it. There was no good reason why the few conquerors should go hungry because the conquered masses were desperately hungry or near starvation, but eating an abundance of superior food in this place at this time, even though it had necessarily been imported, gave me an uneasy feeling.

My store of information was increased by interviews with two Army majors. They regarded the too hasty demobilization of the American Army in Europe as one of the great blunders of the postwar era. They conceded that much of the pressure came from the "We Want Daddy Movement" at home, but they also blamed General Eisenhower for encouraging his soldiers to write "gripe letters" to the Army newspaper, *The Stars and Stripes*. Evidently the folks back in the States did not want their boys to be engaging in such menial tasks as waiting on tables in the occupied zone, and for this reason the Army was forced to employ such help as ex-Nazis and displaced Poles.

The Balts and Poles in particular presented a difficult problem. The former, once independent and then taken over by Stalin, had naturally fought with the Germans against the Russians, and consequently they could not go home again. The Poles were either released German prisoners of war, refugees, or expellees under the new order that at Yalta had guaranteed Stalin's title to roughly the eastern half of Poland. These uprooted people could not go home again either, and thousands of them served with the American forces. I often saw the lonely men of the Polish Guard in their black uniforms standing guard duty or otherwise engaged. General Huebner denied that they were mercenaries, but two of the subordinate American officers told me of their suspicions. Each Pole, they felt, was looking out for himself, as was not unnatural, and some were believed to be concealing a former intimate association with the German enemy.

Jews, or what Hitler's genocide had left of the Jewish population, greatly complicated the refugee problem. General Lucius D. Clay, U.S. Commandant in Berlin, estimated that about twenty thousand remained in Germany. American officers, alluding to anti-Semitism, remarked that if the Jews were not present in such numbers, the United States and other nations would probably accept a general quota of displaced persons. One American colonel told me bluntly, probably with some anti-Semitic bias, that the Jews could not get along with other people and consequently had to be put off somewhere by themselves.

The Jews had their own camps for displaced persons, one of which I was to visit later in the American zone. Unsympathetic sources in Frankfurt told me that the Jews were obtaining more calories than non-Jews, partly because they were operating a flourishing black market. They were also receiving packages of food from coreligionists in the United States and were even peddling some of these gifts clandestinely. The American headquarters in Frankfurt seemed fully aware of what was going on, but did not want to stir up Jewish or pro-Jewish Congressmen and others at home. The displaced Jews reputedly had their own espionage ring and, I was warned, would attack a visitor to one of their camps if they suspected him of spying on them. Some of these tales seemed incredible.

Another mistake, I heard in Frankfurt, was for the United States to send over so many black soldiers and then keep them in Europe so long. But nobody, the explanation ran, had the "guts" to speak out on this subject lest he stir up the antiracist "bleeding hearts" at home. In 1945 General Patton had remarked that the Nazis had formed a political party just like the Republicans and Democrats, or words to that effect, and as a result he was slapped down and shifted to a less conspicuous command.

White officers generally had a low regard for Negroes as combat troops, largely for the reason that many of the blacks had been assigned to commissary work. There they were in a position to steal food with which to buy the favors of the German girls. A few of the blacks had formally applied for permission to marry Germans, but the suspicion prevailed that these young women were merely scheming to escape war-torn Germany and move to America. Divorces could be secured there with relative ease. Somewhat the same story could be heard in England, where the girls had been urged to be nice to the visiting Yankee troops, whether white or black, and some of them had rather overdone the welcome.

A visitor to the American zone had to make allowance for white prejudices, particularly with respect to the allegation that oversexed Negroes had even lured women out of hospitals that were treating female patients for venereal disease. During my stay in Germany I had access to the services of several white and two black drivers. One of the whites remarked that the Negroes tended to their own business; one of the blacks indicated to me that he was dating a German girl.

On several occasions I had to stay overnight at one of the Army outposts, and my hosts expressed their displeasure that the people at headquarters were continuing to send out Negro drivers. The atmosphere sometimes became quite disagreeable. Evidently the accommodations were crowded and the white soldiers, especially those from the South, were unwilling to share their limited bed and board with blacks. The kind of integration ultimately established in the armed forces under President Truman was making only halting progress. My several black drivers were not as skilled as the white drivers, but I supposed that the Negroes had not been privileged to drive many cars in the States.

Primary objectives in the American zone of Germany were the five "ds": demilitarization, denazification, democratization, de-industrialization, and decartelization of the giant industries. The Germans were to be purged of Hitlerian ideology, and then the seeds of American democracy were to be planted, fertilized, and watered. This ambitious and onerous program was designed to turn Germany into a peaceful democracy that would stand as a bulwark against the aggressive and expansionist ideology and military might of Moscow. As subsequent events proved, the political goal ultimately achieved far greater success than many observers had reason to hope for in that dreary Marshall Plan summer of 1947.

High-quality leadership by Germans would have to be enlisted if all these objectives were to be achieved. But where could it be found? Hitler had already executed the several hundred anti-Nazi leaders involved in the bomb plot of July, 1940. The cream of German energy, talent, and enterprise had been attracted to the Nazis or had been coerced into their ranks. The United States itself had faced somewhat the same problem after its great Civil War, for most of the Southerners of enterprise and spirit had supported the Confederacy. Much of the reconstruction had to be carried forward by "whitewashed rebels" and other men of second-rate or third-rate capabilities.

The Russians, it became clear, had openly used second-drawer ex-

Nazis in their schemes from the first. Perhaps the Soviets felt that they could employ this knowledge to blackmail turncoat Germans into doing their bidding. The reasoning also seems to have been that Nazi totalitarianism could be changed easily into Communist totalitarianism through brainwashing. The British, for their part, were not too particular about past misdeeds. But the Americans were reluctant to permit ex-Nazis to hold responsible offices. The policy adopted was to allow them to fill such menial jobs as truck drivers and waiters but not to permit them to lord it over others. Even so, a few of them managed to wind up in highly responsible places. The American program of denazification inevitably led to a vast amount of unfairness, backstabbing, injustice, envy, and other forms of bitterness. A report was current that some anti-Nazis reacted by quietly becoming Nazis at heart.

One of the Army officers in Frankfurt told me that General Clay, the supreme American military commander in four-power Berlin, had initially tried the policy of being as friendly as possible to the Russians. He offered to let them enter the American zone of Berlin freely, but they refused on the grounds that they were forbidden to reciprocate. The Russians have traditionally been hesitant to accept favors without being able to return them.

At the end of the war the American authorities wanted to send some displaced persons to their Russian homes in surplus carrier planes. Moscow refused. The Americans assumed that the Soviets did not want their people to witness the contrast between the fine American aircraft and the ordinary Russians plodding to their homes on foot. My informants were also sure that the USSR wanted a depressed (and weak) Germany on its western border; too high a standard of living near the Russians might invite invidious comparisons between communism and democracy. Further, a depressed Germany would presumably be a more fertile field for Moscow's ideology. Actually, many of the Russian troops who had seen modern plumbing in Germany and Austria, to say nothing of other conveniences of a highly civilized society, were subjected to ideological "delousing" before they were allowed to return to their homes. A current explanation of changing attitudes was "The Red Army has seen Europe and Europe has seen the Red Army."

My sources were frank to confess that they did not know what the secretive Soviets were scheming in the Russian zone. But the Americans were sure that whatever the Russians were doing was antagonizing the Germans and spurring the creeping progress toward denazification and democracy. Among other disagreeable ploys, the Soviets were delaying for years the return of tens of thousands of

German prisoners of war. One colonel believed that the populace of Frankfurt was less friendly to the American occupiers than it was in Berlin, where the Russian presence presented a glaring contrast at first hand.

It was as obvious as the Rhine River that the most pressing problem of all was food for the hungry Germans, whatever their sins may have been under Hitler. Gnawing hunger knows no ideology or age. Democracy would have been difficult enough to teach to well-fed people, but to attempt to do so to those who could be thinking of little but their stomachs was uphill work. More than that, hunger invited the acceptance of Communism, because when people are driven to the desperation of starvation they will grasp at pie-in-the-sky promises.

Thus far, one could observe, Soviet propaganda had proved ineffective in the American zone; in fact, it had boomeranged. The Russians told too many lies, and the Germans were intelligent enough to see through them. In addition, this conquered people had heard too many tales from German occupants of the nearby Russian zone, directly or indirectly. The rumor was current that the Soviets may have deliberately driven various expellees from eastern Europe into western Germany with the intention of debasing the local population and making them more susceptible to the siren call of Communism. One of my informants said that he was quite willing to see the Soviets keep up their backfiring propaganda; another was not so sure. The Germans were a hungry people for whom almost anything would be better than the present situation, and they might be seduced. Their basic problem was that at this time they had no real hope for the future. A great ray of sunshine came nearly a year later, in June, 1948, when the occupying Allies instituted currency reform and permitted the Germans to enjoy a viable monetary system of their own. The Russians used this overdue reform as a pretext for inaugurating the crippling Berlin blockade.

Civilians on the streets of Frankfurt and elsewhere in Germany did not look at all well. The gray-faced older people and the small children alike showed visible signs of undernourishment. The personal appearance of the women was clearly worsened by the absence or shortage of the makeup that was currently in vogue in America. One even heard of instances in which gaunt civilian employees fainted at work because of hunger. The problem was not only one of calories but also one of prolonged malnutrition resulting from the desperate shortage of fats for some two years. Alarming reports had been coming in for many months of the large number of children in the British zone with swollen bellies caused by hunger edema. One of the numerous ironies was that these youngsters could not conceivably have had anything to do with the rise or rule of Hitler, yet they were suffering for his sins. The dismal thought occurred to me that a whole generation of undersized and even deformed children was growing up, as had happened during the Allied hunger blockade of Germany throughout World War I and after the Armistice of 1918.

An interesting example of an attempt to alleviate the food problem and also undercut the black market was the Barter Exchange in Frankfurt. There German civilians and GIs would line up with much junk, but also such personal valuables as paintings, dishes, and cameras. These items were exchanged for points that could be used to purchase coffee and cigarettes. Fifty points would buy a carton of cigarettes (worth a dollar and a half). I saw no Leica cameras being bartered, but was told that when one was presented it would fetch from eight hundred to twenty-three hundred points. The German women in line looked bedraggled and woebegone, and one of them glanced enviously at a well-dressed American woman, probably the well-housed and plump wife of an officer in the occupying forces. She may have been feeling a little "guilty" and somewhat "piggish," as one American wife in Berlin had put it some months earlier.

In another area, a visit to the University of Frankfurt provided a sobering illustration of the problems that confronted higher education in a denazified Germany. The physical plant was badly knocked down. The prewar library of about one million volumes had been destroyed, as well as about half the rooms. But this misfortune was not as severe as one might suppose, because before the war the university had enjoyed the luxury of considerably more space than it needed.

The rector of the University was a Professor Hallstein, a thin man in his forties with an intellectual face. As a former prisoner of war who had been taken to Rhode Island, he not only knew something of the United States but had been exposed to a course in democratization. He declared that the students now enrolled were superior, since they had been chosen from many unusually serious applicants. They generally did not want to go into politics, even though Germany was desperately in need of first-rate, non-Nazi minds in government. Professor Hallstein was attempting to attract exiled professors back, but without success; many chairs remained vacant because of Allied denazification and the disruption of war. Salaries were no problem because money—inflated paper currency—was one of the most plentiful items in a Germany that was short of about everything else.

A vexatious problem was the scarcity of printed materials. Foreign journals were difficult to obtain, primarily because of the monetary problems of foreign exchange. Textbooks were so scarce that students were forced to attend lectures to get the material that they had been able to derive from printed sources before the war. A further complication grew out of the ugly fact that because of inadequate diet there was much illness, with a consequent inability to attend the lectures. Professor Hallstein placed much hope in the Fulbright exchange, initiated a year earlier by the Fulbright Act of 1946. He could hardly have envisaged at that dreary time the magnitude and subsequent success of the Fulbright program, and I have since then regretted that neither of us could have peered this far into the future.

On Wednesday, July 2, pursuant to arrangements made for me by the Army officials, my black chauffeur called in a somewhat battered Chevrolet to drive me to Wiesbaden, some twenty miles west and south of Frankfurt. My objective was to visit the imposing American headquarters in that city and to make contact with a number of informed persons, mostly civilians associated in some way with the occupation of the American zone. Altogether I talked with eight or ten people, most of whom provided me with interesting insights.

At the outset I noticed that a considerable number of German girls were working at the headquarters of the American Military Government. They had all been carefully screened, with the result that no ex-Nazis were knowingly employed. The opinion was being voiced that they would suffer some ostracism from other Germans when the occupation ended; a few of them were actually being warned, "Just wait until the Americans go." But some of this adverse reaction was probably based more on envy than on a complete distaste for any collaboration with the former foe.

An American civilian journalist in charge of press relations detailed some of his difficulties. One of his problems was to familiarize German editors with the concept of a free press, already crushed to earth under Hitler. One of the many evil byproducts of Naziism was that the regimented masses were too prone to believe everything they saw in print. The Americans were imposing no censorship, with one exception: the Germans were not to criticize the occupying Allies adversely. The old Nazi newspaper establishments had suffered severely from aerial bombing, and the editors had to be screened carefully to determine the depth of their pro-Hitler sympathies. My American informant complained that German journals were too prone to present a full quotation without developing the proper background, and that all too often they served as the tools of the parties, as in France. The few struggling newspapers published mostly four-page affairs, like a single-sheet broadside folded over once, and the print was small and crowded.

In one important particular, this journalist remarked, the German newspaper accounts differed from the copy turned in by the American correspondents in Germany. The Germans published information that they judged to be of basic importance, while the American newsmen tended to be police-court types who stressed rapes and murders. A good headline story would be the killing of two innocent German civilians by some deranged and displaced Pole, for such lurid accounts were the result of pressures to turn in a quota of copy each week. A significant but dull development in German self-government would meanwhile pass by unnoticed.

At Wiesbaden the American official concerned with German education had some interesting information to impart. One pressing difficulty lay in procuring non-Nazi textbooks, owing partly to a glue bottleneck, but such printed materials were now beginning to flow in from Switzerland, both in English and in German. Teachers presented yet another problem. Many were overloaded with sixty or so pupils, and some were well past the statutory retirement age. Time would have to pass before a new and adequate crop of instructors could be trained, but there was some hope that this goal could eventually be reached. Teaching guaranteed more than ordinary job security. One unique problem related to the school lunch program. The children from the farms, where food was less scarce, did not urgently need it, while the underfed teachers, some of whom fainted on the job, could not stand the smell of food being eaten by others.

This American expert on education was working to modernize the German curriculum, but he had found that the teachers were too much wedded to traditional Teutonic ways. My own reaction was that this individual was wedded to a kind of progressive education that was better suited to the temperament of free-wheeling Americans than to that of the beaten Germans.

Of special interest were the reactions of a fellow historian and his wife, Professor and Mrs. Landin, who hailed from Ohio State University. He remarked that there was a tendency among the Germans to blame everything on the Americans, including the scarcity of food, the recent frigid winter, and the current dry summer. He pointed out that the clever thing to do, if a German national came from another zone, was for him to complain bitterly about the treatment of Germans in the other zones. This tactic provided the newcomer with a good scapegoat and ingratiated him with his new neighbors by making them feel better. I also learned that many Germans, especially ex-soldiers, had been in Russia as invaders and did not swallow the Communist line about superior industrialization and civilization under the Red regime.

The Landins, among others, reported that the Germans bitterly resented the occupation, as Americans would have, and as the ex-Confederates actually had after the Civil War. There was little direct sabotage, but Mrs. Landin had found mud and gravel in her gasoline tank. She agreed, however, that some mischievous child may have acted in response to motives that were unrelated to anti-Americanism.

Unrepentant Germans could not be convinced, Mrs. Landin observed, that Hitler had bombed Coventry in England; to them, all such accusations were Allied propaganda. Nor did this conquered people believe that Americans had electric toasters and refrigerators, as were advertised in various journals now circulating in Germany. High-caste Germans in particular looked down their noses at the United States. The Landins were entertained by a count who wanted to sell some jewels, and he was visibly angered when his valuables did not command the high prices he had anticipated.

Intimate details of the social and economic life of the American conquerors were frankly revealed by the Landins. The head of the household received a salary of $10,000, at a time when $8,000 was an excellent salary for a full professor back in the States. Yet the Landins could not live on this stipend. They were residing in the sixth best house in Wiesbaden, which had no doubt been requisitioned, and were paying $120 a month for it. On one occasion Mrs. Landin ran up bills totaling $190 to entertain one group of guests. And in preparing for them she was forced to stand in line, presumably at the Post Exchange, although she had received supplements from home.

The Landin house was so big that its mistress needed several servants, although she received an allowance for only one. One German housekeeper turned out to be a neurotic who spread fantastic tales; another came from such a good family that Mrs. Landin could not ask her to scrub floors. The conclusion was that a satisfactory servant was not easy to find among this conquered people. An ugly story going the rounds was that the American occupiers were taking butter and eggs from the mouths of the Germans. Actually these particular commodities were being brought in from Denmark, in line with the American policy of importing the supply of food needed by the occupiers.

What Mrs. Landin had to report contrasted sharply with a sensational article published some four months earlier in the best-selling *Saturday Evening Post* (February 15, 1947) entitled "An Army Wife Lives Very Soft—in Germany." I repeatedly heard indignant references to this exposé among the occupying employees of the American Military Government. The listed author of the article, who was stationed in Berlin as the wife of an Army Air Force captain, lived with her husband and two children in a nine-room house with three servants. She enjoyed ample quantities of the best food and plenty of coal, gas, and electricity—all for $225 a month. Such largesse enabled her to bank $300 a month of her husband's salary. She gained ten pounds while living on the fat of the land—that is, of foreign lands, for the choice cuts of meat she received seven days a week at about thirty-five cents a pound were all imported. But the requisitioned housing did come out of German hides; the former owner of the lucky flyer's house, or one like it, lived huddled on the concrete floor of a nearby garage. One German woman was heard to vow that she would hang herself if her home was not returned within a year.

After further visits in the American zone and also in the American sector of Berlin, I concluded that this fortunate magazine writer was more favored than most occupying wives, especially those with civilian status. Oddly enough, she mentioned none of the obvious drawbacks. But so much "embarrassing" plenty in the midst of such misery did seem a bit like rubbing in the defeat. Stock defenses were "They started it," and "They asked for it, didn't they?" Even the luxuriating flyer's wife wrote, "I keep wondering how this sort of occupation can teach them our brand of democracy."

During my Wiesbaden visit, Professor Landin was rather pessimistic about the future. Some of the best American administrators had already gone home, and he feared that the Russians would outlast the United States in Germany. In their zone they were reportedly feeding well those men who were engaged in heavy labor; in one place the Soviets had forced the local Burgermeister to conscript labor to repair the town hall. On the other hand, so an American major in Wiesbaden observed, the Americans in their zone were having scant success with the local farmers. These traditional German husbandmen bullheadedly refused to do what the American agricultural expert advised regarding the production of food, and as a result the foreigners, instead of the farmers, were being unfairly blamed for the acute shortages.

One of the highlights of my visit to Wiesbaden was a luncheon at the house of James R. Newman, a New York lawyer-educator, who was the leading civilian administrator in this area. Present were about seven grim-faced members of the German cabinet of Hesse, including the Minister President. Some of these men seemed to be sober and taciturn business men who succeeded admirably in covering up their inner feelings. Dr. Landin explained that the new constitution for this area had been threshed out at his house in about three weeks of sessions, and that the document had been floated through on a generous flood of liquor.

Newman evidently was handicapped as an administrator by not being able to speak German. But fortunately he had the services of an attractive young German woman as interpreter. She relayed to the stolid visitors Newman's instructions about how they should run their government under American democratic supervision, and she then repeated to him in English their solemn responses. One could only speculate about the thoughts that must have flitted through the minds of the conquered as the conqueror, who obviously did not know much about Germany, told them how to make democracy sprout in this inhospitable soil.

My observation has been that Americans, by temperament and background, have not revealed unusual talents for governing conquered peoples, whether Indians, Filipinos, Puerto Ricans, or Mexicans. By common report the British colonialists, who had centuries of experience in ruling the "natives," were doing the best job of the Big Four in administering their zone. Moreover, they had a vested interest in resurrecting Germany, for British policy in the generations before and after Napoleon had been to keep any one power, at this time the Soviet Union, from becoming dominant in neighboring Europe.

During the luncheon conference at Mr. Newman's house, much of the discussion turned to the problem of what to do with the hordes of hungry Germans fleeing from the adjoining Russian zone to the U.S. zone. They often came first to the British zone, and then headed south into the American, probably in the hope of finding more to eat. The Americans had adopted the policy of refusing to admit them because there was not enough food for those already present. Mr. Newman's German visitors recognized the seriousness of the dilemma: there was not enough food for the people already under foot, and even if there were, newcomers would flood in to take up the slack.

The German officials at this lunch seemed to be aware of the fact that harsh Soviet policies were driving people out of the Russian zone into the American zone. One of Mr. Newman's guests reported that he had seen papers being served on the Germans by the Russians for forced labor; either the victim would work for the Soviet occupiers, or a member of his family would be drafted. Elsewhere an American colonel expressed the view that there was something highly suspicious about this influx of other Germans into the U.S. zone. He wondered if many of these footloose people were not trained Communists being sent in by the Russians to stir up trouble.

One of my most poignant memories of this visit to Wiesbaden involved the human flotsam of displaced persons, who at full tide had numbered about five million in West Germany alone. Conspicuous among them were expellees from German-inhabited Poland, from Austria, and from the Sudetenland of Czechoslovakia. Forced to leave almost overnight with no more than fifty or sixty pounds of personal belongings, they were not wanted where they came from and they were not welcome when they arrived in Germany. Many of them had been forced into German homes, where they were sharing a stove with two other families, plus one clogged toilet. The Germans, so I was told, were not temperamentally fitted for such communal living, and much friction developed. The intruders had come with practically nothing, not even the tools of their trade, but they did have empty stomachs that only worsened the food problem. The American woman in charge of the DP section at Wiesbaden complained that these unfortunates were not getting the publicity they deserved.

A revealing experience was a trip to the Center for Displaced Persons near Wiesbaden. About two thousand persons were present, mostly Ukrainians and a sprinkling of so-called White Russians, all of them supposedly anti-Communist. Some ancient German barracks had evidently been utilized for their shelter, and each family lived in a single room. Their food intake each day was reported to be 2,000 calories, compared with the theoretical 1,550 for the Germans, and these DPs were actually receiving their full allowance; at least this was the report. A visitor could see them lining up in orderly fashion for their ration of bread, oatmeal, cheese, and coffee.

These luckless people were showing considerable signs of enterprise, partly no doubt because of their reasonably adequate diet. They seemed energetic and clean, as was attested by the rather disagreeable antiseptic odor that pervaded the atmosphere. As evidence of their industry one could see a shoe shop, a dressmaking establishment, a dental office, and a dispensary for drugs. One of the many problems was a shortage of raw materials that could be handcrafted into useful articles.

More impressive in some ways was the Jewish camp near Wiesbaden. An American major gratuitously advised me that there were two sides to the Jewish problem, but that one should always bear in mind the ordeal that these victims of Hitler's malice had suffered. They were not living in barracks, like the DPs, but in houses, with one family to a room, and they were permitting these buildings to fall into disrepair. They refused to work, because they understandably did not want to rebuild Germany after what Hitler had done to them. Also many were waiting for the Promised Land of Israel, which was to be launched the next year on a sea of bitterness by the United Nations. These Jews looked better fed than the Germans, but this seemed only just in view of what Hitler's genocidal sadists had done in attempting to achieve "the final solution."

Lingering anti-Semitism may have been partly responsible for tales that the Jewish traders were deeply involved in black-market activity. But in view of the fact that they were businessmen rather than farmers, one should not have been unduly surprised that some of them were eking out a living by under-the-counter methods. My American major guide remarked that there was truth in the charge circulating from the British zone that a conspiratorial Jewish ring was smuggling contraband items into the U.S. zone.

Like other visitors, we were taken on a guided tour of the recreational and religious facilities of this secluded Jewish camp. American dollars, whose source was not detailed, had financed a modest recreation room, where equipment for table tennis was in evidence. We also entered a Jewish synagogue, newly constructed with fresh-smelling lumber, that was most unpretentious. We removed our hats, as American gentiles customarily do in church, but then noticed to our embarrassment that the grey-bearded Jewish elders standing around were keeping their headgear on. We had no way of knowing whether they were taking offense.

Nearby stood a most impressive monument. It was a small, simple, squarish pile of red bricks erected, as the inscription stated, to the memory of the six million Jews murdered by Hitler and his sadistic fanatics in the "holocaust." Beside it, the pretentious Tomb of The Unknown Soldier at Arlington, Virginia, seemed relatively meaningless. Six million Jews, if lined up at arm's length, would stretch roughly from New York to Chicago.

Returning to my villa headquarters near Frankfurt, I had an opportunity to reflect on these recent experiences. A traveler in Germany was out of touch with the big daily newspapers, but the European edition of *The Stars and Stripes*, the official journal of the occupation forces in Europe, was available. On June 29, the day of my departure from France, it reported that General Eisenhower, who had recently accepted the presidency of Columbia University, had testified on June 28 before a Senate subcommittee. He had declared that the U.S. Army was "a poor second" to that of Russia and that Army planners did not "entirely exclude" the possibility of war in the next twelve months—that is, war with the USSR. The Chief of Staff had added to Eisenhower's testimony that war was not "a probability" but that all contingencies had to be anticipated. These statements do something to explain the rather uneasy feeling that the American officers in Germany felt toward the increasingly unfriendly Soviets.

As for the meeting of the Big Three foreign ministers in Paris on the proposed Marshall Plan, from June 28 to July 2, *The Stars and Stripes* considered this event front-page news. On July 2, the day before I left for the British zone of Germany, the Paris conference broke up in disagreement, as did so many top-level meetings with the Soviets. On the morrow, *The Stars and Stripes* published a banner headline: "RUSS STAND WRECKS BIG 3 AID PARLEY." The next day another banner headline proclaimed: "22 NATIONS CALLED TO EUROPE AID PARLEY." Germany was not invited, partly because that four-piece country was not again a sovereign nation, but readers were advised that the commanders of the four zones would be consulted about German needs. A visitor could testify that such necessities were overwhelming.

5

The British Zone of Germany

Those who fight Germans fight a stubborn and re-
sourceful foe, a foe in every way worthy of the doom
prepared for him.

Prime Minister Churchill
December 11, 1941

Early in the morning of July 3, my Army driver picked me up at the Victory Guest House and we headed north into the British zone of Germany. Our first stop was at Bad Oeynhausen, the British military headquarters, about 150 miles due north in the North Rhine area. From there we pushed on to Minden, and then turned left, continuing for about 115 miles southwest to much-bombed Düsseldorf. On the return trip we stopped at shattered Essen and Cologne, and touched on the outskirts of Bonn, Beethoven's birthplace. En route, revealing interviews were arranged with about twenty knowledgeable and co-operative people, most of them British civilians and military officials, including two generals and one brigadier. A few were U.S. officials and German administrators.

My Negro driver proved reasonably competent, although his color caused something of a problem when the time came to procure proper sleeping accommodations for him. I cut several hours off the end of this tour because he was impatient to return for a rendezvous with a friendly *Fräulein,* and to this end he apparently contrived to bring about a shortage of gasoline. My chief objection to him as a chauffeur was that he had developed the dangerous and noisy habit of relying more on his horn than on his brakes. He presumably derived satisfaction, even a sense of power, in forcing Hitler's once proud and racially conscious *Herrenvolk* to scramble out of his path as he blared his way down the thoroughfare.

Hitler's famous divided highways, known as autobahns and de-signed in part for military purposes, made for smooth driving. As we sped along we could see the large number of blown-up road bridges on either side of our route. Built of concrete, they all had neatly assumed a "V" shape, for obviously a charge of explosive had been placed near the middle of each and then methodically detonated to slow up the advancing Allies. Even footbridges over streams had not escaped Hitler's "scorched earth" policy. In addition, more than eight hundred railroad bridges had been destroyed, although I personally observed only a few of them. Occasionally one saw dead and rusting tanks pushed to one side of the road, for such was the waste of war.

Not much German traffic flowed on Hitler's autobahns, primarily because of the acute shortage of gasoline. On the highway, or stalled beside it, were a few automobiles of the Volkswagen type—also a lasting heritage from Hitler. They were being powered by some kind of substitute fuel, probably charcoal. It required a large, stove-like device that, judging from the number of immobile cars, did not oper-ate reliably.

The British representatives at their headquarters appeared to be unusually open and frank, partly because the administration of the American zone had recently been joined to that of the British zone to form a single economic unit, effective in January of the present year, 1947. This was a step of major importance, not only because it eased the heavy financial burden of the British but also because it led to the formation of what was called Bizone, or Bizonia. The merger in turn proved to be a giant step toward Trizonia (with the French zone), and then toward the Federal Republic of Germany in 1949 (West Germany), with its capital at the ancient Rhine city of Bonn.

Near Marburg, off the autobahn, a disagreeable incident occurred. The road was rather narrow and we had the misfortune to find ourselves behind a slow-moving truck that was hogging the center of the highway. My driver sounded his horn in the expectation that the larger vehicle would pull over and permit us to pass. But in spite of insistent blasts, or perhaps because of them, the truck held its position for perhaps as much as a mile. It finally veered to one side and we passed with a burst of speed. Looking out the rear window I noted that the driver, evidently a German civilian and possibly a former tank operator, was convulsed with laughter, as though he had perpetrated an immensely funny practical joke. I could not resist the impulse to shake my fist at him and go through the motions of recording the number of his truck in my pocket notebook. The prospect of his being reported to the conquerors of Germany may have had something to do with wiping the smile off his face. Incidentally, his was one of the few smiles that I saw in all of a gloomy, grim, and dispirited Germany.

British and American officers subsequently remarked to me that the Germans were the world's worst drivers. According to these biased sources, they lacked "road manners" and loved to lord it over others, Nazi-like, while behind the wheel. Before the war the German people had owned relatively few automobiles per capita, and consequently had not developed exceptional courtesy or expertise in maintaining or handling motor cars. A British expert on food later told me that hunger and malnutrition could affect coordination, especially when dizziness was involved.

Those American representatives who had to deal with the British, especially following the bizonal merger, spoke well of them. One colonel confided to me that the British were just like the Americans when a stranger penetrated their reserved exteriors. Even so, there was clearly not a complete absence of friction. The British occupiers had at first feared that the United States would run out on its obligations in Germany, but now they believed that Uncle Sam was so deeply involved that he simply could not extricate himself. How right they were.

The American colonel who had me in tow confessed that the United States was about as bad as the Soviet Union in agreeing to something in principle and then doing nothing. He said that his colleagues would invite the British to their zone, and they would come. But the Americans were always too busy to accept a return courtesy. The British had ceased issuing such invitations, evidently because they resented being regarded as poor relations who no longer counted. In England I had already noted some British feeling against the Yankees for their attitude of superiority toward a once-dominant world power that had fallen on evil days.

My escorting American colonel advised me to equate my VIP civilian rank with that of a major general when signing the register at the official hostelry that night. This high-flown designation is my only claim to military fame, though it was a hollow and transient one. At all events a British brigadier mistakenly thought me important enough to invite to a dinner with about eight other guests. The food was excellent and the wines, especially the champagne, were superb. Probably the cost matched the high quality of the cuisine, for my taciturn host scowled menacingly as he surveyed the bill. I assumed that he would not have to pay all of it out of his own pocket because, so my official escort reported, the British government, though badly pinched at home, was generous in keeping up appearances abroad. It had recently provided some $50,000 for the entertainment of the American forces of occupation. The total cost to the British of administering their zone was reported to be about $700 million annually; the cost to the Americans in their zone was about the same.

The wife of the hosting brigadier provided some interesting conversation, even though it was shocking. She remarked with some glee that she sat there in Germany and got fat; in fact she had gained a stone (fourteen pounds). While lying in bed in the morning, she would ring her bell and have the "damned German maid" step around for her. Why not? The Germans under Hitler had brought down on the British all the blackouts, bombings, killings, food shortages, and other inconveniences. Now let the "master race" suffer a bit. I could sympathize to some degree with her point of view, having recently visited bomb-blasted Britain, but the poor servant girl was obviously no more responsible for Adolf Hitler than I was for Franklin Roosevelt. The unfortunate impression created by this brigadier's wife was erased somewhat by the spouse of one of the generals; she made a point of giving surplus items, including dresses, to her German domestics.

Female German servants in the British zone were obviously not happy about their lot. The outspoken wife of the brigadier declared that there were no good ones, and I noticed that the British raised their voices sharply in rebuking them. There seemed to be little doubt that German civilians lost caste with their friends and neighbors if they worked for the conquerors. Some of the resulting bitterness was no doubt envy, because British employers paid in money and also in kind, including scarce items such as silk finery. Moreover, extra food was often more available in the employing household and hence represented a strong attraction to applicants for jobs. The British even employed ex-Nazis in various capacities, but no German civilians were knowingly allowed to enter the headquarters building.

German domestics were evidently satisfactory if an employer managed to get a good one. One British general spoke well of them, and referred to a German woman who was about to have a baby but was almost prostrated with the fear that she might be sent to the Russian zone. My own contacts with servant girls were severely limited. The British naturally exported some of their traditions to Germany, and I was agreeably surprised to be awakened in the morning by a sturdy but businesslike German girl who served me a cup of tea in bed.

My accommodations at Bad Oeynhausen in the British zone were quite comfortable and incredibly inexpensive; my notebook records the figure of two shillings a night, including breakfast. In Düsseldorf I stayed briefly at the York House, before which the Union Jack flew conspicuously on a tall mast. Formerly the Park Hotel, and reputedly the finest in the city, it is notorious in history as the place where Hitler had struck his ill-fated bargain with the industrial magnates of the Ruhr. They provided much of the financing that boosted him to dictatorial power, and he in turn permitted them to wax fat. My bill at the York House amounted to two shillings and sixpence for a fine suite with a sitting room, including twin feather beds, plus one breakfast, one dinner, and two sandwiches to take out for lunch.

On the appropriate day I was invited to an impressive Fourth of July party, under the auspices of a Colonel King, who was presumably the chief American liaison officer at the British headquarters in Bad Oeynhausen. The quantity and variety of refreshments, both solid and liquid, were amazing. After all the visible food shortages, I could hardly believe that my host had managed to assemble so many and such appetizing viands from outside hungry Germany. During the ceremonies at midnight the American flag was lowered and an orchestra (probably British) played the *Star-Spangled Banner* badly, although the musicians did much better with *God Save the King (America)*.

This gala affair was held out-of-doors in a festively lighted and attractive garden. The crowd included many young British army officers, most of whom probably had never heard of the glorious Fourth. But they quickly caught the spirit of the occasion and engaged in good-natured banter about George III and the Boston Tea Party. A reference to such defiance of law and order seemed to exhaust their knowledge of the American War for Independence. A barbed American response to such good-natured jollity was that the Yankees thought they had gotten rid of the British 171 years ago, but now Uncle Sam still had the ancient foe on his hands.

At this festive party, one young British officer made a disparaging remark about non-British officers in the army, and some embarrassment resulted when a listener, possibly of Polish background, overheard the jibe. Reference was also made to the spendid work that the soldiers from India had done in the recent war under the Union Jack. This praise rasped one of the British officers, who pointed out that the Indians had been led by white officers and supported by white troops. I sensed that there was considerable racial feeling in the British army.

In the British zone, as in the American, the desperate shortage of food was an overshadowing concern. The German people were literally half-starved, and generally had been in such a state for about two years, ever since the end of the war. In Düsseldorf, as in the industrialized Ruhr, the inhabitants presented a sickly yellow appearance, although they seemed healthier in the Cologne area. In the Ruhr one heard that the unmarried miners, with their larger rations for heavy work, were in passable shape, but the married miners had to share extra food with their families. In some cases their children came to the mines at noontime to get a snack. Renewed food riots had erupted a few weeks prior to my arrival; chalked on the sides of an underpass were these German words: *"Wir Wollen Keinen Kalorien—Wollen Brot"* (We do not want calories—we want bread).

Food rationing, with its lines and red tape, was not working well; if an office girl went for her ration, she was lost for much of the day. An added difficulty was a lack of community spirit. If the Germans could get food for themselves and their blood relatives, they seemed indifferent to the plight of their neighbors. Cases were reported of German children being sent to Switzerland to be fattened up; one of them reportedly gained ten pounds rather quickly. An American major told me of a stenographer who had taken her extra ration home to share with the family; the British ended that practice when they forced her to eat it on the spot.

As was only natural, many hate-filled Germans were inclined to blame wealthy Uncle Sam for their plight. They read in the daily press about the grain crops in America, and could easily conclude that if the Yankees could only show as much zeal in shipping over food as they had shown in shipping over tanks during the war, then the worst would be over.

A key to the food problem was the small-plot German farmer. If he owned only a few acres of wheat, two or three cows, and a small flock of chickens, he and his family would be self-sustaining in food, probably with some left over for black-market barter. Cows were being used in lieu of oxen to pull mowing machines and other relatively light farm equipment. One of the oddest sights in Germany was the spectacle of a cow and a horse yoked together.

The methods of the small German farmers were generally primitive; tractors were virtually unknown, and women were sent out into the fields to wield wooden rakes and other relatively clumsy tools. In the absence of commercial fertilizer, dung from horses and cows was highly prized; large manure piles in front of houses were a source of satisfaction, even a status symbol. Horse droppings were eagerly scraped up off the streets for fertilizer. Mixed with prized human excretions, the animal manure was taken out into the fields in barrel-shaped wagons and flung around with a long-handled dipper. The American GIs irreverently labeled these odiferous conveyances "honey wagons."

German farmers were producing food, but most of them flatly refused to turn in all their products for the low prices offered and the ruinously inflated paper currency available. Laws and machinery existed to force producers into line, but the local German officials were either unwilling or unable to crack the whip effectively. My British hosts were in agreement with Herbert Hoover, who reportedly had placed some blame on the self-serving German farmers for the critical food shortage.

The problem of hunger was complicated by the fact that even before the war Germany had been only 80 percent self-sufficient in the production of food. Of all four zones, that of the Soviets happened to be the richest in agriculture, and the Russians were keeping that food for their own purposes. One result was that the three non-Soviet zones now needed to import about 50 percent of their calories. Yet in the three-power Potsdam Protocol of 1945, the Soviets had agreed that "During the period of occupation Germany shall be treated as a single economic unit." The United States subsequently violated this principle by establishing currency reform in 1948 without Russian consent, but by that time previous Soviet infractions had rendered the Potsdam Protocol a dead letter.

German city dwellers somehow managed to live with the existing economic system. They would venture out to the farms, especially on Sundays, and barter for food with their more valuable personal possessions, such as jewelry and silverware. As a consequence of these forays, many Germans looked better fed than their limited caloric ration warranted. In one place people were out gleaning heads of grain dropped by the harvesters, and elsewhere the scroungers were picking wild berries or using sickles to gather what appeared to be rabbit food. Such excursions into the countryside were especially important in the sprawling Berlin area; they may in fact have spelled the difference between gnawing hunger and outright starvation.

From numerous sources in the British zone, one received mixed impressions about the denazification and democratization of Germany. When the British troops first arrived, they found the populace sullen and bitter, yet dazed and docile, somewhat like leaderless sheep. Perhaps the *Herrenvolk* rejoiced inwardly over being reconstructed by the British rather than by the vengeful Russians. The occupying officers remarked that they were able to preserve order with fewer troops than they had anticipated. One was reminded anew of the ancient saying, used by Winston Churchill during the war, that "The Hun is always either at your throat or at your feet." A British major remarked in my hearing that if you gave a German an inch, he would quickly grow insolent and take a foot.

In the British zone, as in the American, the poison of Naziism was being purged with inevitable injustice and inequities. Many Nazis, even those who had joined the party under duress and had behaved reasonably well, suffered punishments of various kinds. On the other hand, some of the more militant Nazis had escaped the Allied dragnet and were even awarded positions of considerable power and prestige. Such miscarriages of justice did nothing to remove the resentment and rancor of the vanquished. Slogans of 1945 still current in the British and American zones were: "Once a Nazi, always a Nazi" and "They are all Nazis." Some Germans were so badly handled that they secretly reverted to Naziism and became renazified.

German war criminals, declared my sources, were receiving fair trials, at least by British standards of justice, and at least some of the former foes were thought to be aware of their good fortune. A case in point involved a village of about 850 persons, some 500 of whom had been killed by Allied bombers. The townsfolk were being tried for having murdered a shot-down parachutist, possibly with their pitch-forks. Also, one place to the north had been demolished, and the survivors grimly resented their fate because this area had strongly opposed Hitler's initial attack on Poland.

Fear of armed resistance by the Germans was not completely absent among these British overlords, for many hidden arms were still un-reported. About two million German troops had been demobilized in the British zone, but only five hundred thousand rifles had been sur-rendered. A few minor incidents had already occurred involving civil-ians and British troops. At first the Germans had engaged in minor sabotage by deliberately misdirecting the road signs and giving out false information to inquiring travelers. But that time had passed. Yet the British officials dared not leave their houses unoccupied and un-guarded, for the premises were liable to be raided by Germans for cigarettes, whiskey, and even furniture. The capture of such looters was not easy, but it was facilitated by the cooperation of the people. Encouraged to inform on one another under Hitler, some would turn state's evidence in the hope of a job or some other reward from the occupying forces.

Despite such grave obstacles, denazification was proceeding with some success in the British zone. Progress toward democracy was being achieved, one British general reported, although the Germans were not taking to it like penguins to water. He believed that the Americans were inclined to throw the defeated into the depths too soon and that the Hitlerian leaders were being discredited, not so much because they had started and prosecuted the war but because they had lost it. Losing was the great crime, and few Germans would admit to having been aggressive Nazis.

A British general from Lübeck, on the Baltic Sea, remarked that the iron-fisted policy of unconditional surrender had not worked out well.

German civilians were arguing that since they had been denied a
negotiated surrender, they had been forced to throw themselves on
the mercy of the victor. They felt that the duties of feeding and governing them had clearly passed out of their hands into those of their
conquerors. Many of the early Allied advocates of unconditional surrender had not looked that far down the road, for total victory spelled
total responsibility.

As for the future, the British officers left me with the impression that
they were sitting on a powder keg. No one could foresee what would
happen when the Germans became uncontrollably desperate. German youths now in their teens would remember that they had eaten
well under Hitler, and they would probably react accordingly. Fear
was expressed about the generation between the ages of twenty-five
and thirty-five; some attempt would have to be made to reach them
through adult education, including the retraining of older teachers.

One British view was that the Germans would resort to war for a
third time in the century if given the chance; the strongest deterrent
was the chilling possibility of a sweep westward by the Russian colossus to the east. Anticipating this dire eventuality, the occupiers were
earmarking available transportation for their own women and children. At a lunch in Düsseldorf, a British colonel and two journalists
expressed the additional fear that if and when the Soviet hordes
poured in, the Americans could not be relied on to stand and fight.

In later years so-called revisionist historians, many of whom were
not adults when all this was happening, were to insist that there was
no likelihood whatever of Soviet armed aggression. Perhaps there was
not, but it should be noted that the aggressive conduct of the Soviets
since the victory in Europe had inspired great fear, especially among
those Britons and Germans living in the path of a prospective thrust to
the Channel by the Russian juggernaut. Some weeks later, a high-
ranking general at the National War College told me that the high
command in Washington was much concerned with making plans for
evacuating Germany if the dam should break.

German militarism, allegedly absorbed with mothers' milk, was also
a current but less immediate source of worry. Critics of Germany
pointed out that even the children in school and at play seemed too
docile, too well-behaved, too orderly, too rigidly disciplined, too help-
less while on their own. Youngsters at parties seemed strangely quiet,
possibly awed by the abundance of the occupiers' food. I had earlier
noticed a game being played near the Victory Guest House on the
outskirts of Frankfurt. The participants would line up in semimilitary
formation, and at a command would jump either right or left. If they
moved prematurely, they were disqualified. Everywhere one heard

of the German love of uniforms and of marching, all of which had reached a goose-stepping climax under Hitler. When Britons went for a walk in the country, as one of them observed, they often walked alone; when Germans went for a walk, they proceeded in a gang.

The victorious Allies had put a damper on German militarism and nationalism by breaking Germany into four zones and Berlin into four sectors. In addition, the Poles and the Russians had chopped off large annexations from Hitler's Reich in the east. Such divisions and mutilations were designed as bulwarks against the threat of a united, militarized, and aggressive Germany in the predictable future. In this respect the Soviets and the Western Allies were in agreement from the outset.

Fears of a Russian invasion westward were deepened by the lack of cooperation shown by the Soviets in implementing the zonal agreements. The barbed-wire fence on the western reaches of their zone was relatively easy to penetrate, and many Germans were fleeing from Russian overlordship to the British or American jurisdiction. The influx of these starving people gravely worsened the already desperate food situation, for the number of calories to be rationed per capita went down proportionately. The Russians had also been coming into the U.S. zone in search of reparations and other loot. My American informants confided to me that after the Allies had printed German military marks, the Russians had agreed to use them if a duplicate set of plates was provided. Much confusion was created when the Soviets ran off millions of dollars in such marks without ever rendering an accounting, although they had agreed to do so.

A further report on the progress of democratization in the British zone came from an interview with the German Minister of Education in Düsseldorf. Upon being ousted by the Nazis in 1933, he had retired to read books. He conceded that the worst problem lay in the bad effect of Hitlerism, which had rolled back liberal currents in the schools. He was certain that despite the existence of a long and deep-seated military tradition, the democratic spirit was indigenous in Germany, as seen in the developments of local government and labor unions.

As we were leaving this office of education, one of the functionaries present took me to one side and, without my solicitation, gave me a vivid lecture on the German national character. He turned out to be an Englishman who had lived for many years in Germany and who spoke the language fluently. With great earnestness and precision he related to me that he had lost two sons in the war—I presume on the German side—and that he knew the German character like an open book. He had escaped the Gestapo, he said, by ten minutes.

The Germans, this British expatriate felt, were an honest and decent people, but many had been forced into the Nazi camp to protect businesses or families. Even so, they had a cruel streak (like the Scots) that was accentuated by Naziism. He believed that German atrocities had been greatly downplayed. Before Hitler took over, the people did not inform on one another, but the Nazis turned them into paid informers. They loved to put on a uniform and buckle on a sword—to give commands and see them obeyed with clicking heels. Echoing Rudyard Kipling's observation that the female is the deadlier of the species, he declared that the German women were largely responsible for what had happened, because they trained their children from the cradle to adapt themselves to militarism.

My own observation has been that glib generalizations about national character, especially those involving racially and culturally mixed peoples, are suspect. The myth of inborn and ingrained German militarism, of infants who goose-stepped out of the cradle, was not borne out by subsequent events. When the victorious Western Allies tried to induce a defeated Germany to arm itself against a menacing Russia, they encountered an alarming reluctance among the young Germans to don uniforms and shoulder rifles as their fathers had. Despite the dehumanizing mesmerism of Hitler, my brief observations provided abundant evidence that basically the Germans were human beings, not radically different from the other peoples of northern and western Europe.

Bombed-out schools in the British zone, as in the American, presented a dreary picture. In some places the damage to buildings and libraries required pupils to attend in shifts, despite shattered windows and gaping holes in roofs. The maximum time allowed in many of these schools was about two hours, and this meant that the children were receiving a half-time education or less. There were shortages not only of space but also of teachers and textbooks. Shoes were in short supply and fuel was desperately scarce, ironically in or near one of the world's richest coal deposits. A partial and pathetic solution of the problem during the recent savage winter was to have each child bring a lump of coal to school so that enough would be available to reduce shivering for a couple of hours. The British had introduced hot lunches of soup and bread, which added up to about three hundred calories daily per pupil.

A few undernourished teachers were burdened with almost impossible loads. As many as sixty to seventy pupils were assigned to a single instructor, and in one case seventy-five were enrolled. Tales were prevalent of teachers who had fainted in their classrooms, presumably because of malnutrition, hunger, and fatigue.

British authorities were hopeful of some progress in teaching democracy, while conceding that the schools might have to be closed during the forthcoming winter. Like a lingering disease, the influence of Naziism persisted, conspicuously in the textbooks. One arithmetic manual posed this problem: "If a Jewish shopkeeper asks 4.50 marks for a vase worth only 3.75 marks, by how much has he swindled his customer?" A history text on World War of 1914–1918 concluded: "Towards the end of 1918 the German Army came home after more than four years of fighting, victorious on all battlefields of Europe and Asia, but still not as a victor." Ironically, after the Confederacy lost the Civil War in 1865, Southern textbooks did much the same thing.

My impressions of the German children were quite favorable, despite the sad state of the schools and the grim statistics on the rising rate of tuberculosis among the youth, to mention only one affliction. Youngsters were actively at play in the streets and on the playgrounds, where they gave noisy evidence of enough caloric energy to stir about. My itinerary took me through the Düsseldorf-Cologne area on a Sunday, where I noticed a large number of people on their way to church. Carrying their Bibles and decked out in such finery as had survived wartime devastation, they evidently retained some faith in a God that had permitted such hellish things to happen to them. The accompanying children seemed well scrubbed and smartly dressed, some of them like little Lord Fauntleroys.

Near Düsseldorf trucks passed by filled with chattering children displaying banners. Packed in like sardines, they were standing and swaying with the movements of the vehicles. Probably they were the beneficiaries of a British-sponsored democratization of the Hitler youth movement. The Americans in their zone had inaugurated a German Youth Assistance program, which embraced six hundred thousand boys and girls at its peak and was coordinated with other German movements of a similar nature. General Lucius D. Clay records in his *Decision in Germany* (1950) that the Soviet Marshal Sokolovsky, speaking in the Allied Control Council in Berlin, accused the Americans of teaching German boys baseball to keep alive their military spirit.

For the women of occupied Germany, life—or rather existence— was undoubtedly rugged. Oftentimes they were to be seen laboring in the fields beside beasts of burden. The women in the cities were better dressed, even better than one would have expected after seeing the heaps of rubble that had once been their homes. Standards of cleanliness had obviously deteriorated. Soap was in painfully short supply, as one quickly discovered when there were German women (and men) in the room or in the automobile. In one place, a German-operated public building, there was a complete absence of toilet paper. This widespread deficiency was all the more disagreeable because the food and water in Germany caused a high incidence of a common intestinal affliction known in Army circles as "the GIs."

Despite various discouragements, there was considerable contact with the German civilians, especially the younger women, in the American and British zones. The ban on fraternization had been lifted for all areas as early as September, 1945. The British officials were keenly aware of the temptations to which their young soldiers and others were subjected as occupiers. Many hungry females would do almost anything for a few cigarettes or candy bars; and the rate of venereal disease among these occupying troops was distressingly high. There were some marriages, but such unions were discouraged by the short tours of military duty, prolonged waiting periods, and precautions against disease. I was not surprised to learn that three-fourths of the German girls marrying British soldiers were pregnant; in fact, the presumption was that they had deliberately chosen to have babies as a means of escaping from their blighted land. Many of the same problems with German girls existed in American jurisdictions.

In another field of endeavor, the German newspapers were faring reasonably well under British auspices. At first the paper shortage was desperate, but now the daily journals were appearing twice weekly, some of them boasting four pages. A prominent German editor told me that paper was being allotted on the basis of party, and that the Communists had expanded their quota from 9 percent to 14 percent. He rather apologized for devoting so much newsprint to food shortages, but he explained that this subject was closest to the people's hearts—and stomachs. He also volunteered the surprising information that the German masses were or had been quite skeptical of Hitler's big lies.

At a different level, British military officials had informed me that the German press was freer under their auspices than it was in any of the other three zones, and the German editor agreed. One Communist paper had suffered suppression, to the accompaniment of shrill objections. Among its alleged sins, it had harped incessantly on the evil intentions of Uncle Sam. A British brigadier also reported that there was much ill-informed comment about the Allied occupation in the newspapers of Great Britain. These inaccurate or exaggerated commentaries fell into the hands of the Germans, as might have been anticipated, and did much harm. The Americans, I had already learned, were confronted with a similar problem with regard to their home press, especially stories that stressed the theme, "We never had it so good." Taxpayers in the United States were annoyed; the German people were resentful.

In the British zone, as in the American, my informants reported that some factories of giants such as General Motors and Ford had apparently escaped severe bombing or any bombing. The Russians were spreading tales, doubtless false or exaggerated, that the American capitalists had deliberately looked to their own investments rather than to the goal of defeating Germany. I also heard that Hermann Goering's plant, large enough to employ some twenty-five thousand workers, had escaped unscathed. It was of recent construction, and the Allies reportedly did not know it was there, especially since it was protected by elaborate smoke screens.

Many factories in truth had proved to be difficult targets to knock out, partly because of concrete shields erected around the patched-up machinery. They were also protected by dispersal and effective camouflaging. One of the most amazing aspects of the war was the capacity of presumably destroyed plants to turn out twenty-five or so tanks a day apiece. Near Minden, one report ran, an underground factory had escaped the bombers altogether. Postwar figures proved that the bombing alone had not brought Germany to her knees: cities and towns were flattened, but metallurgy suffered only 10 percent plant destruction, chemicals only 10 to 15 percent, and engineering only 15 to 20 percent.

Havoc inflicted by Allied bombers, both British and American, was as frightful in the area from Essen to Cologne as any that I was to observe in Germany. The Germans, though traditionally doers, had been slow to clear the rubble out of the streets, but by now had made substantial progress. One reason for the early apathy was a feeling that a war between Russia and the Western Allies impended, and that there was no point in rebuilding structures that would soon be blasted into rubble again. The Americans and British were not alone in fearing a Russian assault. Incredibly wrecked were the famous arms-producing factories at Essen, which had been a particular target of Allied bombardiers. I was certain that not a soul could be living at this spot until a ray of light beamed out from a hole, possibly a cellar, over which slabs of concrete had fallen.

At Essen, in the once-smiling Ruhr Valley, I inspected the heart of the famed Krupp steel works. From the top of what was left of a seven-story Krupp building, one could survey the tangle of metal that had once been a famous, even notorious, industrial complex. Also revealing was a conducted tour through the palatial Villa Hügel, the home of the Krupp dynasty and a famous showplace. Among its other reputed wonders was the third largest carpet in the world, as well as majestic rooms, including the enormous bedroom in which the twin villains, Kaiser Wilhelm II and Hitler, had slept.

The crucial coal industry of the Ruhr, at first a heavy liability to the occupying British, was struggling to get back on its feet as the summer lengthened and memories of the past arctic winter faded. Production in mid-1947 was about half of what it had been during the last full year before Hitler invaded Poland. Manpower had been depleted by the war, and those men who wanted to work were so poorly fed that there was much absenteeism. Those who did report were unable to produce up to capacity, although they received a higher caloric ration than white-collar workers.

Unfortunately for the Ruhr, economic problems were complicated by political maneuvering. One of the British administrators confided to me that there had been considerable friction between the Americans and the British over the operation of the mines. The socialist Labour government in London wanted them nationalized, in line with the nationalization of Britain's own coal industry in 1946, but the "capitalistic" United States was able to sidetrack this radical scheme. In American circles there was a feeling that the British had managed the German mines badly.

From the beginning, the Ruhr coal-steel complex had been a major bone of international contention. The Russians had wanted a large hand in its control and exploitation, and here they failed. They bluntly accused the American and British experts of trying to revive Hitlerian cartels, although in a sense all Russia was a giant cartel. The French for their part were adamant against an unrestricted return of the Ruhr to the same type of industrialists who had backed Hitler and who had built the powerful German war machine in the last two world wars. On the other hand, the recovery of this vital industrial center was tied in with the economic recovery of all western Europe. A former German industrialist complained to me that the British were deliberately delaying the recovery of Germany by pursuing their own goals.

As events turned out, the Ruhr was largely British dominated from 1945 to 1949, when the International Ruhr Control Authority was established by agreement among the Western powers, with its headquarters at Düsseldorf. Its major aims were to allocate Ruhr products and to guard against the revival of German war industry. In 1952 the multipower authority was disbanded with the removal of all restrictions on German industry, preparatory to the emergence of a sovereign Federal Republic of [West] Germany in 1954–1955.

Cologne Cathedral, April 28, 1945

(U. S. Army photograph)

South of the Ruhr, Cologne had suffered frightful destruction. The famed Gothic cathedral, whose two sky-piercing spires could be seen for many miles, had suffered considerable damage, but it was being painstakingly repaired. The Allies had not embarked upon a policy of bombing cathedrals, despite the damage the Germans had deliberately inflicted on the historic British cathedral at Coventry in 1940. But the proximity of the Cologne edifice to the key railroad yards, which were also hit, virtually guaranteed that this famous landmark would not escape unscathed. There probably was no real danger at this late date of a visiting American being roughly handled by a crowd of vengeful Germans, but we took the precaution of not getting out of the car when we stopped for a look. While driving through Cologne I chanced to see smoke coming out of a pile of rubble, and concluded, since this was summer, that someone was cooking a meager meal, perhaps in a cellar, from scraps salvaged from a British garbage can—a frequent occurrence in the occupied areas.

Before returning to the American zone, I gathered further evidence that one of the greatest obstacles to German economic recovery was the uncertain state of the depreciated currency. In the British zone at this time, one cent of American money on the black market would buy a twenty-cent mark. Cigarettes served as a currency of sorts. In the British zone one of them was reckoned to be worth about a twenty-cent mark. At Minden, north of Bad Oeynhausen, an American civilian complained of having been overcharged by a shoemaker when he was required to pay five cigarettes for a pair of heels. An American colonel, the one who had me in charge, reported that he could not persuade a tailor to make a suit for him unless he offered a bribe of cigarettes, and then the job would be done with surprising speed. The same was true if one needed a technician to repair a refrigerator.

The British were less favored than their American colleagues; they received only ninety cigarettes a week compared to about two hundred for the Americans. A German youngster near Bonn gave us directions at our request and then asked for a cigarette as a reward. An American in Bremen, the American seaport enclave in the British zone, had organized the children to play but had been fired. His sin was that he arranged for his pupils to carry banners proclaiming, "Don't Make Beggars of Us."

Such were some of my recorded gleanings in the British zone as my driver picked up my few belongings and we headed back to our headquarters in the American zone on July 7, 1947. Representatives of the sixteen accepting nations—twenty-two received invitations—were simultaneously preparing for the Paris Conference on the so-called Marshall Plan, to be held July 12–15. The delegates duly met, without Soviet sabotage, and appointed a sixteen-member committee. Its labors, as we shall note, would represent another giant step in the fruition of the historic Marshall Proposal.

One conclusion was meanwhile inescapable. Divided Germany—a gigantic slum—was in such desperate shape economically that she threatened to pull down with her into bankruptcy all the major nations of western Europe. Dollars for the Marshall Proposal would have to be rushed to the rescue, and fast, even to the ex-enemy Germans. They finally came to Germany in the amount of $1.39 billion spread over the four years 1948–1952, but no funds were allocated to the Russian zone or Soviet sector of Berlin. So it was that the former German foe fared better than America's wartime Russian ally, which had spurned imperialism-tainted Yankee dollars. The sum poured out to truncated West Germany ranked only below the outlays that were made available to Britain, France, and Italy, in that order.

6

Four-Sectored Berlin

*We cannot and we must not take the risk of losing
western Germany and having all of Germany become a satellite or even an ally of the USSR.*

General Lucius D. Clay
Nov. 3, 1947

On a glorious seventh of July our plane took off from an airfield near
Frankfurt for the hot spot known as Berlin, some 275 miles distant.
The somewhat battered Army airplane, a twin-engine C-47, was
scheduled for regular flights on this direct route through the Soviet air
corridor to the isolated city. We were all required to don parachutes,
presumably because of engine failures in the past, and this announcement evoked audible protests from the women passengers, who were
probably the wives of officers. Amid considerable confusion they retired to a crowded restroom to exchange dresses for trousers so that
they could fasten the bottom strap of the safety contraption. On the
numerous other flights that I took on this summer odyssey, parachutes
were not obligatory, and fortunately so, because I probably would
have been too petrified in an emergency to jump out and jerk the rip
cord. Most of our flight spanned the Soviet zone of Germany, and an
added hazard was the prospect that the ever-suspicious Russians
might imprison parachuting Americans as spies.

I caught my first bird's-eye view of Germany from this airplane, and
the view proved to be almost breathtaking in its beauty. The countryside was emerald green; the roofs of the dwellings were russet red;
and the small, one-family farms were cut into neat squares or rectan-
gles that resembled a gigantic checkerboard. I was reminded of an
observation that I had heard in Frankfurt from an American Army

officer. He wondered why the German people, blessed with such an enchanting country, could not settle down in it and live in peace.

At this time, pursuant to the basic arrangements made at the Yalta Conference and confirmed at Potsdam in 1945, Germany was sliced into four zones. Deep in the Russian portion lay the city of Berlin, itself carved into four sectors. This compromise arrangement was so clumsy as to be a sure-fire guarantee of friction, and friction certainly did develop in full measure. Someone cleverly remarked that Berlin resembled four pieces of pie lying on a Red tablecloth.

Fortunately for the Western Allies, Berlin's main airport, Tempelhof, lay in the American sector of Berlin. As we circled and then descended for a landing, I noticed that the field seemed more closely hemmed in by buildings than most airports I had previously encountered. The next year, when the Soviets cut off all access to Berlin by water and land, the Allies responded with their gigantic airlift. One could only marvel that this "Operation Vittles" could be sustained with so few casualties in such a cramped airport, especially in all kinds of around-the-clock weather. The Russians must have been similarly impressed.

Upon landing I was driven in an Army car to the Wannsee Club on the shores of serene Lake Wannsee, on the opposite side of which lay historic Potsdam. My quarters proved to be pretentious, including the feather beds, for the place reputedly had housed Walther Funk, Hitler's Minister of the Economy from 1936 on.* The rumor was that the invading Russians had stabled their horses in an outer clubhouse once used for the press.

Battered Berlin, which was about three-fourths destroyed, fully lived up to its billing as the biggest rubble heap in the world. Estimates were that the task of cleaning up would take two hundred men forty years. An unknown number of dead lay entombed beneath the piles of broken brick and twisted steel, all of which served as macabre gravestones. Occasionally one saw a wooden cross on a pile of debris with the name or names of the presumed deceased nailed on, sometimes accompanied by a few pathetic flowers. Even Hitler's Germans had loved ones, including innocent children.

Aside from the saturation bombing by the Allies, the vengeful Russians had inflicted terrible destruction when they fought their way into the city, house by house. The outskirts had fared somewhat better. Some of the worst wreckage had already been carted away, but

---

*Funk was condemned to life imprisonment by the Nuremberg Tribunal in 1946 but was released in 1947 because of poor health.

there were enough ruins left two years after Berlin surrendered to give the impression of a nightmare. Key parts of the blasted city lay in the Soviet sector, in which the front of the wrecked Adlon Hotel displayed a huge idealized portrait of Comrade Stalin.

Conspicuous among the gutted and twisted buildings stood what was left of Hitler's once-magnificent Reichschancellery, in the Russian sector. Its front was horribly damaged; its interior was a mass of broken stones, mosaics, and other debris. The palatial marble floors had escaped virtually intact, but the Russians were then busily quarrying and removing the slabs, with the obvious intention of shipping them back to Russia under the category of reparations. Scattered about were many pages of neatly mimeographed documents, clearly of a routine nature and connected with some phase of Hitler's government. I picked up and kept a few of these sheets as souvenirs, greatly surprised that they should be lying there more than two years after the surrender.

Brandenburger Gate, Berlin, July 7, 1945

(U. S. Army photograph)

A stone's throw from the Reichschancellery the visitor could see the unimpressive entrance to the burned-out underground bunker where Hitler had spent his last moments with his mistress, Eva Braun, whom he married only hours before they both committed suicide. One would want no better support for the scriptural admonition that those who take to the sword shall perish by the sword, but usually not in such a flaming Wagnerian *Götterdämmerung*.

Nearby nakedly loomed the scorched Reichstag building, which Hitler had allegedly burned in 1933 so that he could saddle the Communists with responsibility for this act of sabotage. Not far from the charred Reichschancellery stood a monument that the Russians had erected to their millions of dead in World War II, the great bulk of them killed by the Germans. An estimated one hundred thousand Soviet soldiers had lost their lives in the furious Battle of Berlin. This fact alone partly accounts for the subsequent orgy of rape and pillaging by the Russians, as well as their feeling that they had a better right to be in Berlin than the Americans, the British, and especially the French. France had not only succumbed to Hitler but a large area of the country had openly collaborated with him.

During my week in Berlin I managed to interview about twenty-five knowledgeable people, mostly Army officers but also German and American civilians who were involved with education, religion, journalism, or business. I saw a number of uniformed Russian officers and men walking about, and can testify that they looked and acted like human beings, not ogres. But they seemed solemn and reserved, as though they feared punishment from Moscow if they made the wrong move. The Russian soldiers in their own sector, wearing their traditional boots and conventionally armed, seemed to be tending strictly to business.

Outward forms of social harmony were being preserved, notably at official gatherings, one of which I was privileged to attend. After a session of the four-power Allied Coordinating Committee, which was a trilingual affair conducted through interpreters, the Soviets served refreshments. It happened to be their turn, and they went overboard in laying out an impressive spread of caviar, ice cream, champagne, and vodka. My Army guide remarked that the Russians were especially good at this kind of thing; they would put on a great show even if their own people were starving, to say nothing of the Germans around them. When the British entertained with refreshments, the pickings were much thinner.

At this lavish affair, I noted the presence of an attractive Russian girl, probably an interpreter, and was tempted to approach her in the hope of learning something. But I finally backed off, thinking that she might not be there the next day if her suspicious employers saw her fraternizing with an American. From what I learned later, this conclusion was fully warranted.

Especially impressive was an opera staged by the Russians deep in the Soviet sector, obviously with some or all German performers. The Army car that took me there developed some radiator trouble, but fortunately managed to hiss along; otherwise we might have been jailed by the Soviets as American spies. The Russians traditionally enjoy grand opera, and they probably wanted to impress their critical allies, if not the fallen foe, by putting on a spectacular display testifying to their devotion to culture.

On this operatic occasion the presentation was *Sadko,* which featured the well-known "Song of India." Appropriately, the composer was the Russian Rimsky-Korsakov, who had drawn inspiration from an old Novgorod trading song. Although not an opera buff, I was greatly impressed. The costumes were glittering and the voices were of high quality. As a visible reminder of the current food shortages, the scantily-clad female performers revealed ribs that in ordinary times would have been covered with flesh—or at least more flesh. During the intermission, Russian officers with military caps in place wandered around the outer edges of the hall munching sandwiches, as I assumed they would have done at home.

Berlin happened to be the one place where intimate physical contact with the Soviets had caused a disturbing degree of friction, and one of my primary concerns there was to see the Russians in the flesh and then draw appropriate conclusions. From the standpoint of the National War College, the USSR was then the only possible major adversary of the United States if a large-scale shooting war should come. As was obvious, the battle was already joined in the Cold War with Russia. President Truman, who regarded the previous Soviet moves as aggression against the West, had opened a counteroffensive in March, 1947, by enunciating the Truman Doctrine. It was followed in June with the suggestion of a Marshall Plan to save Europe from Communism—and America from a depression.

At the outset one must remember that in 1945 the victorious Allies had speedily developed divergent aims regarding the fate of Germany. A major purpose of Moscow was to render the hated Germans so weak militarily and so cooperative ideologically that they would never invade Russia again, as they had done with devastating effect in World War I and again in World War II. At the same time, a satellite neighbor would stand as a buffer against invasion. The French had much the same goal and for the same reasons. On the opposite side, the objective of Great Britain and the United States was to create a democratic Germany, fully cooperative with the West, that would serve as a buffer against the westward sweep of Communism while contributing to the prosperity of the democracies. Given these diametrically opposed aims, friction was inevitable, particularly since the victors had shortsightedly borrowed trouble by marooning Berlin, with its four divided sectors, deep in the heart of the Soviet zone. The situation was made to order for a Moscow-engineered Communist takeover.

With good reason the victorious Soviets felt they had a special claim to Berlin, for they had paid a high toll in blood to capture it. General Eisenhower has been unfairly blamed for not having seized the city first, as he could have done, but the Allies at Yalta had already earmarked East Germany for the Russians. There was no sense in sacrificing the American blood and material necessary to capture Berlin and then having to turn it over to the USSR.

The Soviets paid the frightful price themselves and, as is traditional in warfare, their troops immediately sought informal reparations in the form of looting and rape. The invaders seized all the available liquor supplies and, often under the influence of alcohol, grabbed everything of value they could lay their hands on, including watches, money, jewelry, and silverware. General Frank Howley, who entered with the first United States troops and became the American representative on the Berlin Allied Kommandatura,* later filled in the gory details in his bitter book, *Berlin Command* (1950). What he had to say was confirmed for me by eyewitnesses in 1947. There was undoubtedly an orgy of rape, even though the German women desperately tried to make themselves repulsive by rubbing dirt and filth on their faces. They were even pulled out of churches and raped in the streets. General Howley reports that 230 German girls were treated as victims of the conqueror's lust on one day in the same hospital in Berlin.

From the beginning the Soviets continued their pillaging and raping in the American sector, but General Howley finally managed to put a stop to it, as well as to the kidnapping of individual Germans on the Soviet grab list. There were some ugly small-scale incidents involving Americans shooting Russians and vice versa. Howley, who conducted a kind of one-man war against the Soviets, wrote that he came to Berlin thinking that the Germans were "our enemies," but soon became convinced that the Russians "really were our enemies." He thought it folly to try to "appease" them.

Official reparations on an immense scale were a diplomatic problem of far greater magnitude than the looting. At the Yalta Conference in

---

*The four-power Allied governing body for the city.

1945, Roosevelt and Churchill had agreed that the Soviet Union might have reparations from Germany for the appalling damage inflicted by the invader. The sum of $10 billion was tentatively mentioned, and at Potsdam the details of collection were set forth. But many Americans in Berlin felt that the Russians were not morally deserving of reparations. After all, Stalin had given Hitler the green light for the invasion of Poland, with the consequent launching of World War II. The diabolical scheme of setting Hitler on the Western powers had backfired, and Russia itself suffered a massive surprise invasion by the Germans in June, 1941. The blow fell with crushing force despite repeated warnings from the Western powers that an overwhelming attack was imminent. Stalin's costly initial reverses were partly attributable to his having alienated his own people in the path of the invader and his having executed many officers of the Red Army in the notorious purge trials from 1935 to 1939. These paranoid prosecutions probably had the additional effect of persuading Hitler that the demoralized Soviet armies would be relatively easy to destroy.

Some of the reparations exacted by the Russians were both useless and senseless. One of my informants in Berlin, a foreign-service officer, stated that a gang of Russians had ripped up some railroad tracks in the United States sector. When the Americans remonstrated, the reply was that since the rails were of no use to the occupiers, why should there be any complaint? An impoverished German industrialist told me that the great bulk of the factories seized, dismantled, and scrambled by the Russians for alleged reassembling in the Soviet Union were of no use to anyone. When shipped, they were just a jumble of broken parts, many of them eventually rusting on railroad sidings in widely separated areas. This German manufacturer believed that if the Russians had played their cards right, the Americans would have been willing to supply the dollars and the technicians with which to replace the ruined Soviet factories. He had even said to the Russian despoilers, "Let us Germans build them for you but leave ours." The Soviets shook their heads and replied, "Nyet." They ultimately stopped the dismantling and took their reparations from current production, no doubt realizing that it was wiser to gather golden eggs than to carve up the goose that laid them.

Russian brutality was further exposed by an episode later related to me in Washington by Robert Murphy, who had served with General Clay in Berlin as the U.S. political adviser. The rapacious Soviets not only moved a key optical factory (Zeiss) from the historic city of Jena to the outskirts of Moscow, but also took along the seven thousand skilled workers and their families. At two o'clock in the morning these luckless Germans were given thirty minutes to assemble their belongings. When the American representative in the Allied Control Council in Berlin protested against such inhumanity, Marshal Grigori Zhukov replied, "This is precisely the same thing that we do to our own people. Surely you do not expect us to treat the Germans any better."

Twin goals were obviously dictating the Soviet policy of dismantling factories. One was to strengthen Russia; the other was to weaken Germany. The evident design was to rob the former enemy to the point where he would never again be a menace to the USSR, while debilitating him to the point where he would be willing to turn to Communism as a choice of evils.

In various other ways the Russians, from the American point of view, were continuing to be suspicious allies and uncooperative partners, as they had been during the war. I heard repeated reports of their tapping American telephones and of anti-Western propaganda blaring out from the Soviet radio. Despite Moscow's pledges not to allow the Moscow-controlled press to attack the occupying powers, the Soviets were hurling well-inked barbs at their nominal Allies. The Russians had made promises regarding food that they were openly breaking; they were exporting it from the hungry Soviet zone to the USSR. They not only needed it themselves but they could also use it to force the Germans into the Communist camp with the prod of hunger. The Russians were also active in spreading rumors that would stir up dissent among the Germans, who were almost literally scared to death of the invader. At the same time, Soviet propaganda was ceaselessly making trouble among the Western Allies, all with the same divide-and-conquer goal.

The new Battle of Berlin, so I was told, was reportedly being lost in the three Allied governing bodies. The Russians had recently engineered a deadlock over Ernst Reuter, a former Communist whom they despised but whom the Germans had recently elected mayor or Oberbürgermeister of Berlin. Evidently scheming to force a new election, the Soviets managed to bar him from office for many months, until they finally walked out of the four-power Allied Control Council in Berlin in March, 1948. The Russians were saying that they could not be responsible for his safety, and this warning struck home because his seat of government lay in the Russian sector of Berlin. The Soviets had also exerted enough pressure to bring about the dismissal of the Education Minister. This disturbing turn of events, combined with the blocking of Reuter, had greatly shaken the faith of the Berliners in the United States. The Americans had urged the Germans to stick out their necks against the Russians and now their heads were being lopped off.

In the Allied Control Council, where the four governing generals met, relations were formally correct. The impression prevailed that the Soviet representative dared not make the slightest move unless he communicated with Moscow. I gathered from my informants that the Russian officials often disliked what they had to do in the Control Council but knew better than to fly in the face of orders from Moscow. Siberia was still cold in winter.

The British, my inquiries revealed, were experiencing many of the same difficulties with the Soviets as were the Americans. Great Britain wanted a revived, prosperous, and friendly Germany, not only for its own trade but also as a bulwark against a westward push of Soviet Communism to the English Channel. The French generated less friction with the Russians, partly because they had not signed the governing Potsdam agreement and partly because, like the Russians, they did not want to see the renewed threat of a powerful, united, revived, and vengeful Germany. The Americans generally desired a self-governing Germany so that they could go home; the Soviets evidently desired the same thing so that they could take over.

In the three governing bodies of four-power Berlin, the "rule of unanimity" prevailed or, more bluntly, the veto. Much was being said in American circles about the abuse or overuse of this weapon. By a vote of one to three, the Soviet representative could tie up any substantive proposal, and he was the one most frequently condemned for using this technique. The Russians were doubtless much concerned about the tyranny of the (Western) majority, in Berlin as well as in the fledgling United Nations. At this stage in Germany they were listening patiently, even stoically, to the argumentation. The British in general were evidently content to let matters remain in deadlock, on the assumption that delay was a game that two could play. Yet Soviet "approval in principle" often meant rejection in practice. One American general told me that the four-power sessions used to be discussions among gentlemen; now there were no longer discussions and no longer gentlemen.

Another American general reassured me by saying that he was not greatly concerned about the way the deadlock was developing. The Russians were admittedly difficult when dealing with the larger issues, but on secondary or minor questions they had proved to be surprisingly cooperative. There had been much exchange of war criminals by extradition. In the four-power Allied Kommandatura, the Soviets had used the veto freely, but more than nine hundred decisions had been reached by unanimous agreement. He was not at all worried about the one vulnerable railway line to Berlin through the Russian zone that was at the disposal of the United States; he dismissed as exaggerated the rumors that the Soviets might blow it up.

Fortunately, arrangements were made for me to attend a session of the Allied Coordinating Committee, which consisted of four deputy commanders in Berlin. (The Control Council, at a higher level, involved the four commanders themselves.) Present were the four deputies, with their aides (the Russians were in uniform), as well as the three interpreters. The Soviets declared that their decision blocking the election of Dr. Reuter as Oberbürgermeister was final, and they quoted against General Ryan, the American, a statement he had recently made in a press conference relating to this hotly disputed case. The British spokesman appealed for a change of vote on the grounds that he had recently yielded when he was a minority of one. The word "approved" in English evidently has two meanings in Russian, and the question of an "approved" paper was dropped after some quibbling. General Frank Keating, then the American deputy commander, ended the discussion on a lighter note by making a quip about blowing up the building. One frozen-faced Russian never cracked a smile. The Soviet deputy on one occasion yawned when he was being urged to change his vote; evidently he had no intention of flouting his orders from Moscow.

Even more memorable was an open meeting of the City Council, held in a large hall before an enthusiastic audience of several hundred people. Dr. Reuter was still being barred from assuming his seat, and his place was being taken by Frau Luise Schroeder, a noble-appearing woman who spoke passionately and evoked warm applause. One pro-Russian speaker blamed the Allies for using the veto to block desired Soviet objectives. In truth, all four Allies, including the French, had at one time or another been on the solo end of the three-to-one vote. Yet there was strong anti-Communist sentiment on the Berlin City Council, and when one pro-Communist speaker began to make extreme charges, he was shouted down, while the presiding officer vigorously clanged the bell for order. Even some of the Russians present laughed at the scene; they must have been mystified as well as amused by the wondrous workings of democracy.

As for strained Russo-American relations, I remember a disquieting interview with a junior American foreign-service officer. He pointed out that there was only a single railway line connecting Berlin with the American zone, and that if the Russians blockaded it, Berlin would fall completely into the hands of the Communists. A short time later I mentioned this dire possibility to two U.S. Army officers, both of whom scoffed at such an eventuality. One of them said that the Russians, without the atomic bomb, were weak militarily but that their leaders were smart; they would pull out of Berlin when they had a Communist regime organized to their satisfaction. The next year, after the Soviets clamped down the starvation Berlin blockade, I often recalled how right the young foreign-service officer had been.

My overall impression was that the Soviets were grimly determined to stay in both Berlin and East Germany, either in person or through their Communist puppets. They had taken over the schools, including the University of Berlin, which was located primarily in their sector. They had heavily infiltrated the labor unions. The enormous Berlin wall did not spring up until 1961, fourteen years later, but that was to keep East Germans from leaving, not the Russians. The Soviets thus achieved their goal of a guaranteed western defensive buffer in the shape of a Communist satellite inescapably rotating in the Russian orbit.

The nerve-taut Americans, as well as the British and French, suffered in 1947 from the uneasy feeling of sitting on a bulging powder keg. I learned that the United States Army then had only one piece of artillery in Berlin; the Soviets had scores of such weapons, as well as thousands more troops in the city or in their nearby zone. Even so, the Russians in Berlin were reasonably cooperative in some dealings that did not intimately involve their central objectives. One should also add that much of the trouble in Berlin was caused by carefree American troops who did not share the Soviet concern about photographing military installations or invading places that were clearly designated off limits. The U.S. Army major who served as my guide reported that an American soldier, presumably intoxicated, had sold a light tank to the Russians for an unspecified amount of currency. Whether he was preying on Soviet gullibility or treacherously selling military secrets were questions that remained unanswered.

One of my most revealing contacts in Berlin was with a German civilian, Richard van Tongel, who had been the president and half-owner of a steel company in Güstrow, about ninety miles to the north and west of Berlin. He was now employed by the American Military Government. His comments were the more valuable because he knew America and spoke cultured English, for as a youth he had been sent to the United States for his upbringing before the outbreak of World War I. He had married a remarkable American woman from Utah whose relatives in the United States were much concerned about her welfare, especially in view of the grave shortages of food in Germany. One of them, a close friend in California, had asked me to look in on this refugee family and see how they were faring.

Preparatory to my visit I stopped at the Army Post Exchange, one of those oases of plenty in a desert of poverty. My purchases consisted of a dozen or so candy bars and other items of high caloric content. The refugee family, consisting of the father, mother, and attractive, teen-age, twin girls, was living in a small apartment, crowded almost to the ceilings with expensive furniture, including a grand piano. The major who had driven me there remarked, "These people aren't too badly off," as indeed they were not, in relation to the bulk of the population.

Fortunately for these refugees, the invading Russians had extended favored treatment to the entire Van Tongel household. At the time when Hitler's all-conquering armies were invading the Soviet Union, the man of the house had treated certain Russian prisoners of war with exceptional humanity. For this sin he had been prosecuted, convicted, and fined. When the Russians finally came, the Soviet officer or officers in charge, at great risk to themselves, sought to reward Van Tongel by piling his furniture onto a railroad car and shipping it to Berlin. Gratitude for this favor was somewhat weakened by the harrowing experience of the two young Van Tongel daughters. When the enemy neared their home, the girls were sent up onto the roof to spend a terrifying night in the darkness and thus foil the lustful attentions of the soldiers who came searching for them.

My interesting interview with Van Tongel was conducted under curiously embarrassing conditions. When I arrived at his apartment like a midsummer Kriss Kringle laden with goodies from the Post Exchange, I expected that all four faces would light up with joy and gratitude. After all, the Germans were on the semistarvation ration of fifteen hundred calories, which, they complained, was often not obtainable in full—sometimes the ration card was just a license to hunt. To my distress Van Tongel's face turned so red that I feared he was going to suffer a stroke. Perhaps he felt humiliated by having to accept charity (commissioned by a relative) or by having to expose to a stranger the lowly state to which a wealthy German aristocrat had fallen. But he did say that the one GI meal a day that he ate was the biggest thing in his life, and that he had never expected to see the time when so little would mean so much to him.

Furious though he appeared to be, Van Tongel related how the Russians arrived and ultimately removed his entire steel mill as reparations. He was sure that the orphaned parts never reached Russia in such shape as to be put together again, in which case the name of the game was retribution rather than reparations. When the invaders first arrived they asked to see his workers' quarters, and when he showed them the neat cottages they responded, "You lie, capitalist." The American-born wife of this once wealthy industrialist resorted to her American citizenship as a shield when the invaders arrived, and she may thus have cooled off potential rapists. She had foresightedly pinned a small American flag to her dress, but the Russians, who in her opinion liked Americans even less than they did Germans, responded with "Amerikanski nicht gut, Kapitalist."

The Van Tongels had suffered many months of misery and deprivation, but they looked far better than most haggard Germans. The past winter, during which hundreds froze to death in Berlin and beautiful trees were cut down for fuel, had proved to be a frigid ordeal. The family had been forced to barter belongings for fuel until their nerves almost gave way. One of the girls had applied for admission to the Sovietized University of Berlin, but had been rejected, she felt, because she and her family were not in sympathy with the Communists.

Van Tongel referred bitterly to the Russian practice of taking away what little the Germans had, and then doling back a small part of it in a manner that was supposed to elicit gratitude. He was confident that the Soviets were working to infiltrate France through the indigenous Communist party there, and he greatly feared that the Soviets would ultimately take over Berlin bodily. If they moved in, he declared, he would move out on foot toward the Western zones, together with about 750,000 other Berliners.

This high-born German freely criticized the mistakes of the Americans in their attempts to rehabilitate, denazify and democratize Germany. One blunder, he felt, was to foist political parties prematurely on the recently one-party Nazi Germany. Such a policy, in his opinion, would only create the kind of confusion on which Communists were best able to capitalize. Another blunder, he believed, was to try to teach democracy from books rather than from working examples. Perhaps remembering his happy boyhood years in America, he remarked that the need was to send hundreds of the best German youths to the United States for their schooling. The big defect in this scheme was that many of them probably would never return, especially if they managed to marry American girls.

The Van Tongel story had a curious sequel. The lady of the house, having retained her American citizenship, managed to return to Utah with her husband. Positions as presidents of steel companies were not available to ex-enemy expatriates, and he was forced to resort temporarily to gardening and other kinds of manual labor. He ultimately rose to a white-collar supervisory position.

7

Life in the Berlin Ruins

While I personally discount the prospects of early war, I cannot forget for a moment that this is possible and that if it occurs we must not be caught as we were at Pearl Harbor.

General Lucius D. Clay
December 27, 1947

While in Berlin I chanced to meet a young woman, a journalist, I believe, who had just left Moscow after eleven harrowing months. What she had to say threw some light on why the war-weary Russians were behaving as they were in occupied Germany.

My informant had gone to the USSR thinking that the Communists might be on the right road, and that perhaps the future had already arrived there with all its glory. Now she viewed the whole country with horror, although she still believed that the Soviet leaders were idealists who would sacrifice for the cause of the downtrodden by creating more downtrodden. She declared that the people were starving, a condition that could have explained the current Soviet practice of shipping German agricultural products to Russia out of their own hungry zone. The Moscow subway, she related, was even more jammed than the one in New York. Water had to be obtained from pumps, and the people were crowded in their cramped housing, with little soap and no toilet paper.

This woman reporter was perhaps most impressed by the deadly fear that prevailed regarding the NKVD—the ruthless secret police who came with a knock in the night. A Russian version of the exposé by the defecting Victor Kravchenko, *I Chose Freedom,* had been bootlegged into the USSR, but one Russian woman scoffed at it. She labeled it old stuff and was astonished to learn that people outside Russia paid good money to read such stale fare. The Moscow government would not let Soviet citizens leave the country unless there were members of the family who could be left behind as hostages. Despite anticapitalist propaganda, my journalistic source believed, the Russian people had great admiration for America's technological advancement.

Up to this point, my inquiries in Berlin had brought me in touch mostly with diplomatic officials and military officers. Most of them were primarily involved in the denazification, democratization, and feeding of the prostrate Germans, with special concern for the intrusive presence of the Soviets. Being a university professor myself, I was especially interested in the education—or rather re-education—of the Germans, and to that end I managed to gather some revealing information.

A valuable contact in Berlin was Dr. Thomas Alexander, head of the Education Branch of the United States Military Government in Germany. An academician long associated with Columbia University in New York, he was a specialist on the German educational system and had published a number of books relating to formalized education.

Dr. Alexander remarked that he was putting twelve students through the University of Berlin for one semester by selling cartons of cigarettes for 1200 marks each. The twelve cartons that he was using for this purpose had cost him only $9.40 in American money. I could hardly believe that such a quantity could be parlayed into 15,400 marks, or about $700, but that is what he told me and what I dutifully recorded.

Dr. Alexander invited me to meet at his house with about thirty-five German students, presumably all or virtually all from the University of Berlin. He scheduled me for a brief talk, which probably involved American foreign policy as it related to the reconstruction of Europe. The students seemed to be exceptionally bright, and during the question period they impressed me with their ability to understand and speak English.

Germany's younger generation could claim something of an apologist in Dr. Alexander. He said that some of the youths had been taken into the Nazi party automatically without their having made application. So much pressure had been applied to many others that large numbers had finally signed up. He added that the Russians did not want the Americans to have the records of former Nazis, especially of those who had recently turned Communist in response to Soviet inducements or threats. At the same time, Moscow condemned the

American practice of giving a clean bill of health to small-fry Nazis, some of whom were not so minor.

College-age Germans, Dr. Alexander concluded, were generally pessimistic about the future, and this state of mind was understandable in view of the almost hopeless chaos. The University of Berlin lay primarily in the Russian sector, where classmates would suddenly disappear without a trace. A reasonable assumption was that Russian agents had kidnapped them. In this atmosphere the students developed "the German look"—a quick and furtive glance over the shoulder. Many of these young people recalled with nostalgia the glory days of the departed *Führer*. The Hitler youth movement, Dr. Alexander felt, had much to commend it as a form of boy-scoutism. He believed that Hitler had promoted some worthy ideals, despite his unspeakably evil doings. The German people were not sheep, in his view, and Germany could be democratized.

As the students asked questions at Dr. Alexander's house, one realized more fully that Germany was being fought over ideologically by the occupying powers, and that these young people, like all Germans, had to live with this ugly reality on a day-to-day basis. A young man present remarked with complete frankness that the conquerors were all bad, but that the Americans were the least bad of the lot. Another student asked what was becoming of America's vaunted freedom of speech; a German national had allegedly been jailed near Frankfurt for merely spreading rumors. Why did not the American press play up the dire need of the seventy million Germans and their importance to the United States in the long run? Why had the United States Army requisitioned German furniture at its uninflated prewar value in marks?

From this alert student group I also heard that the Soviets, ordinarily vigilant, had not yet carefully screened students entering the University of Berlin. Many of those routinely admitted were actually being allowed to go on through. On the other hand, one of the students complained that a valuable picture had been stolen from him in the Russian sector, but that the Soviet police would not help him retrieve it. Perhaps they were too short-handed or too indifferent at this time to bother with such petty crimes.

Two embarrassments occurred in connection with this student gathering. At one point Dr. Alexander scolded the entire group harshly for some minor offense, perhaps inattention resulting from hunger. The other incident involved the enlisted man who drove the Army automobile that was at my disposal. As we were leaving, someone—perhaps Dr. Alexander—asked if we could transport four or five students to the general area of my destination. Regarding this as a legitimate manifestation of goodwill, I naturally consented, and we fell to chatting as we drove along. After we had traveled a mile or two, the driver turned to me and in a stern voice demanded, "Are these people enemy aliens?" I replied that technically they probably were, because no treaty of peace with a united Germany had been signed. He then declared that their presence was contrary to Army regulations and that they would have to get out. I was reluctant to dump these passengers at night in the heart of Berlin, but on the other hand I did not want to expose the driver to disciplinary action. With great embarrassment and sincere expressions of regret, I explained to the students that they would have to leave, and this they did without undue demur, no doubt thinking less well of Americans in general and of me in particular.

The next day I mentioned this disagreeable incident to the Army officers who were in charge of my mission. The consensus seemed to be that the enlisted man was technically right, but that the regulations could have been stretched a bit without anybody getting into trouble or even hearing about my embarrassment. Looking back on the affair, I probably should have pulled my assimilated rank of major general on this private, and then proceeded as planned. At the very least I should have returned the students to Dr. Alexander's house.

My legalistic driver nevertheless did give me an insight into the seamy side of Berlin. One night, in a tough district, he pointed out nine streetwalkers gathered in front of a place that he called a "cat house." He declared that if a male driver slowed down, these harpies would rush out and drag him from his car. I suspected that he was exaggerating, yet I felt somewhat relieved when our automobile sped safely on down the street.

A somewhat different picture of the University of Berlin came from two faculty members at that once prestigious institution. The first was a woman scientist who told me that the students were exceptionally earnest; they were immersing themselves in their studies to escape from the unpleasant present and the unpromising tomorrow. The University of Berlin was widely dispersed, but most of it, as I noted earlier, was located in the Russian sector. Many more students were applying to the badly damaged institutions of higher learning, particularly this one, than could possibly be accepted. The university was now requiring stiff entrance examinations. Among other questions, the students were being asked what they thought of Marx and Lenin. If the answers did not square with the Moscow party line, the applicant was rejected—at least this was the general belief.

This woman faculty member spelled out some of the difficulties under which higher education was then laboring. All of the top scientists in nuclear physics had escaped to the West, she explained, but some German chemists were now working in the Soviet Crimea. One professor had been robbed of his X-ray machine by the Russians, and since he could not get another, his work was languishing. Scientists at the university could not replace the back files of scholarly periodicals that had been destroyed during the war; when they ran experiments they had no way of knowing whether or not they were duplicating the labor of others. Desirable textbooks were difficult or impossible to obtain.

Another professor at the University of Berlin, this one a man, likewise deplored the absence of learned journals and the impossibility of securing needed books. He and his wife denied that the Germans were basically cruel or that they lacked a community spirit. German character, he felt, must be considered in the light of the gnawing hunger, as well as of the demoralizing practice of spying on one's neighbors that Hitler had promoted. Countless Germans had followed the hope-giving Hitler largely because they wanted to escape Communism.

Yet the information I received about the University of Berlin was not all depressing. Dr. Alexander reported that the Russians dealt harshly only with incompetent instructors; they wanted superior ones whom they could trust to be left alone. As for the few exchange professors from the United States, the Soviet officials did not go out of their way to seek scholars with strong pro-Communist sympathies. Even so, during the next year advocates of complete freedom broke away from the Communist-dominated University of Berlin and established in the American sector the Free University of Berlin. With the help of funds from the United States, it became a large, flourishing, and prestigious institution.

A brief visit to the Berlin Technical University also proved rewarding. The destruction was frightful, for about 80 percent of the once imposing buildings, including the library, had been blasted into rubble. Heavy fighting had occurred at this spot in the last days of Hitler's Berlin, when the Russians had flushed out their foe with flame-throwers. The scorchings were still visible. Ironically, a monument to the German dead of the World War I remained standing beside the jumbled piles of bricks, themselves unwitting monuments to the recent dead of World War II. Corpses were still being dug out of the ruins; fourteen days earlier five bodies had been exhumed.

To their credit, the Russians had started to put the Technical University back on its feet, and they had remained there for about three months. They could have blocked these initial steps, just as they now dominated the University of Berlin. My information was that they had been invited back to the Technical University but did not respond, presumably because they had received no word from Moscow through the bureaucratic chain of command.

Soviet soldier embraces U. S. soldier at link-up near Grabow, Germany, May 3, 1945

(U. S. Army photograph)

Staff members at the Technical University further explained that they were trying not to duplicate the work then being done at the University of Berlin. Some attempt was being made to squeeze in a few courses on the humanities, but this step was difficult because of the tight scientific curriculum. Concern was felt for the whole man, and the Rector remarked that the catastrophe that had befallen Germany was in large degree the work of the narrow and gullible specialists who had enchained the German people under Hitler.

While visiting the Technical University, I sat in on one of the lectures, which went way over my head. The instructor read from some kind of book, whether manuscript notes or printed pages I could not ascertain. He was more fortunate than the Rector, who had lost all of his books and notes and had to reconstruct all his lectures from memory. At the end of this presentation the students tapped their pencils noisily as a sign of approval, in the traditional German manner. In earlier days they had shuffled their shoes, if disapproving, or had stamped their feet, if approving. But this practice was abandoned when the ill-shod students discovered that they were wearing out their already shabby shoes faster than necessary.

Standard equipment at the Technical University was in critically short supply. The professors were forced to use the blackboard instead of nonexistent projectors and lantern slides. Salvaged from the ruins was a lone turbine, forty-two years old, the only one of any vintage remaining intact. It was so antiquated that the Russians did not bother to cart it off as reparations. One other reason for the scarcity of equipment was the prevalence of hungry thieves, the worst kind, and what still remained was carefully locked up. The shattered windows were being temporarily replaced with translucent paper.

In conversing with three students at the Technical University, I picked up some revealing insights. About 12 percent of the enrollees were married, and these, as well as many others, had to scrounge around for food and fuel to supply their homes. Nourishment was the oppressive problem, for students fell into the lowest category in food rationing, that is, number three. Manual laborers received more calories, but even so some had fainted or were fainting on the job. One professor testified that the students who were desperately hungry could not remember information that they had already absorbed. They could recall it, or recall it better, when their stomachs were not blotting out their brains.

Students often studied until two o'clock in the morning, and some labored an eighty-hour week on their courses. This stint was difficult to believe because it amounted to more than eleven hours a day for seven days a week. In one class there was only one book for one hundred members. Students were forced to copy down the lectures as furiously and completely as they could, as their forebears had done during the Middle Ages and before the invention of movable type in the fifteenth century, ironically in Germany.

Tennis balls and soccer balls were also needed so that the students could engage in limited but vigorous exercise. Although they had little energy for such diversions, some stirring around was thought necessary to improve the circulation of blood and hence enliven the brain.

Despite all these handicaps, the rector at the Technical University insisted that the institution was doing good work. His faculty members were at pains to point out that they were better off than their colleagues at the University of Berlin, which the Russian-sponsored Communists now dominated. At this sister institution the Marxist-Leninist professors were promoted more rapidly than the others, many of whom suffered dismissal. A notable exception was a prominent Catholic professor of law, who was retained. The Soviet overseers required an abstract of each lecture so as to make sure that the gospel according to Marx was being properly presented.

Also at the Technical University, the word was that there were twice as many applicants for entrance to the University of Berlin as there were places. Students were screened after oral examinations, and those were eliminated who answered incorrectly or insincerely questions about Marx and Lenin. The Russians then made sure that only Communists of the true faith were added to the list of the lucky. Moreover, trade unions with Communist orientation were strong in the Russian sector, and they exerted considerable influence at the University of Berlin.

Elsewhere in Berlin an Army major complained that the United States was not supporting the local educational program adequately. A prominent German educator had been dismissed, for he was so tactless that he antagonized the French as well as the Russians. The Soviets were cleverly jockeying to get their men into key spots. The American major further observed that a serious problem for the universities was the shortage of shelf space. Countless books and surviving professional journals, all urgently needed, had been gathering dust in basements for two years because lumber and other needed materials could not be obtained for shelving.

Churches, no less than the schools and other public buildings, had suffered severely from Allied bombing. In one large town in Germany only one house of worship had been left with a roof, and the various denominations were using it in shifts. I was curious, therefore, to learn something about the state of religion in Berlin.

One of my best sources was Father Powers, a U.S. Army chaplain and a graduate of Notre Dame University, where he had been a member of the boxing team. His skill with his fists had recently been put to a severe test, according to newspaper accounts he personally confirmed. Thievery was then rampant in a hungry and devastated Germany, and when Father Powers found his quarters invaded by a gang of young thieves, his rugged Christianity asserted itself. He knocked out three of them in a free-for-all fight. In modestly commenting on his fistic prowess, he remarked that German children fought dirty, with kicks in the face. The Bavarians, he claimed, were especially bellicose, and would fight at the drop of a hat.

Father Powers believed that the beaten German people were now

showing more interest in religion. It was one of the few sources of
solace for the demoralized masses, but this was not saying a great deal.
The hungry victims of war were too much preoccupied with thoughts
of their stomachs to be thinking primarily of their souls. The two-
fisted priest criticized the cruelty and lack of community spirit among
Germans, but he also praised their good qualities, including their
traditional cleanliness, which, one should add, was not now conspicuous in a land where soap was a rarity. Father Powers pointed to
the young, pinch-faced secretary in the building who, he said, was
literally starving. I was sufficiently touched to leave a traveler's check
with instructions to this man of God to use it where it would do the
most good.

Another interviewee, a German priest, declared that he had served
the Lord under wraps during the Hitler nightmare. The moral tone of
the people was low as a result of the war, and there was only a slight
increase of interest in religion. To me such information came as no
surprise, for the humiliating defeat must have weakened faith in a
personal God who had permitted a proud people to rise so high and
then fall so low. As for the vengeful and atheistic Russians, this German priest gloomily reported that they had made off with his personal
belongings, including watch, pen, and pencils.

A pleasanter memory of Berlin involves a luncheon in the French
sector. My host was the deputy commander, General Roger Jean
Charles Noiret, who had escaped to England while France was falling
in 1940 and who had continued the uphill struggle. He said that his
personal contacts with the Russian representatives in Berlin were
good but his official relations were bad. Actually, his official relations
were often annoyingly good from the American standpoint. As might
have been expected, the numerous and noisy Communist party in
France was pressuring the Paris government to pursue a policy toward
defeated Germany that conformed with Soviet objectives, especially
those that did not relate to such crucial issues as control of the Ruhr
and separation of the Rhineland. General Noiret had no confidence
that the hated Nazi leopard would change its spots after a forced dose
of democracy. He favored a policy of indefinite occupation of a weakened Germany and control of its government, with a special eye to at
least partial French jurisdiction over the Ruhr and the coal-rich Saar
basin.

General Noiret reported that Germans disguised as Russians had
seized goods in transit on trains passing through the Soviet zone.
There had been some minor incidents, including the shooting of a
Soviet captain by a U.S. sentry that was evidently the result of mistaken identity. Before I departed, the general asked me for my im-

pressions of Paris, which, I gathered, he had not seen for some time. I naturally praised the famed city and added some remark about the attractively dressed women. As a true Frenchman, he was obviously amused and pleased by my observing eye.

Leaving Berlin in mid-July, 1947, on an Army C-47 for the return flight to Frankfurt, I carried away a jumble of impressions. Among them bulked destruction, destitution, poverty, hunger, and four-power friction. Berlin was a sick city in a sick sector of a sick zone of a sick country.

Poverty and hunger stalked everywhere in this city of the dead. A few months earlier a German had captured and killed a fat dog belonging to an employee of the American Military Government, obviously with intent to eat it. He was sentenced to imprisonment for several months by an American military court. I personally saw people in the streets scrounging for stray lumps of coal and eagerly scooping up horse droppings in tin cans for fertilizer. But food was the omnipresent and pressing necessity, and on various occasions the occupying Russians would take away even the tiny supplies laboriously acquired. Sometimes the conquerors would give a little of it back, expecting gratitude that was never forthcoming. I was told that the numerous wives of the Army officers arrived in Berlin hating the Germans and then wound up feeding them. But these good ladies, who did much charitable work, were advised not to wash dishes for the defeated.

Berlin, one quickly learned, was a vast black market that included the swapping of valuables for food. Little wonder that this situation should prevail when three hundred inflated marks served as the monthly wage of a worker—or the price of one pound of butter. Obviously the black market was about all that kept the city from complete collapse; no less obvious was the stark truth that there could be no economic recovery unless and until the nearly worthless currency was established on a solid basis. This was finally done in 1948 to the great benefit of the Germans and the great displeasure of the Russians.

Much of the friction in Berlin was generated by the unflinching determination of the Russians to remain. They were clearly laboring to communize not only Berlin but also their entire zone, with the presumed objective of creating a friendly buffer on the west. To this end the Soviets were using all the parliamentary tricks possible to achieve their purposes in the quadripartite governance of Berlin. The Sovietized and communized German Democratic Republic of [East] Germany was finally formed in 1949, following the creation of the Federal Republic of [West] Germany by the Western powers in the same year. The use of the word "democratic" in the official name of

East Germany is yet another example of the differing connotations in Communist countries and in the West.

As for beleaguered Berlin in 1947, the position of the Western Allies in this terrifyingly exposed spot was weak and steadily growing weaker. Lines of communication and supply by land from the American zone of Germany depended on the jugular vein of a single railway line. The Soviet army, either in the Berlin sector or near it, was overpoweringly strong. The United States was so short of troops that it was employing ex-German soldiers to guard military installations, although they were outfitted in uniforms that had been dyed black. The Americans were also using black-uniformed Polish refugees of the so-called Polish Guard. Berlin continued to be a great whispering gallery for the rumormongers, and the newsmen who came here from America were becoming increasingly nervous. One current barb was: "The Russians keep their threats, whereas the Americans break their promises."

Five days before I reached Berlin came the collapse of the three-day conference in Paris of the Big Three foreign ministers, meeting to discuss preliminaries of the Marshall Plan. The monkey wrench was the unwillingness of the Soviets to participate in this dollar-baited program. Berliners were deeply depressed by this disappointing turn of events, but by the time I arrived their vain hopes of Russian cooperation had largely faded. An American foreign-service officer, the one who had worried aloud about the possible cutting of the single railway line, took what comfort he could from this turn of events. He said that as long as the Paris conference was destined to fail, he could rejoice that it had broken up in only three days without the bitterness of prolonged wrangling.

As for denazification and democratization, a number of Germans told me that many of the Nazi party members had been inducted against their will or enticed by prospects of better jobs or other advantages. The great secret of Hitler's success was that under his system millions of people had the smug feeling of outranking someone else. No German was willing to admit that he was in any way personally responsible for the rise of Hitler, whose hypnotic appeal was to the masses rather than the intelligentsia. One German professor assured me that he had been highly embarrassed by the fanatical rantings of *Der Führer*.

An observer repeatedly heard the German people referred to as sheep politically but as individualists culturally. The argument was that they had some feeling for democracy but that it had withered from a period of disuse lasting more than ten years. One American remarked that the Germans were afraid to embrace American-style democracy for fear that they would be punished as collaborators when the United States pulled out its troops and the Soviets took over.

Whatever generalizations one might make about German cruelty and militarism, one fact stood out as plainly as Berlin's Brandenburg Gate. The Germans hated and feared the Russians, and the feeling was reciprocated. With good reason a prostrated and divided Germany feared Russian vengeance, and with equally good reason the Germans had no stomach for exchanging the dictatorship of Hitler for that of Stalin. They had lived next door to the Soviet brand of Communism for more than two years, and they wanted none of it. Many of them had enough of a memory of the democracy that had existed before Hitler came to power in 1933 not to want totalitarianism back. This fact alone does much to explain why they endured the added hardships and tensions of the harrowing Berlin blockade of 1948.

8

The Italian Interlude

It can be frankly said, therefore, that Italy is on the verge of a dollar crisis, which if allowed to break, will . . . cause an inflation, with attendant political upheaval, so far unmatched in Italy. . . . While the Marshall plan is still a light of hope on the dismal road Italy walks, it is a dim and distant one for the weary traveler.

James C. Dunn
U.S. Ambassador to Italy
telegram, September 17, 1947

After an uneventful return flight from Berlin to Frankfurt, the opportunity arose for me to pay a three-day visit to Rome, departing July 14, 1947. General Robinson's two-motor C-47 was flying to the Eternal City on a special mission, and there were a scant half-dozen passengers on board, all of them traveling on official business. One of the party was Colonel John D. Millett, who in civilian life taught political science at Columbia University, and I had no difficulty striking up a shoptalk conversation with him. Six years later he was selected to be president of Miami University in Ohio.

At some point in this interchange with Colonel Millett, reference was made to my having written a letter a few months earlier on behalf of Admiral Arno Spindler, the German naval officer and scholar who had published extensively on the German submarine campaigns of World War I. In the mid-1930s he had generously sent to me photostatic copies of revealing documents relating to the torpedoing of the *Lusitania*, which was then my special interest. At or near the end of World War II he had fallen into the hands of the invading Americans, who evidently suspected him of being too closely connected with the Nazi regime. I was able to write to his captors in good conscience that nothing in my extensive epistolary exchanges with him had indicated that he was a Nazi, although he was naturally a German nationalist. In any event, he was released, and although our paths did not cross, I did send him a CARE package of food and other necessities. It was most gratefully received, as his thank-you letter revealed, all the more so because by sheer coincidence the gift arrived on his birthday.

As we Rome-bound passengers chatted, our plane sped over southern Germany; then over Austria's Innsbruck (subsequently the site of the Olympic winter games); and then over the Brenner Pass (elevation 4,494 feet), the historic route over and between the Alps. The pilot descended disturbingly low, with the result that we caught a stunning view of the snow-clad peaks on each side of the aircraft. Below we could glimpse the tiny valleys, in which the cottages of the villagers seemed cuddled comfortably close together.

In overflying Italy I saw for the first time the blue-white coastline of the Adriatic Sea. We passed Florence, on the winding banks of the Arno River, and I noted what seemed to be the lopsided tower of Pisa in the far distance on the right. The farming country below was clearly less lush than that of Germany; the strips of cultivated land were narrower and the country appeared more brownish, evidently as a result of the continuing summer drought. The sun that had scorched much of Europe during this starving time had caused the recently harvested crops to fall dismayingly below expectations. This abnormality was the most distressing because cereals represented about two-thirds of Italy's normal intake of calories.

Conditions were especially grim in southern Italy, where the fertility of the predominantly Catholic population far outran that of the soil. At this time the annual surplus of births over deaths in Italy amounted to about four hundred thousand souls a year. The Catholic hierarchy, for religious reasons, wanted no birth control; the Communists, for political reasons, saw eye to eye with the Vatican on this issue. Misery and poverty, often the results of oversized families, were fertile seedbeds for Communism; food, fecundity, and land distribution were among the most pressing problems.

As our C-47 approached the landing field, I was somewhat prepared for this visit by a foreknowledge of the major events that had unfolded since Hitler burst into Poland in September, 1939. But I had to guard against drawing conclusions about Italy from its legendary capital city. Just as Paris is not France, so Rome is not Italy, all the more so since the fabled capital had luckily escaped the wholesale devastation that had cursed many other urban centers in Europe. From the beginning of hostilities, the belligerents on both sides had regarded Rome as an open city, and the retreating Germans, whatever their motives, must be given credit for not having destroyed both Rome and Florence, those priceless monuments of Western civilization.

In June of 1940, while France was collapsing under the fury of Hitler's *Blitzkrieg,* dictator Benito Mussolini of Italy had stabbed his French neighbor in the back by joining Germany as a cobelligerent within the Axis alliance. These jackal-like tactics backfired disastrously, for in subsequent months the inept Italian armies were destroyed in North Africa, and Italy itself suffered invasion by the Americans and their allies in the summer of 1943.

After the Allied invaders had swept over Sicily and successfully bombed military installations on the outskirts of Rome, Mussolini fell from power on July 26, 1943. The king asked the Fascist-tainted Marshal Badoglio to form a government, and on September 3, after much squirming, this new premier consented to what was nominally an unconditional surrender. The next month the recreated Italian regime, striving to work its way back to respectability, declared war on Germany and became a cobelligerent of the Allies. In this way the turncoat Italians hoped to buy more lenient treatment in the eventual peace treaty than they finally received.

But if Italy dropped out of the war against Germany, the Germans did not drop out of Italy. As they grudgingly gave ground northward, they fought tenaciously against the Allied invaders and also against their Italian ex-allies. In the industrial areas of northern Italy, where the Communist workers in factories were well organized and anti-Fascism was strong, the Partisans organized an underground resistance movement. They fought with outstanding courage and skill—qualities for which the regular Italian soldiers had not distinguished themselves in this war. Mussolini had declared in 1940 "To make a people great it is necessary to send them into battle, even if you have to kick them in the pants."

The deposed Mussolini, daringly rescued by the Germans from prison, had maintained a weak puppet government in the north until April, 1945. He finally fell into the hands of his own maddened people, who shot and then hanged him upside down, along with his mistress, who was similarly treated. Elongated Italy thus became the victim of a confused civil war, in which she was trampled underfoot by friend and foe alike. The devastation and destitution were frightful. Earlier in the conflict British aerial bombs had blasted Turin, Milan,

Cassino, Italy, destroyed by air attack, March 16, 1944

(U. S. Army photograph)

and Genoa, all important manufacturing centers in the north. For their part, the slowly retreating Germans had wreaked havoc, notably in Naples. When the shooting finally ceased, the Italian people were desperately short of almost every necessity, especially food, including seed for planting and fertilizer for fatigued soil. The Germans had so planted mines in thousands of acres of the already sterile fields that the peasants had to plough them at the risk of life and limb.

Italy was rescued from starvation and complete prostration by foreign aid, mainly from the United States. Help was sent at first on an emergency basis, and then through the United Nations Relief and Rehabilitation Administration, formed in 1943 and better known as UNRRA. Relying heavily on American dollars, it was an international organization created by forty-eight nations and designed to succor war victims in the liberated areas. This stipulation excluded Germany and Japan, both of which were defeated enemies, but Italy had become eligible for handouts by prudently switching sides in 1943.

All told, UNRRA distributed about $3 billion in supplies to various beneficiaries, or about 25 million long tons. The United States, the wealthiest nation of the group, was by far the heaviest contributor, and its humanitarian hand was crucial in helping Italy back onto its feet, albeit shakily. To the dismay of many Italians, UNRRA closed up shop in Europe in June, 1947, about two weeks before I reached Rome. Yet, partly because of the presence of so many millions of Italian-Americans in the United States, Washington continued to send substantial stopgap aid. It served to alleviate hunger and also slow down the feverish inflation of the sick lira. By this time the cost of living had rocketed to roughly fifty times the prewar level; the budget deficit in mid-1947 was about 600 billion lire, at a time when the lira was worth about one-third of a cent in American money.

Armed to some extent with this foreknowledge, I sought contacts with people in Rome who knew Italy and who could speak with some confidence about its current problems. Special items of interest were the nation's progress toward recovery, both physical and financial; the state of the food supply; the willingness of the people to help themselves; the eagerness of Italians to cooperate in the implementation of a Marshall Plan; and particularly the probable outcome of the struggle for power between the Communist left, chiefly in northern Italy, and the conservative right, deeply entrenched in the south.

After we touched down bumpily at the Rome airport, we were driven in an Army automobile to our hotel. My first impressions remain vivid. Unlike the cities of Germany, the ancient capital displayed little or none of the devastation caused by the recent war. Such ruins as existed in the inner city, notably the decaying Colosseum, owed their sad state to the ravages of time and the elements, as well as to the hand of man. A newcomer could not help noting the side-by-side scrambling of architecture, ranging from the ancient times through the Renaissance to the modern period. What especially struck me was the fresh appearance of the ancient but colored marble columns, even those that were prostrate or semiprostrate. They looked as though they had been quarried only yesterday. I thought then—and still think—that if our textbooks in high school, whether for Latin or ancient history, could have presented colored pictures of these monuments instead of the drab black and white, those dreary subjects would have taken on more life.

My quarters were centrally located at the Excelsior Hotel, which the Army had evidently requisitioned. Food and lodging cost me a trifling ninety cents a day, including sitting room, bedroom, and bathroom. All of my meals except one were consumed at this convenient center, where one excellent dinner, complete with orchestral music, cost only twenty-five cents. The exception was at a nearby Italian restaurant, where I enjoyed a traditional spaghetti-type pasta and topped off my repast with a rosy-cheeked fresh peach that had floated about temptingly in a dish of water. My retrospective enjoyment of this delicacy was dampened when I returned to my hotel and noticed a sign above the bathroom mirror warning visitors of the prevalence of amoebic dysentery and of the dangers of eating uncooked food. Happily, I escaped this miserable affliction, which evidently had been on the increase since the arrival in Italy of thousands of displaced persons.

During working hours in Rome I interviewed about a dozen informed people, most of them connected in some way with the U.S. Embassy. This building, centrally located, was far more spacious and pretentious than I had anticipated. The rich Washington government, traditionally penny-pinching in such matters, had never gone overboard in providing housing for its servants abroad. As might have been expected, the large official structure in Rome, as in London and Paris, had burst out of its seams and was overflowing to additional quarters. The official list of the personnel connected with the Rome Embassy contained nearly sixty names.

Whenever the Embassy and other sources were closed, I strolled many miles over the streets of Rome. The days were warm, as was usual in July, and my conspicuous Panama hat was fully appreciated. The various structures ranged from the "noble slums" to the raucously ornate Victor Emmanuel Monument, which fronted on a central square, Piazza di Venezia. From the balcony of a nearby building the strutting Mussolini had delivered some of his famous jut-jawed harangues to the cheering but misled masses below. I know virtually no Italian, so when I lost my bearings I would accost a native Roman, pronounce "Piazza di Venezia" in my best high-school Latin, and gesture in the direction where I thought it lay. With voluble understanding the hospitable Roman would steer me in the right direction.

One after-hours outing to a tourist attraction introduced me to one of the horse-drawn cabs, of which there were quite a few shabby specimens, as in Paris. I do not recall specifically how the horse looked, but many of those on the streets made a pathetic display of their ribs. At that, I supposed that on the whole these animals were better fed than many of the people.

The closest resemblance to a bombed-out building of any size was the ancient Colosseum, where the gladiators had fought and the hungry lions had received their quota of Christians. Civic pride in this ancient ruin was evidently strong, for at night floodlights bathed it. Yet more than pride was involved. Postwar housing in Rome was so scarce and crowded that young lovers, seeking precious moments of privacy, would resort to this dreary place for what Americans of that generation called "necking." Odors emanating from the ruins gave proof that others had sought the seclusion of this ancient ruin for other purposes.

Somewhat to my surprise, the Italians in the streets did not appear to be in bad shape physically; they certainly looked better than the half-starved Germans I had recently observed. Many of the women, as in Paris, were attractively attired in the bright summer colors of print dresses, more of them in fact than one had reason to expect in view of the shortages of almost everything material.

Pregnant women were much in evidence, as was not surprising in a country in which the ruling church frowned on birth control. More mothers were breast-feeding their babies in public than I was accustomed to seeing in the United States. The birthrate, according to my sources, had increased markedly since the war, as is common in times of stress, privation, unemployment, and returned soldiery. Children roamed the streets, even late at night, some of them picking up soggy cigarette butts from the gutters for reprocessing and sale or barter. Overpopulation, combined with unemployment and various shortages, was causing the government to encourage emigration to other countries, especially the Americas, without conspicuous success.

As for sin, I spotted only one woman who was obviously on the prowl, although there must have been many sisters of her ancient profession in the city. One shop was openly displaying venereal pills, which seemed curiously out of place in the shadow of the Vatican. The ugly truth is that these unmentionable afflictions had become rampant in the later stages of the war and its aftermath.

In roaming the streets of the great city, I encountered only a few merchants of the black market, although everyone knew that a small army of these harpies was loose in the land. This abnormality was inevitable in a situation where the currency was dangerously inflated, where the cost of living was skyrocketing (about forty to sixty times that of the last prewar year), where unemployment was endemic, and where luxuries and necessities alike were scarce. Rumor had it that the big money in the black market was to be made in sugar and grain, but at the sidewalk level the operations were conducted on a small scale and were much less brazen than in Paris. One of these furtive Romans approached me for a deal in currency, while on another street two of them tried to sell me a suit of clothes. My interest was in looking and listening, not in buying; as in Paris, a visitor had no desire to run afoul of the authorities.

In Italy, as in Germany, the scarcity of food continued to be the overshadowing problem. Despite desperate shortages, only a few staples were being rationed, including cereals. In the south of Italy, an overpopulated area that urgently needed grain for its pasta, this scarcity was inflicting severe hardships, which were being alleviated somewhat by the flourishing black market. Many of the hungry peasants were turning in desperation to Communism and becoming, in the phrase then current, "Communists of the stomach." Disorders had erupted in the south, notably in Sicily, which had recently suffered a "May Day massacre." According to the press, the police had been goaded into firing upon an enraged mob, at a cost of ten lives among the workers and peasants.

At the U.S. Embassy, the agricultural attaché had just returned from a conference in Rome on cereals. He reported that there simply was not enough grain to go around for a stricken Europe, even with help from the bumper crop of wheat in the United States. Moscow-leaning Communists were capitalizing on this untimely disparity to make new converts. They did not relish yellow corn in their white bread any more than did the Americans who were recommending it, and Italian propagandists were featuring pictures from the United States that showed the farmers dumping their surpluses of potatoes. The food problem was being aggravated by the clandestine bootlegging of wheat to Communist Yugoslavia at 10,000 lire a quintal (220 pounds), and the Yugoslavs for their part were reported to be counterfeiting the badly inflated Italian lira. Another complication was arising in the overcrowded south of Italy, where some farmers were turning to raising sheep. The result was the production of less grain and a further rise in unemployment at a time when a harsh winter loomed ahead.

The same agricultural expert at the Embassy complained that the United States should be doling out its food on a more selfish ideological basis, as the Russians were then doing with their "political wheat"—and continued to do. He believed that his country should help only people who rotated in a common political orbit, especially since there was not enough food to go around. At the same time, America should exclude heavy beneficiaries, notably Poland, that had already been forced into the Soviet camp. (He evidently did not know much about the pressures that immigrant minorities in the United States could exert on the government in Washington.) He concluded that the American people were generous, but generous in the mass. Some Italians, he reported, gave the United States credit for the postwar helping hand provided by UNRRA and other generous grants, but many others, especially the local Communists, did not.

Another American official, who generously shared his experiences with me, was a former member of recently expired UNRRA. He was then involved with the displaced persons, who numbered about forty thousand in Italy alone. They were mostly Jews, Poles, and Italians from the Adriatic territory, Venezia Giulia, that Italy had been forced to cede to Yugoslavia in the peace settlement of February, 1947. The Italians were unhappy about this sacrifice. They felt that since they had overthrown Mussolini and switched sides, they should have been treated as a cobelligerent rather than as a fallen enemy forced to yield territory to Yugoslavia and to assume a burden of reparations for several of Mussolini's lesser victims.

The former UNRRA man further believed that on the whole the Italians thought reasonably well of the United States, despite the unpopular peace treaty of 1947. They may not have been overflowing with gratitude, but at least they had some awareness of what Washington had done to promote their interests. This American official believed that UNRRA, with Uncle Sam carrying the heavy end of the financial log, had operated rather intelligently, more so than the Americans were then doing under their substitute relief efforts. The old organization had required reciprocal obligations on the part of the

Italians. My informant knew of one village that had formerly been ultrarightist and conspicuously friendly to the United States. Yet it had recently voted Communist, presumably in protest against the weakness of the conservative De Gasperi government in Rome. As to whether Italy would be taken over politically by the Communists within the next few years by sheer numbers, he remarked that one could best answer that question by tossing a coin.

On one point this American official was emphatic. These heirs of Michelangelo and Galileo were an ingenious people, and with the proper tools and materials they could work wonders. They had already rebuilt many railroads, culverts, and bridges, not only solidly but with remarkable artistry. He had taken a trip shortly after hostilities ended, and on the outbound journey had noted that all the bridges had been blown up. When he returned somewhat later, they had been substantially replaced, with the help of Americans who, of course, wanted the main lines reestablished.

Elsewhere I gleaned further details about the progress of Italian reconstruction. The slowly retreating Germans had deliberately wrecked many factories, in addition to those already destroyed during the war. Yet the output of textiles had made some recovery, largely because the Italians had rolled up their sleeves and pitched in. Early in the present year, industry as a whole had reached better than 50 percent of capacity. With the coal and raw materials that were envisioned under the Marshall Plan, the people could stage a remarkable recovery, as in fact they eventually did. At the time of my visit, unfortunately for them, the cutoff of supplies from UNRRA had not only lessened the food supply but had also deprived the Italians of other imports necessary to turn the wheels of industry. All the misfortunes had come at a time when former markets had largely dried up, notably those in Germany, Austria, and Czechoslovakia.

Yet the Italian people were not a sullen, dazed, beaten folk, like so many of the unfortunate Germans recently observed. While circulating among the Romans, I did not have the feeling of being in an enemy camp, as one so often felt in Germany. Yet the Italians must have had confused feelings: despised as enemies before 1943, they were unappreciated cobelligerents after 1943.

One of my most fruitful contacts was the distinguished Don Luigi Sturzo, a well-known priest, the author of many important books, a prime organizer of the Christian Democrat movement, and an anti-Fascist whom Mussolini had driven into exile for twenty years. He stated categorically that the two gravest problems at the moment were the scarcity of calories and the inflation of the lira. Food and finance alike were complicated by the uncertainty of coal imports, which before the war had amounted to about a million tons a month. In normal times the supply would be coming in from Germany and Britain, but now the Italians had to import much of it all the way from the United States—a costly operation indeed. The coal-rich Saar basin, formerly in German hands, was now in the grasp of the French.

Not only was the lira inflated, Don Sturzo told me, but it fluctuated wildly, thus complicating the problem of foreign exchange. He referred to a man who had come some weeks earlier to work for UNRRA. The new arrival had to rent housing at 36,000 lire a month; and even though there were ceilings on rents, he had just managed to make ends meet.

The future of Communism in Italy, Don Sturzo felt, depended primarily on economic recovery—or rather the lack of it. In the near chaos that prevailed, the chances were good that the country would embrace some form of the Moscow-connected ideology. From an economic standpoint, he believed that such a course would be neither catastrophic nor completely novel. Italy had already nationalized many of her important industries, some of which were then being run at a loss, to the distress of the taxpayer. The brand of Communism being advocated was primarily political, and its outstanding leader was the gifted Palmiro Togliatti. An anti-Mussolini exile for some twenty years, he had spent much time in Moscow. Yet he was not a complete visionary, for he favored an indigenous brand of Communism rather than the type dictated and directed by the Soviets. He was committed to taking the Italian road to democratic socialism. As for the future, Don Sturzo reckoned as 50–50 the chances that the Togliatti Communists would win control of the government in the crucial general election that was to be held in April of the next year, 1948.

My learned informant, perhaps hoping to flatter his American visitor, assured me that the Italians in general thought well of the United States. The occupying American soldiers, he added, had shown real savoir faire, unlike the cold and distant Britons. This characterization was a little hard to swallow, for I had already learned that many of the GIs, with money to fling around, not only had become involved in the black market but also had taken full advantage of the vulnerable Italian girls. Many of these females, suffering from hunger and other deprivations, had been willing to sell their favors for a chocolate bar or a few cigarettes, like their sisters in Germany. A few of the soldiers, to their credit, had actually married Italian women and brought them home. Yet many of the American invaders had assumed an air of superiority toward these Latin people, who were being forced into poverty and its attendant squalor. The British, remembering the bullying Mussolini's attempts to make war on the Allies, cherished much bitterness. One officer was quoted as saying, "The bloody bahstards tried for years to do us in; now let them suffer." Actually, some Italian aircraft had joined in Hitler's bombing of London.

My private poll of ninety-seven ex-GIs, taken just before I left Stanford University for Europe, indicated that the American servicemen who came in contact with the Italians during the war disliked them more than any of the other Europeans they encountered, even more than the French. One complaint was that the turncoat "dagoes" had not shown real "guts" during the war in fighting the enemy, and that in this respect they somewhat resembled the people of France. Like the French, the Italians seemed interested only in what they could get out of the United States. They were personally dirty and their general standards of cleanliness were low. They were always begging candy and cigarettes or stealing. One ex-veteran reported that many youngsters had hung around the encampment and on one occasion had cleaned out his tent, down to the floor mats, while the occupants were on a brief leave.

The same GI reported that after the invading Americans had strafed the streets of Foggia, the people were so resentful that it was the only city in Italy not "overflowing with prostitutes and eight-year-old pimps." He also wrote that in Bari, near the heel of the Italian boot, "the inflated price for an overnight shack-up with a woman reached $35.00," which was quite a jump from the days when a candy bar was supposed to suffice.

Few of the American servicemen seem to have realized in retrospect that they had not themselves cut a heroic figure with the local folk by taking advantage of their starving females in this fashion. Another veteran delicately wrote, "The impression received by Europeans during the war of the 'typical' GI could perhaps be represented by a phallus at uneven keel."

In a revealing interview in Rome, this one with an American academician then serving as a cultural attaché at the U.S. Embassy, I picked up some interesting but somewhat contradictory information. He believed that the Italians thought of the Americans in their native habitat as sophisticated barbarians. One writer, who had rather recently visited the United States, had written a book about America that was both constricted and jaundiced in viewpoint. He had seen only New York and then Chicago, where he had been the victim of a holdup that probably colored his judgment.

On the other hand, the same attaché reported that the happy-go-lucky GIs, many of them of Italian background, had made a reasonably good showing. One U.S. colonel told me that a number of Italian-Americans in his outfit had secured leaves so that they could visit grandparents and other relatives in Sicily and Italy. One should note that the policy of Washington during these postwar years was partly shaped by the millions of Italian-American voters in the United States, especially in regard to the relief for Italy provided under UN-RRA and the Marshall Plan. Similarly, the zeal of Roosevelt for establishing a non-Communist government in postwar Poland had Polish-American roots. He was probably influenced more by what he referred to as the six or seven million Polish-American voters than by any hope of regaining or retaining the free markets of Poland and eastern Europe. Some revisionist historians have either ignored or slighted the hyphenated Americans.

The GIs in Italy, whether Italian-American or not, had not become too drunk at the many beckoning bars, so I heard, but they had impressed the Romans as being naive. The American "boys" were friendly with children and, as good Boy Scouts, they had helped old ladies cross the streets. The Italian press was at pains to give its readers the stereotypes about the United States that they wanted and expected, especially such absurdities as flagpole sitting and being married in bathing suits. All this the Italians regarded as rather amusing *Americanata*.

Also enlightening was a press attaché at the U.S. Embassy. He observed that there were currently many restrictions on the newspapers, in which an anti-Catholic campaign, probably inspired by Communists, was being resisted by the Vatican. The Italians were more than 90 percent Catholic, at least on paper. Yet many of the Communists, though nominally Catholics, were anticlerical. Few of them tangled openly with the Church, however, largely because they feared excommunication. A Catholic could be a Communist but not a "good" Catholic at the same time. Catholicism was the last great bulwark against the atheistic Communism of the Soviets, and if the Papacy did not stand in its path, this attaché concluded, Italy would already have gone down the road to Moscow. Like other visitors to Rome, I was constantly reminded of the power and presence of the Church by St. Peter's Cathedral in Vatican City, as well as by the many Catholics, male and female, going about their business in flowing black robes.

This press attaché had a generally low opinion of American foreign correspondents, most of whom, he judged, served in Europe as glorified police-court reporters. They were often more intelligent and better grounded in European history than their reports revealed, but they were at the mercy of the home office in America. If they wrote too much high-brow stuff about Premier Alcide de Gasperi and his government, which was then floundering, they probably would receive a cablegram from their employers to go easy on these dull think pieces and cover some dramatic kidnapping in southern Italy. Further, the American newsmen were aware that cabled wordage was highly expensive, and that if they wanted to keep their jobs, they would do well to send in brief stories devoted to subjects that appealed to the more sensationalized standards of the home office. Correspondents would not admit that they slanted the news, but some of them evidently did so unconsciously. The most talented reporters, such as William L. Shirer, tended to become high-priced, with the result that they were often brought home, seated behind desks, and replaced by men who were younger, greener and lower paid. The press attaché concluded that the *New York Herald-Tribune* had the best foreign coverage at that time, and that the *New York Times* sinned less than most.

My Embassy press source further stated that a recent trip to Europe by prominent American editors and publishers was a step in the right direction, especially for the editors. But the publishers were successful businessmen like Frank E. Gannett, head of an influential newspaper chain, and they had already hardened their ideas. They were too old to learn new tricks, and they seemingly did not want to be taught. Arriving weary from their overseas plane trip, they spent much time on such frivolous missions as trying to locate scarce silk goods and other luxuries for their wives.

British correspondents, so this press attaché concluded, were much abler than their counterparts from the United States. They knew Europe as Americans know baseball lineups and batting averages. Britons were keenly aware of their military and industrial stake in a continent that was only twenty watery miles away; hence they were continuing their intense concern with reshaping Europe. The representative in Rome of the British Reuter news agency was consequently a more perceptive journalist than his opposite number employed by the Associated Press.

Elsewhere in the U.S. Embassy I managed to secure an interview with the military attaché, Colonel John M. Willems, who was quite willing to speak frankly to an accredited representative of the National

War College. The Allies had permitted Italy to retain a small regular army, he said, but it was low in morale and poorly equipped. Limited to three hundred thousand men, it would be wholly inadequate to stop an assault by the Communist leader of Yugoslavia, Marshal Tito. Fears then prevailed in Rome that Tito was preparing to lunge into the disputed area of Trieste and on into northern Italy with a formidable army of several hundred thousand men well equipped with Soviet weapons. Yet despite all these discouragements, the Italian armed forces were fairly loyal to the conservative government of Premier De Gasperi, as the Communist uprising of the next year was to demonstrate. Indicative of the lowly station of the army was the status of the Chief of Staff. His salary was about $75.00 a month, and the smallness of this stipend was in keeping with the unimpressive appearance of his uniform.

From all the information thus gathered, I concluded that the Communist party was gaining momentum. It might well oust the Washington-backed Premier De Gasperi and his leading Christian Democrats in the crucial general election scheduled for April, 1948. Political posters, generously plastered on the walls and buildings of Rome, already gave mute testimony to the mounting political fever. The criticism was widely heard that the rightists should be compromising more, but the response often came in the form of a question: How does one compromise with a Communist? The labor unions were controlled by the Communists, and their leaders, some of them Moscow-trained, worked full-time as agitators. The opposition, much less fanatical, gave the rightist cause only part-time attention.

Many of the impoverished Italian peasants who supported Communism did not have the faintest idea what they were letting themselves in for. The list could include collectivization of farms and the installation of secret police. Yet these Communist dissidents were more conspicuously hostile to Italian rightists than to capitalistic Americans. I learned that Ambassador James C. Dunn, speaking for the United States, had recently addressed large groups of workers in a Communist center of Sicily, and that he had received an exceptionally enthusiastic welcome there.

After boarding General Robinson's C-47 for the return flight to Frankfurt, I could reflect at length on what I had seen and heard in Rome. Foremost in my thinking was the peril to the so-called Free World of a takeover in Italy by the Communists, who were presumably Moscow-directed or at least Moscow-inspired. Up to that time I had assumed that the real danger lay in the ballot rather than in the bullet. Yet some twenty-five years later the Washington government published highly classified documents indicating that in 1947–1948 the bullet was perhaps more to be feared than the ballot.

On June 18, 1947, almost a month before my arrival in Rome and about two weeks after Secretary Marshall's epochal speech at Harvard University, Ambassador Dunn had cabled a disquieting dispatch to Washington. The Italian press, he reported, was publishing alarmist reports of activity by veteran Partisan fighters in the Communist strongholds of the industrialized "Red Zone" of northern Italy. Many of these former members of the hard-fighting Resistance were bringing their weapons out of hiding. Fiery speeches were urging armed revolt against the De Gasperi government in Rome, from which the Communists had been completely excluded the previous May. Dunn added that he had himself received reports of the activities of military or paramilitary organizations under Communist control. He discounted the rumors that 150,000 armed men were thus available; he put the figure at a more reasonable 50,000, plus some sympathizers. Yet he was hopeful that all these threats were supplements to political measures. It was to the advantage of the Communists, he believed, to keep the country in a "state of jitters."

In mid-September, 1947, the press announced a gigantic Communist rally at Rome. An impassioned Palmiro Togliatti, the Italian Communist leader, delivered a speech to a crowd numbering a reported one hundred thousand Communists. He denounced the United States as a "world dictatorship" that was "trying to spread another war." From the assembled multitude came the angry cry, "Death to Truman!"

Some of Ambassador Dunn's worst fears were realized the next year, shortly after the De Gasperi government, aided by unabashed verbal and financial support from the United States and the Vatican, soundly defeated the Communists in the heated general election of April, 1948. The campaign left countless hammers and sickles scrawled in red paint on walls and buildings. One should note that representatives of the millions of Italian-American voters had made their influence felt, monetarily and otherwise. Two months after the election, a Sicilian student shot and severely wounded Togliatti, the Communist leader. His aroused following, which dominated the trade unions, thereupon called a paralyzing nationwide strike. In some cities of the north, notably Turin and Genoa, angry workers brought out weapons hidden since the Resistance, rushed into the streets, and opened fire. With unexpected vigor the government called up some three hundred thousand police and troops, and in three days of disorders at least twenty-one people were killed and two hundred injured. The fighting ended when the Communists called off their general strike and opted for the ballot instead of the bullet.

The crushing of this small-scale civil war, combined with the electoral setback for the leftists, made possible the successful implementation in Italy of Marshall Plan aid, beginning in 1948. This starving country received in all $1,508,800,000 from the United States under the European Recovery Program, ranking below only Britain and France. In 1949 an alarmed Italy joined the United States and other democratic nations in the twelve-power North Atlantic Treaty Organization, designed as the military bulwark against the westward thrust of Moscow.

9

Occupied South Germany

*The march westward of communism and world rev-
olution has been stopped in central Germany.*

General Lucius D. Clay
October 27, 1947

Bright and early in the morning of July 17, 1947, a new Army driver
called for me at the Victory Guest House near Frankfurt to take me on
the first leg of an inspection tour of southern Germany. Our con-
veyance was a Plymouth sedan, slightly the worse for wear, and the
chauffeur was a Caucasian whose presence would not create racist
difficulties with regard to food and lodging.

After driving some fifty miles through lush green country, we made
our first stop at Heidelberg, picturesquely located on the Neckar
River. Aside from a ruined castle, the most famous tourist attraction
was probably the famous University of Heidelberg, founded in 1386
A.D.. and widely regarded as the leading institution of its kind in nine-
teenth-century Germany. To Americans, especially those familiar
with Sigmund Romberg's operetta, *The Student Prince*, it conjured up
memories of duels, songs, beer drinking, and romance.

Nestled comfortably among the hills, Heidelberg differed from
many other German cities in that it had suffered practically no damage
from bombing. The obvious major reason for such immunity was the
absence of vital war industries. The unbombed streets were crowded,
although one noticed relatively few men in their middle or late twenties. This age bracket had been decimated by the recent war.

Heidelbergians naturally looked healthier and better fed than the
inhabitants of any of the other places I had thus far visited in Germany. I would almost say "happier," were it not for the fact that

previously I had noticed few German smiles. But there was probably considerable laughter in this favored city, for one theater was advertising *Charley's Tante,* which was presumably an adaptation of the thigh-slapping English stage comedy known as *Charley's Aunt.*

Passersby in Heidelberg were better dressed than their northern counterparts, although an observer could not help seeing a good many of the short leather trousers common in Bavaria and known as *lederhosen.* They were said to be handed down from father to son, and this tale could be believed in view of the begrimed appearance of many of these durable garments. By contrast, the women, especially the girls, were the best-dressed lot that I was to see in Germany. Many of them sported lipstick, a scarce article at this time that reflected the presence of American soldiers, who also dispensed cigarettes and chocolate bars. GI generosity, one assumed, was not without its price.

My arrival at the university did not bring out any brass bands or even red carpets. On the contrary, the man who served as liaison for the Army scowled as he complained that the people "up there" persisted in sending down VIPs to pester him. His chief grievance appeared to be that he had to dispatch his pretty young secretary as a guide; he did not want to interrupt his work by doing so, especially since he was paying her out of his own pocket. He finally relented with ill grace, and although I was embarrassed to be caught in the middle of this dispute, I availed myself of the services of Hanneliese, a young university student who spoke excellent English and otherwise proved most helpful. She had been living in Cologne until the bombing became too hot, and then she had moved to Vienna for the remainder of the war. From her and others close to the scene I picked up some insight regarding the status of the university, now more than five centuries old.

Shelter was not the problem at the University of Heidelberg that it was in bombed-out Berlin, but the U.S. Army had not helped when it appropriated a large room for a movie theater. About twenty of the faculty chairs were unfilled, and during a period of sixteen months one of the professors had received no contract and no salary. Of special interest to those who looked forward to the denazifying and demilitarizing of the German people, the traditional duelling was now strictly *verboten*—at least under existing conditions. No longer could the faces of German militarists legally bear honorable but disfiguring scars.

Estimates were that about 80 percent of the former teachers in the Heidelberg schools had been Nazis, and that about half of these had been activists for Hitler. Many prominent ex-Nazis were now teaching in the institutions of this area that were not under American control. Germans were more critical than they had formerly been of the U.S. Army of occupation, and this attitude was not altogether bad. The conquered people were evidently learning the ways of democracy that had been stifled during the dictatorship of Hitler.

Among the lower-level U.S. Army officers at Heidelberg I found considerable cynicism about the prospects of retooling the Nazi mind. One of them, echoing General Patton, observed that the Germans were in roughly the same plight that American Democrats would have been in if the Democratic President Roosevelt had lost the war. The claim that many of the Nazis had been blackmailed or otherwise forced into the Hitler camp no doubt was true; hence a feeling prevailed that the victor should not be too rough on the vanquished. One complaint that I heard involved the difficulty of recruiting an adequate police force in view of the strict policy of excluding Nazis from such responsibilities.

These Army sources in Heidelberg assured me that the Germans were great whiners and self-pitiers. They had a strong tendency to "squeal" on one another, as they had been encouraged to do under Hitler. As the military occupation continued, they were showing less servility and greater contempt for the Americans. A part of the problem was the behavior of the young and naive Yankee soldiers who were being sent over to serve as occupying soldiers. An ugly incident had occurred some weeks earlier when they had beaten up a German girl on the street, probably for reasons that related to her unwillingness to "fraternize." Fortunately, my sources concluded, the newer arrivals were proving to be more intelligent and more mature.

Pushing southward, we headed next for Stuttgart, about eighty miles distant. The officers in the American headquarters here were quite willing to have me continue with the trusty Plymouth, but an enthusiast for air transportation began to sing the praises of his one-passenger L-5. His big talking point was that one could travel faster and perhaps more safely. After some hesitation, I permitted myself to be talked into going by air, and this decision proved to be questionable. We saved many hours in getting all the way to Munich, and we saw countless treetops and rooftops, but we met no people. What interested me most was how the Germans looked, acted, and reacted, with special reference to the conditions imposed by the conquerors.

This flight southward was a scary experience. We flew at a height of about one thousand feet, and the pilot, an ebullient lone eagle, liked to swoop and tip his wings at a sharp angle, or what seemed to me to be a sharp angle. I was strapped helplessly into the single passenger seat with no real flooring below me—except solid earth. We did see at low levels much beautiful green country, laid out like giant golf courses and intersected with tiny streams. Somewhat surprising was the great expanse of scientifically cultivated forest, from which lumber was then being extracted to help replace the bombed-out housing of Germany. Here and there were scattered neatly clustered villages, as well as a number of relatively small and isolated factories that had escaped mass bombing.

At Frankfurt the Army headquarters had not arranged any contacts for me in Stuttgart; hence I was unable to secure information from individuals. About all that my journal records is an overnight stay at the Graf Zeppelin Hotel. Yet I could see that this formerly beautiful city lay in a charming green valley, with houses dotting the surrounding hillsides. The bomb damage was heavy, comparable to that at Frankfurt and other major cities to the north. I had a special interest in the great Stuttgart library, which contained mostly materials relating to World War I. This depository and the Hoover War Library (now The Hoover Institution) at Stanford University were generally regarded as the two richest collections of their kind in the world. The sad tale was that when war came the priceless materials at Stuttgart had been moved to a remote castle, which unfortunately suffered heavy enough bombing to destroy about one-fourth of the documents. Yet today the library is still a world-famous center.

My lone-eagle pilot next flew me in his two-seater to Nuremberg, which lies about one hundred miles northeast of Stuttgart. The historic city had suffered frightful bombing—scarcely one house in ten stood undamaged at war's end—for it was a major producer of engines for submarines, airplanes, and tanks. Nuremberg had special attractions for the historian because it had been the site of Hitler's great "Sieg Heil" rallies and more recently the scene of the war-crimes trials. These proceedings, begun in November, 1945, had resulted in the conviction of nineteen big-name Nazis in September, 1946, although the trials of lesser fry were still dragging out and were to continue to do so in the American zone until April, 1949.

As a spectator and auditor, I was present with earphones in the galleries of the courtrooms in which five war-crimes trials were in progress. But before being permitted to attend any one of them, I had to follow the routine of presenting myself, even as a representative of the National War College, to the chief prosecutor, General Telford Taylor, a distinguished lawyer. His brief remarks do not linger clearly in my memory, but he impressed me then, as later, as having an exceptionally keen mind. My officer-guide told me that Taylor not only formally opened and closed each case, but that he prepared his own presentations in an era when ghost-written performances were becoming increasingly common.

General Taylor indicated to me that the defense was deliberately protracting the proceedings. This strategy of delay obviously was governed by two lines of reasoning. First, because time heals wounds, the passing of another year or two might create a climate of opinion more favorable to the imprisoned Germans. Second, a dreary logjam of unfinished cases might help to persuade the weary prosecutors to drop the whole sordid business.

One of the most pressing problems for the prosecution was to round up enough competent American judges. Qualified jurists were generally reluctant to leave their families and firesides in the United States for a protracted stay abroad, especially in this cold, hungry, bitter, crowded, and ravaged country. An effort had been made to enlist enough competent federal judges, but in the end the Washington government had to settle for a number of state jurists. The problems involved were later laid bare with rare fidelity in the movie *Judgment at Nuremberg* (1961), which starred Spencer Tracy as a confused, lower-level jurist.

My own impressions at the time were that some of the judges were too old for such strenuous business. Many of them undoubtedly had grave misgivings about getting involved with ex post facto litigation, for the Constitution of the United States specifically ruled out prosecution for crimes that were not clearly contrary to law at the time they were committed. Hermann Goering and the other top-flight German war criminals could argue that the "crime" of waging aggressive war was not a clear-cut personal crime under international law when Hitler burst into Poland on that fateful September morning in 1939. Such charges as "crimes against peace" and "crimes against humanity" were vague, particularly at a time when all civilized nations had specific laws against murder.

Two of the most memorable lessons taught by the Nuremberg trials were clear. First, if a nation goes to war, it had better not lose; second, the victor makes the rules for punishment. In a sense, losing was the real crime, and undoubtedly the greatest source of genuine regret to most Germans. In all great conflicts atrocities always occur on both sides; in truth, war is the greatest atrocity of all. Later that year at the National War College many of the American officers voiced concern over this brand of victor's justice. Their feeling was that if the United States lost the next war, the Nuremberg trials would have established a boomeranging precedent which one day might result in wholesale hangings of Americans. Even while the prosecutions were in progress, the suggestion was heard that if the Germans had won, they might then be hanging Americans for violating the laws of war. Both sides, including the Americans, had torpedoed numerous unresisting merchant ships without warning, contrary to international law as of 1939. Like the German U-boat officers, the Allied submariners were only carrying out orders from their superiors and did not regard themselves as murderers.

Conspicuous at the Nuremberg trials were Soviet prosecutors and judges, but no German judges. By the elementary principles of logic and fairness, Stalin and other Russian officials should have been in the dock along with accused Nazis. In terms of crimes against peace, one should note that Stalin had connived with Hitler to start this war of aggression, then had plotted to come in for his share of Poland, which he had simultaneously assaulted from the rear.

As for crimes against humanity, although not directly connected with this war, one should remember the millions of dissidents whom Stalin had condemned to death in the labor camps of the Gulag Archipelago, as well as the millions of peasants (kulaks) whom he had liquidated by displacing them from their land. More directly related to the recent conflict were the innumerable Russian atrocities and barbarities committed against the Baltic peoples and especially the Poles during the war. The deliberate execution and burial in mass graves at Katyn of some forty-two hundred uniformed Polish soldiers, mostly officers, pointed more than a finger of suspicion at Joseph Stalin. Yet there is an ancient principle in Anglo-Saxon jurisprudence that he who comes into court must come with clean hands.

At the five Nuremberg trials then progressing, the galleries were occupied by concerned citizens, presumably mostly Germans. Admittance was by a special pass, and friendly Germans ("white Germans") were able to secure the necessary tickets. "Gray Germans," or those properly denazified, were being considered acceptable risks. Local interest in the trials was keen, as attested by the presence of many spectators, some of whom came long distances and often had to go without food all day. Germans of university age were conspicuous, especially those taking notes on the mysterious workings of democratic justice and the lessons to be learned by the losers.

German witnesses for the prosecution needed considerable courage. Naturally they were not popular with former Nazi neighbors, and they were exposed to various pressures, including threats against their lives. The Allied prosecutors were obliged to go to considerable pains to protect their witnesses, and my information was that at least some of them were lodged in jail alongside ex-Nazis.

The German counsel for the accused was chosen by the defendants themselves, and these learned German lawyers appeared in the conventional judicial garb. They seemed to be quite human, for I saw one obviously asleep and another smiling at the sallies of a voluble witness. One plausible explanantion for prolonging the trials was that the counsel for the defense was receiving American food rations, plus soap and a carton of cigarettes each week. Ordinary Germans were faring much less well.

The small-fry trials that I witnessed at Nuremberg were anticlimactic, for Hermann Goering and eighteen other Nazi big fish had been convicted some ten months earlier. Of the secondary prosecutions now proceeding, one involved a half-dozen well-fed industrialists, whose uniforms seemed to be prison garb. Only one of them looked like an evil character to me, but I must add that the all-purpose mask known as the human face is often misleading. Another simultaneous trial involved eleven generals, nine of them in uniform and two of them in civilian clothes.

Of special interest to me, though of only slight interest to the partially full gallery, was the trial of some twenty doctors who allegedly had performed inhuman experiments on human subjects, to say nothing of other atrocities. Some of the medics looked like ordinary Germans, but others presented stony faces. They were all obviously concerned about their fate, as was further evidenced by their passing notes on to their counsel. An attorney for the defense was reading his brief from the dais, and I caught a bit of the translation in the earphones available to the auditors. The familiar argument advanced in these trials was that the medical defendants were merely carrying out the orders of their superiors or practicing euthanasia. I heard of an incident involving an attack on one of the doctors by a mentally retarded patient whom the same doctor had sterilized—all in pursuance of eugenic orders. This authentic outburst was later featured in the movie *Judgment at Nuremberg.*

While at Nuremberg I was escorted with some other visitors on a guided tour of the formidable jail in which some lesser Nazis were then awaiting trial. The entrances and exits were well guarded, and dozens of vigorous and well-muscled prisoners were walking around briskly, presumably for exercise. As a lot they not only appeared to be vigorous, but some of them had a pronounced military bearing. One of our guides informed us that their daily ration was 2900 calories, far above the nominal 1550 for Germans at Frankfurt, and this abundance no doubt did much to account for the impression of physical wellbeing. One of these stalwart inmates stepped up briskly in line for his kitful of food, which consisted of a large serving of what looked like white cereal mush. He received it with evident relish and most likely washed it down with his daily ration of coffee.

Our guides showed us the cells of the inmates, including the vacant one formerly occupied by the late Hermann Goering. It was small, cramped, dingy, and depressing. Conspicuously in one corner stood an all-purpose toilet bowl; in the other a bedlike cot. In between was a chair, which served as Goering's dining table when he laid out the mess kit containing his prison fare. In the big door was a small hinged door through which the prisoner's mess kit could be shoved. Here were the basic elements of a Greek tragedy. Once a glitteringly be-medalled war hero and one of the most powerful men on earth, Goering had tumbled from his dizzy height into a dingy death cell, where he had awaited his ignominious end in drab prison garb.

As all the world knows, Goering was condemned to death but cheated the gallows at the last moment by taking a cyanide pill or capsule that he had cleverly concealed, presumably on his person. The story then current was that he had left a note informing his captors where they could find another such capsule. He had an engaging personality and an exceptional mind, which he used at his trial to embarrass what he regarded as hypocritical prosecutors. My guide told me that the German people were shocked and dismayed that so famous a man could not face his end with composure, but instead had to do away with himself in a cowardly fashion. Yet I remembered that the American press had reported considerable joy in Germany over the way "Foxy Hermann" had outfoxed his captors.

Reflecting later on this visit to the jail, I concluded that it was a foolhardy thing to do. With dozens of able-bodied men within a few feet of us, nothing could have prevented them from suddenly jumping us and overpowering our Army guard. Our protector might have been able to pull out his forty-five and squeeze off one or two shots, but even that seems unlikely. Of course, the escaping prisoners would have been captured ultimately, but there was really nothing to keep them from seizing the dozen or so visitors as hostages and holding them for promises of amnesty or some other favorable terms.

Before leaving Nuremberg I encountered an American colonel who, at one stage of the war or after, had something to do with the management of about fifty thousand Russians. Whether they were prisoners of war taken by the Germans or displaced persons of some kind my notebook does not say, but I assume that they fell into either of these two categories. The colonel referred to these unfortunates as "animals" who had to be taught to use latrines rather than the corners of rooms. The Russians, he gathered, were cruel, even brutal, and had little regard for human life. He told of a Soviet officer who had shot his driver because this luckless person had dented the official car. The murderous Muscovite then allegedly remarked that it was easy to get a new driver but not a new automobile. My American colonel concluded that the Soviet government, like the Russians themselves, understood only the language of brute force. To top it off, they were extremely distrustful of the United States; in fact, partly as a result of Communist propaganda, they seemed to be fearful and distrustful of everybody.

There was truth, probably mixed with exaggeration, in these eyewitness observations regarding the behavior of the fifty thousand uprooted Russians. But the views expressed were common among American military men who had been privileged to see the Soviets at close quarters.

My trusty L-5 next carried me under the clouds for nearly one hundred miles from Nuremberg to Munich. Once known as the Paris of Germany, this city was now notorious as "The Cradle of National Socialism," from which Hitler had launched his Nazi conspiracy. Comparisons of degrees of rubble are not especially useful, but Munich impressed me as being about as badly smashed up as any place I had thus far seen in Germany. We circled in over the smokestacks of the notorious crematoria at Dachau, which was pointed out to me by my daredevil pilot.

No red carpet awaited my arrival; in fact, no carpet of any kind. In cutting loose at Heidelberg from the Plymouth car and taking to the air, I had evidently disrupted the more leisurely schedule worked out for me at Frankfurt by an extremely efficient woman officer (WAAC). (One male officer told me that a good WAAC did five times the office work of one man—and ate less.) In any event, the word had not come through that a VIP was arriving, and instead of being met by a limousine or even a dented Chevrolet, I was greeted by an enlisted man with a sturdy jeep. The ride to my hotel was a teeth-chattering experience, and I felt an increased admiration for the GIs who had bounced their way across Germany in such an invention of the Devil.

My hostelry proved to be the famous Four Seasons Hotel, which was a far cry from the Victory Guest House near Frankfurt or the Wannsee Club near the heart of Berlin. But it had its good points; it cost only thirty-five cents a day and it was eerily quiet. The reason for the second blessing was that one side of the structure had been blown off, leaving a gaping hole, and consequently there seemed to be no other guests to disturb my slumbers. The disquieting thought crossed my mind that a prowler might enter my room during the night through these bomb-created entrances. But all that I lost was a pair of leather bedroom slippers, which I overlooked in my haste to depart but which I am sure became valued footwear for some shoeless German.

As was my practice, I picked my way through the rubble-strewn streets of this once proud nursery of Nazidom. The Germans had made a beginning, but only a beginning, in carting away the debris and in undertaking some repairs and a little new construction. In places the terrible smell of decaying corpses assailed the nostrils; the dead were too deeply entombed under the rubble to be easily exhumed. But life does go on, as I was reminded in seeing several children busily engaged in making a playhouse from the multitudinous loose bricks.

Munich, April 30, 1945. U. S. 7th Army units prepare to enter heart of city.

(U. S. Army photograph)

Further light was shed on the younger generation by two incidents. In the badly damaged railroad station in Munich a little German girl, about ten years of age, panhandled a lighted and partly consumed cigarette from a Negro trooper; she then extinguished it on the floor with her heel and made off triumphantly with the butt, probably for reprocessing. On another occasion I was being driven by one of the American Army officers when we had to halt at a stoplight. A young boy nine or ten years old, his handless arm in a sling, darted up to our car to beg "cigarettes for my fader [father]?" Quick as a rapier, he reached in with his good hand, pressed open the ashtray, and scooped out three or four cigarette butts. Meanwhile the officer-driver was vainly trying to slap away the arm of the youthful intruder.

On the streets of Munich the Bavarian types with grimy leather knee pants were much more in evidence than I had noticed elsewhere in Germany. The supposedly fun-loving Bavarians were more commonly of the brunette type than the Prussians of the north, who were reputedly more addicted to duelling and militarism. These southerners had traditionally harbored considerable antipathy for their countrymen to the north, so much so that separatist movements had surfaced from time to time. Rather recently, so I learned in Munich, signs had appeared demanding "Bavaria for the Bavarians."

As was the case elsewhere in Germany, the people of the Munich area looked gray and undernourished. A British medical man remarked that the Germans were slowly starving, and that there was no real cure for tuberculosis, which had already reached alarming levels. The Army people reported that traditional German cleanliness was now a myth. There were terrible animal odors in the nearby town of Freising, and there had been a real problem in keeping the kitchen cleaned up in the jail at Nuremberg.

Much fraternization with the former enemy was going on in the Munich area, largely because the military government had lifted the ban on it as early as September, 1945. While restrictions were still in force the servicemen had sought the company of undesirable types of women, with a consequent sharp rise in venereal disease. One major spoke of a German girl who refused to go out with American officers; another of good family married an officer in spite of strong objections from her parents.

One of my Stanford students, a veteran once stationed in postwar Germany, had reported to me shortly before I took off for Europe that he had been in contact with the Displaced Persons Camp at Feldafing, about twenty-five miles south of Munich, where the Jews allegedly had little food and no money. According to his written report, which seemed hard to believe, a Jewish female had vainly offered him $10,000 in cash if he would marry her and bring her to the States.

A depressing feature of my stay in Munich was a visit to Dachau, about twelve miles by motor car northwest of Munich. This was the famous concentration camp, equipped to handle some 30,000 victims at a time, where many luckless souls were done to death. Although about 230,000 human beings were murdered here, the toll among Jews and Poles was far greater at places like Auschwitz, which was an extermination camp rather than a concentration camp. My guide, Colonel Clio Straight, chief prosecutor in this area of lesser German crimes of a military nature, said that Dachau was cynically known as the country club among concentration camps. Indeed, Pastor Martin Niemöller, the dissenting Protestant cleric whom Hitler failed to break, had survived incarceration here.

Colonel Straight wondered aloud why the Nazis had gone to all the trouble to ship so many emaciated victims from afar, only to cremate them. His view was that it would have been much cheaper and more humane to dig trenches with bulldozers, dump the bullet-riddled corpses in, and then bulldoze dirt over them. He scoffed at the standard excuse that the German people did not suspect or know what was going on at Dachau, especially what was rising from these belching smokestacks. At the time of my visit to this charnel house, more than two years after the last cremation, one could still detect the offensive death smell, which Colonel Straight remembered as having been really bad as recently as a year earlier. A good many Germans must have feared that something evil was going on below those busy smokestacks, but wisely concluded that they might be coming out of them in the form of smoke if they spoke out of turn. Individual Germans did not cross Hitler in those days with impunity; it was best to look the other way, as Americans probably would have done if similarly imprisoned within totalitarian walls.

Near the entrance to the main building at Dachau I noticed the scattered fragments of bones, including some neatly sawed sections of large wrist bones two or three inches in length. I was a little surprised that some of the less squeamish visitors had not picked them all up as souvenirs of Hitlerian horrors. My attention was also drawn to one or two wreaths placed here under French auspices to honor the many French citizens who had perished in this charnel house. Few inmates ever escaped; attack dogs had been specially trained to recognize the prison uniforms and to sink their fangs into escapees. When recaptured, the prisoners were often subjected to inhuman kidney-beating, administered in front of the other prisoners and depicted by gruesome wax figures carved by former Polish inmates.

Inside Dachau, splattered bloodstains still appeared on the walls of one reception room. A visitor could also see the cells in which the inmates were kept in tandem to discourage suicide, as well as a gas chamber, resembling a shower room, in which lethal fumes poured out of the pipes. There were also execution places used for both hanging and shooting, in addition to the grisly crematoria, big and small.

Here were the small and big trays, with the latter accommodating three bodies. What remained was scraped off and saved, if of any commercial value.

After visiting the Dachau hellhole, I understood better why the German doctors were being tried at Nuremberg. The Nazis had not only abused the prisoners, but had exploited their labor while living and then their bodies while dead. Tons of hair were shorn from female heads, while gold was "mined" from the teeth of victims. One room, then open to the public, was in the nature of a museum for students of anatomy. Pickled in scores of large jars of clear preservative, probably alcohol, were parts of human bodies of interest to medical people. Presumably these specimens were extracted when the patients were dead, but one could not be sure in all cases. Representative exhibits were a half-head profile of an adult Pole; parts of lungs; and an extraordinarily large varicose vein (varicocele) extracted from the genitals of some ill-starred adult male who was probably starving to death.

My helpful guide, Colonel Straight, proved to be one of the most valuable sources of information on my entire trip. As chief prosecutor at Dachau, he was instructed to bring justice to those culprits, mostly soldiers, who had violated the rules of war. He was not involved with the top-echelon Nazis at Nuremberg who had started and prosecuted the conflict.

The "Malmédy massacre," in which the Germans had shot about ninety inconvenient American prisoners of war during the Battle of the Bulge, December, 1944, had proved especially bothersome to Colonel Straight. Shooting prisoners is an old army game, especially when those captured would hamper the forward movement of an operation or constitute a menace if released in the rear. Colonel Straight remarked that the case was not only a hard nut to crack, but that it got worse the more he probed into it. The German participants were sworn to silence and would not inform on one another, yet American public opinion demanded prompt action. Another problem was that the United States could not conceivably bring to justice all former German soldiers involved in this sort of thing; many of them were in the Soviet zone, and the Russians were highly uncooperative in releasing them.

Colonel Straight's military trials at Dachau were designed to deter other aggressors in future wars. The United States was not attempting here to establish a new international law, as at Nuremberg, but to punish open-and-shut violations of the Geneva Convention and the laws of war. Such progress as was being made, I learned, was due in large part to fearful cooperation by German "squealers," who had been encouraged to inform on their neighbors under the Nazis. A standard German defense was the *tu quoque,* or "you're another," argument; that is, the Allied troops, including the Russians, had also been guilty of ruthless actions. But the loser in such cases does not have as effective a voice as the winner.

Procedures in these lower-level trials differed markedly from those at Nuremberg. All the defendants had American counsel and they could request as many German defenders as they wished. The judges were U.S. military men, many of them near retirement and not judicially minded; they were accustomed to the procedures of a court martial. As good soldiers themselves, they accepted more readily than civilians would the argument that the German culprits had simply been obeying the orders of higher-ups. In any event, whatever the American tribunals ruled would be reviewed later by higher authority.

Colonel Straight stated that he personally leaned over backward to be fair; he preferred to give the benefit of the doubt to the defendants —a trait that later got him into trouble.* To his credit, he wanted the record to look right for posterity. A case in point involved a German soldier who had shot a grounded American airman allegedly reaching for his gun. Colonel Straight had only the German's word to go on, yet he found it convincing enough to warrant dropping the accusation. But there were plenty of other cases. A number of former German soldiers awaiting trial were being imprisoned in small cells with barred doors that, to me, resembled cages in a zoo.

Difficulties with the Soviets were still much on Colonel Straight's mind. He stated that the Russians had been completely uncooperative in providing evidence or witnesses to convict the German prisoners still held by the Americans. The last trial involving Russian assistance had occurred about a year and a half earlier, but after that the Americans had given up all further attempts to enlist Soviet help.

Colonel Straight could only speculate on why the Soviets were unwilling to punish these war criminals, especially since the Germans had inflicted an enormous amount of rape, pillaging, murder, and devastation in the USSR. Perhaps the Russians felt that they had already meted out enough rough justice. Perhaps they reasoned that they had much to gain by blackmail: they could threaten to turn German ex-soldiers over to the Americans if the individuals in question did not become pliant Communist stooges.

---

*Colonel Straight in 1948 was haled before a Senate subcommittee to explain why he had recommended that the life sentence of Ilse Koch, "The Bitch of Buchenwald," be reduced to four years. She was the notorious wife of the German commandant of an infamous concentration camp. Despite the public uproar, General Clay stood firm in commuting her sentence to four years.

Pathological suspicion was a long-recognized national trait of the Russians. It had already annoyed Americans, military and civilian, who were trying to assist Soviet officials, even after the launching of the lend-lease program. In these postwar years the Soviets evidently did not want the American "imperialist-capitalists" snooping around, and they had put all kinds of roadblocks in the paths of investigations. According to Colonel Straight, American agents had to be at a certain place at a certain time on the frontier of the Russian zone; then they were required to fill out elaborate forms. These questionnaires asked who was to be interrogated and where, and also what specific questions were going to be presented. The U.S. Military Government had permitted the Russians to enter the American zone to investigate, but they arrived at the frontier with no identifying insignia, refused to reveal what agency they represented, and then faded out of the picture.

Above all else, the Russians were extremely sensitive to foreign spying—and still are. One American soldier had gone on a private jaunt in his L-5 plane, was caught in the Soviet zone, and then jailed for about three weeks. A comrade who went to secure his release was himself imprisoned for a few days. Snoopers were suspect.

Colonel Straight concluded that the Russians thought differently from the Americans, that they were boorishly unmannerly, and that they were ignorantly ungrateful for what the United States had done for them with some $11 billion worth of lend-lease equipment. An American could never convince a Russian, he said, that Fords and Chevrolets were not of Soviet manufacture.* Many Russians believed that all these vehicles encountered outside the Soviet Union had been manufactured in Russia and then exported to the West. As for manners, when Colonel Straight, all decked out in his uniform, had reached Berlin, he visited the ruins of the Reichschancellery and was handed a book of photographs depicting the place before the bombing. A Russian private seized it from his hands, glanced at it, and then thrust it back.

Before taking leave of Germany, I should record some assessment of the general attitudes of the GIs toward the peoples whom they had encountered during and after the war. The Germans and the British enjoyed the highest rating, and this judgment was confirmed by the poll that I had recently taken of ninety-seven student-veterans in June, 1947. As I have already noted, there had been some friction

---

*Many American GIs, transported to England in the mighty *Queen Mary* and *Queen Elizabeth* could not be persuaded that the British, not the Americans, had built ships of this size.

between the Americans and the British, but the "limeys"* were generally respected or liked because they were clean, spoke a familiar language, shared a common culture, and had shown real "guts" in standing up to an overpowering Hitler. The French, also for reasons I have previously indicated, ranked low on the list, especially for their inferior sanitation, their superior attitude, their ingratitude, and their gouging shopkeepers, who had bilked the GIs.

The suspicious Russians—crude, unmannerly, and ignorant—were generally disliked, partly because they were distrusted and feared. Photographs of American and Soviet soldiers joyously clasping hands or embracing near the Elbe River in Germany are misleading. Early misunderstandings and friction soon led to fistfights and some shooting incidents, especially after an unwelcome Colonel Frank Howley entered the American sector of Berlin before the looting had ended. The raping and plundering Soviet soldiers had been indoctrinated with distrust of the American capitalist-imperialists. They also angered the Americans by stubbornly believing that they had won the war themselves, and they were arrogant enough to think that they were just as good as the capitalist-enslaved Americans—perhaps even better.

All things considered, it is hardly surprising that many American soldiers liked the Germans best of all, especially in the months after Hitler's collapse. The enemy people looked better than those of a France that had suffered German occupation for four years. In sharp contrast with the situation in 1947, Hitler's misled masses were relatively well fed and well dressed in 1945. The Germans seemed more like Americans, especially the attractive females, who resembled the girls left behind in Peoria. The GIs admired German habits of cleanliness (flush toilets), discipline, industriousness, and quality workmanship, especially in binoculars and Leica cameras. The girls soon became intimately friendly, especially in the presence of chocolate bars. Germany rapidly became a black marketeer's paradise in which the cigarette was king.

Dazed by defeat, the Germans were naturally docile and flattering, even obsequious. Eager to please their conquerors, they were intelligent enough to perceive that the stronger their resistance was, the longer the occupation would last. The naive young American soldiers, sent over for occupation chores, were susceptible to the charms of the girls and to the wiles of the ex-Nazis, some of whom spread the Hit-

---

*The nickname "limey" apparently grew out of the earlier practice in the British Navy of issuing lime juice to ward off scurvy.

lerian lie that President Roosevelt was a Jew (born Rosenfeldt). The gullible GIs were told, often by a friendly *Fräulein*, that Hitler had given the Germans splendid new highways, ample food, high employment, new hope, resurrected honor, and national pride. Besides, the individual German did not regard himself as responsible for the *Führer* or his hellish cremation camps.

The results of such seduction were inevitable. After nearly two years of the occupation, many a young GI, often a grade-school dropout, was believing what the local girls may have been whispering in his ear. Their story was that what the Germans had been saying from the beginning was true. The real enemy, as well as the pressing danger, was Communist Russia. Hitler had clearly perceived this menace and had fought Stalin in vain on behalf of Western civilization. Hence America and a revived Germany ought to clasp hands in an alliance against the common Communist foe.

Such suspicions about Soviet noncooperation seemed to be fully borne out by what was happening on the Marshall Plan front. On July 15, two days before my departure from Frankfurt for the four-day tour of south Germany, representatives of the sixteen West European nations hoping to share in the proposed Marshall Plan concluded their four days of deliberation in Paris. They then departed for home to draw up their "shopping lists" for the desperately needed American dollars. The suspicious Soviets, unwilling to be caught in a capitalist-imperialist trap, were taking countersteps to organize their eight Communist satellites as the nine-nation Communist Information Bureau (Cominform). Proclaimed on October 5, 1947, it was openly designed to promote the spread of Communism while sabotaging the economic recovery of Europe under the not-yet-approved Marshall Plan program. At the same time the Soviets, through the rival Molotov Plan, took steps to fight the Marshall Plan by attempting to shackle the satellites together in a Communist economic bloc. In this way they could divert to Eastern Europe much trade that had previously flowed westward.

Thanks to the conflicting rivalries of the victorious powers, the Western Allies encouraged a truncated Germany to rise again. Under the so-called Marshall Plan, the Federal Republic of [West] Germany took form and received $1.39 billion in Marshall aid. Adding in the previously granted gifts and credits, the grand total was some $2 billion. The fallen foe thus played with conspicuous financial success the hoary game of divide and conquer.

10

The Tug of War Over Austria

We cannot afford to let this key area [Austria] fall under [the] exclusive influence of [the] Soviet Union, for if this should happen it would not only consolidate Soviet domination of Danubian and Balkan areas but would also weaken our position in Italy, Germany, and Czechoslovakia.

U.S. Joint Chiefs of Staff to Geoffrey Keyes, U.S. High Commissioner for Austria, May 25, 1947

On July 20, 1947, the official car deposited me at the Munich airport to board another Army two-motor C-47 for a five-day inspection of the power centers of pear-shaped Austria. Our flight spanned some two hundred miles, and much of the time the passengers could view below them the ribboning Danube. Even when I later saw the famed river from the ground, there were no azure hues in "the beautiful blue Danube"—at least not at this time of year. The dominant color seemed to be that of brownish mud.

During the flight I had ample time to reflect on what might lie ahead. The Austrians were known to be in desperate straits, for they were suffering from a scarcity of food and a prostrated economy. I was also aware that this occupied little country was caught in the middle of a tug of war between the democratic West and the Communist East. In comparison with the neighboring Germans, who spoke the same language, the Austrians were no less hungry and economically depressed, but they had certain signal advantages over their former brethren in Hitler's ill-starred Reich. In November, 1943, the foreign ministers of Britain, Russia, and the United States had agreed in Moscow that when the war ended Austria would be treated as a liberated country, not as a conquered foe. On paper at least, the unfortunate

Austrians were assured of their independence and the restoration of their prewar frontiers.

As became painfully evident, the Kremlin chose not to honor these solemn agreements or to respect either the independence or the territorial integrity of Austria. In all fairness, the Russians had reason to feel unhappy about their wartime commitment. Hitler, with an overpowering show of force, had peacefully annexed German-speaking Austria in the dramatic *Anschluss* of 1938. The best guess is that many Austrians had disapproved of this rape before it occurred, but that an overwhelming mass of Nazis and pro-Nazis joyously permitted their country to be seduced.

As a semiwilling part of the German Reich, Austria had contributed substantially to Hitler's military might, and more than one million Austrian men had reportedly served in the German armed forces. Beyond a doubt, thousands of them had participated in the invasion and looting of vast stretches of the Soviet Union. In these circumstances, the Russians refused to forgive and forget, especially since they felt fully entitled to reparations from those nations, whatever their excuses, that had inflicted grievous wounds on them. Yet on the assumption that a liberated people have already suffered enough from their invaders, the liberators do not ordinarily exact reparations from them. Here was plainly the root of much of the East-West postwar friction.

The French, likewise invaded and ravaged by Hitler's Germany, were not represented at the Moscow Conference of Foreign Ministers in 1943, and hence did not regard Austria as an innocent liberated country. They managed to extract their share of reparations from their zone of Austria, although they did so less conspicuously, more cleverly, and less brutally than the Russians. At times the vengeful French in Austria were almost as much a problem to the Americans as were the Russians. In a sense, Austrian independence was saved by the jealousies of the four powers; no one of them would pull out for fear that a rival or rivals would take over. Another paradox is that Austria was probably saved from Communism largely by the presence of Communist Russia, for the Austrians came to hate what they saw.

In many respects liberated Austria was treated like conquered Germany. Both nations were forced to yield what amounted to heavy reparations to the Russians and the French. Both were chopped into four zones, with the French zone in Austria (as in Germany) farthest west and the Soviet zone (as in Germany) farthest east, adjoining Communist-controlled Hungary. The British zone of Austria was near the middle, adjoining the U.S. zone (as in Germany), and the British,

The Postwar Zones of Austria

(Thomas A. Bailey, *A Diplomatic History Of The American People*, 9th edition, © 1974, p. 782. Reprinted by permission of Prentice-Hall, Inc., Englewood Cliffs, New Jersey.)

as in Berlin, were more helpful in supporting American policy against the Soviets than were the French.

The Russian zone bordered the Danube River, which the Soviets dominated. The inevitable result was the development of much friction among the occupying allies over the right to navigate this important fluvial artery. An American officer in Vienna later told me that the Russians would not permit the Americans to swim or fish in "their river"; in a sense, it was not the beautiful blue Danube but the drab Red Danube.

In Austria as in Germany, the Soviet zone complicated the problem of feeding the other three zones. Before the war it had produced about 65 percent of the total agricultural yield of Austria, to say nothing of manufactures and oil. Yet the Soviets, instead of supplying the urgent needs of the three Western zones, shipped out much of the edible produce to the east for their own purposes. With some bitterness, an American general in Vienna later told me that the Russians got the cream of the food-producing areas, whereas the other three powers got only the music and the scenery. This observation was an exaggeration, but it did contain considerable truth.

As in four-zoned Germany, Austria's capital city of Vienna was chopped into four sectors, which also happened to lie deep within the Soviet zone. There was also a small sector in the heart of Vienna known as the International Zone and controlled jointly by all four powers. As was unpleasantly true of Berlin, access routes to the capital were under the control of the Russians. The Western Allies were allowed access to only one airport, that at Telln, about seventeen miles from Vienna. The Russians made a practice of blocking off the one good road to the capital with one excuse or another, and thus forcing the traveler, especially if an American, to take a much longer and poorer route. I was warned in advance to avoid getting a flat tire on this highway, lest the ever-suspicious Russians arrest me as a "capitalistic" spy who was seeking to get a better look at their preserves. One also heard tales of an American officer who had his film confiscated, and of the kidnapping of persons in the American areas by Soviet thugs in broad daylight. A party of American newsmen had been held up at the frontier because they had failed to receive the proper clearance, but as soon as the Americans admitted their mistake, the group was admitted. One oddity was a complete lack of reciprocity. The Americans permitted the Russians to circulate freely in the U.S. zone, but the Russians would not extend the same privilege to their distrusted "capitalistic" allies.

The Soviets not only held the Telln airport and the access road to Vienna, but they also controlled the railroad lines and the telephones. All mail had to pass through the hands of censors, and in addition telephones were routinely "bugged." An American general later related in Vienna that when he picked up the telephone receiver the strong voice at the other end would suddenly grow fainter as the "bugging" device made contact. Not content with such tactics in their own sector and zone, the Soviets "bugged" telephones in the U.S. zone, notoriously in Linz, the largest city under American jurisdiction. The only untrammeled means of communication between Vienna and the outside world was by radio, which naturally had to be used in code.

As partial solace for their other troubles, the Austrians enjoyed one great life-giving advantage, in addition to their being regarded by two of the four victors as citizens of a liberated country. As a result of "unconditional surrender," the Germans had no government when the war ended, but the Austrians rapidly created one. It was initially sanctioned by the occupying Russians, who evidently expected to control it and who installed their own police. But the Austrian Socialists proved to be so strong that in the first general election the Communists won only 3 out of 165 seats in the national assembly. The Socialists, who were blessed with shrewd leadership, proved to be too numerous to be ousted by the Russians, short of a resort to armed force.

Parallel with the new Austrian government, the occupying powers established a four-power Control Council, as in Berlin—"four elephants in a boat," one Austrian statesman put it. The Soviets were unable to retain authority over the Austrian police force, and consequently failed to secure the kind of stranglehold in Austria that had worked so successfully in the Sovietized satellite states. Yet they kept up a drumfire of criticism at the Vienna civilian regime, and issued pamphlets picturing the Austrian authorities as puppets of the Western allies. My official informants in Vienna later told me that the Austrian government could take a strong tone with the Russians as long as it had American support, and that the United States must continue to give the Austrians nourishing food and strong diplomatic backing.

Such was the general background of the complicated Austrian problem, and such were some of my thoughts as we approached ill-starred little Austria. When our plane finally touched down, I was met by a Captain Plum in an Army automobile. He turned out to be most helpful as a guide, escort, and counselor during my brief stay in Vienna. As we rode through the streets of the fabled city to my quarters at the Bristol Hotel, I noted that this great cultural center had not suffered the saturation bombing meted out to Munich, Berlin, and other German cities, although in places the damage to the fought-over city was heavy. Some of the public edifices appeared to be reasonably intact, and the main complex of the University of Vienna seemed to be only slightly pockmarked or battered. But many of the structures had been hit by the fire bombing, which had inflicted great interior damage; other buildings had been badly scorched or blistered when the retreating Nazis set fire to them. The rumor was that the Allied bombers had eased off somewhat in attacking this "captive people."

Much of the destruction was not outwardly visible, for it had been wreaked by the looting Russian soldiers when they captured the city. Captain Plum related that the Soviet officers had allowed their men three days of unrestrained rape and plunder, including the liquor supplies. General Mark W. Clark, Commanding General of the United States Forces in Austria and High Commissioner for Austria, states in his *Calculated Risk* (1950) that the greatest immediate problem was to persuade the Russians to permit him to enter the city and establish his command post. They were still so busy looting Vienna that they did not want to be bothered with him or by him. Two years later, looting at a more sophisticated level was still going on in the Russian zone in the form of reparations, especially the taking of oil from the productive fields at Zisterdorf. The Russians even tried to scrounge in the neighboring American zone, with scant success.

Looting, drunkenness, and rape have traditionally been the rewards of victorious armies, and the Russians evidently felt little mercy for German invaders who had given them the same brutal treatment. Captain Plum recalled the fate of his English secretary, the mother of two children; she had been thrown onto a bed and raped by twenty-seven Russians. The Soviet soldiers were only "animals," he concluded, and he disliked them. He also referred to two Russian majors, both university graduates, who had to be advised by their landlady to use knives and forks instead of their hands. She also suggested to them that they change occasionally to a clean handkerchief when they had to wipe their noses. A visitor could not determine how many of these tales were true, but they squared with the stories that one heard in Berlin from other responsible American officers.

A wristwatch was then a luxury in the Soviet Union, and the Russian looters were conspicuously successful in "liberating" them from the Viennese. As in Berlin, one heard numerous tales relating to this form of rapacity, especially stories involving soldiers who wore a string of wrist watches up to the elbow. The proud new owners, unaware that their prizes had to be wound, would often throw them away as useless when they ran down. One Austrian civilian told me of a Russian soldier who secured a large alarm clock and took it to a local watchmaker with the request that three small ones be made from it. Moreover, the Russians promptly confiscated all of the good cab horses, leaving the poorer ones. Even so, my chauffeur estimated, there were more motor cars on the roads than before the war.

Despite these tales of bestiality, I must in fairness report that the few wooden-faced Russian soldiers abroad in the International Zone were tending strictly to business. As a rule the privates were wearing cheap, dirty, and ill-matched uniforms. One soldier, with a tommy-gun strapped on, casually boarded an electric streetcar in front of the Bristol Hotel. A number of Russian officers, all armed with handguns, were carrying inexpensive cardboard suitcases. I was reminded of the existence of Soviet patrol craft on the Danube by the presence of a bemedalled Russian naval officer on the street. On another occasion I observed an officer with his wife and child, all of them wearing elegant knee-length boots despite the warmth of the late July summer.

Little fraternizing took place between the Russians and the Americans. Soviet soldiers who became too friendly with the Western occupiers were reportedly shipped home, with perhaps a one-way ticket to Siberia. Several American fliers said that they had "softened up" three or four Russians who soon thereafter were sent back to Mother Russia. The ultrasuspicious Soviets were prone to judge the motives of others by their own, in at least one instance with an amusing result. General Alfred M. Gruenther had been recalled from Vienna a year earlier to serve as Deputy Commandant of the National War College, and the Soviet High Commissioner in Austria had given out the story that the American had been brought home because of undue friendliness toward the Russians. This was the same General Gruenther who had recently briefed me in Washington without showing any affection for the Soviets.

Many of the invading Russians came to appreciate the joys of Western capitalistic culture, including electrical appliances, hot and cold running water, and flush toilets. A major in U.S. Army Intelligence (G2) remarked to me that there were currently many desertions from the Soviet army in Austria; some of the fugitives simply went underground. There were some cases of Russians jumping off trains while reluctantly on their way home, as well as a few instances of officers murdering their families and then committing suicide after receiving orders to return.

In one case a reverse situation developed when an Austrian girl married a Russian soldier. Upon reaching his home, she was shocked to find that he was a sheepherder and that she had to sleep on the floor. She wrote for money to return home and she left—at least this is the story my Austrian chauffeur told me. On the other hand, Captain Plum had made some slight contacts with Soviet officers, and although they knew much about Russian art and literature, they were complete blanks when the conversation turned to any subject outside their homeland.

My living quarters were at the well-known Bristol Hotel, in the heart of Vienna and deep behind the Iron Curtain. The door of one of the rooms was damaged, though partially repaired; possibly some rampaging Russians had burst through in pursuance of whatever they had in mind. As usual, the Army accommodations were ridiculously inexpensive, including meals, and the waiters, who were local Austrians, proved most deferential. Captain Plum said that the Viennese regarded the Americans as godfathers, as well they might have, for the United States was the major force that stood between them and a possible takeover by the Russians in the manner of Hungary, Bulgaria, and the other Iron Curtain satellites.

Shortly before checking out of the Bristol Hotel for Prague, I lightened my baggage by giving the middle-aged Austrian porter a spare cake of scarce soap. Never have I seen a face suddenly glow with so much gratitude for so little; he burst out with something in German to the effect that his wife would be overjoyed.

Soon after meeting Captain Plum I told him that my purpose was to make contact with as many well-informed people as possible so that I could report to the National War College what was developing in Austria. He paid me the compliment of saying that of all the dozens of junketing VIPs whom he had shepherded around, from Congressmen up or down, I was the first one who seemed to know what he wanted. In any event, I made useful contacts with about a score of people, military and civilian, victors and Viennese, generals and chauffeurs. There was an official American legation in Vienna, as there had not been in governmentless Berlin, and among others I conversed with Dr. Eleanor Lansing Dulles, financial attaché, who graciously invited me to lunch with some others. She was the well-known sister of John Foster Dulles, who later gained the headlines as Secretary of State under President Eisenhower.

One of the most vexing problems for the United States was the prolonged unwillingness of the Russians to enter into a treaty with the Austrian republic and the other three Allied powers to end the hateful occupation. I talked at length at the American legation with a half-dozen or so experts who were working on this issue or on difficulties closely related to it. They felt that the treaty was already two years too late, and that the Russians were illogical in their opposition. The Kremlin evidently had not abandoned hope of making over all or part of the little republic in the Communist image, despite the formidable political strength of the Austrian Socialists. There was some feeling at the U.S. Legation that the Russians were working for a Danubian federation, and that to this end they were infiltrating Austria economically. Dr. Dulles believed that the de facto split-off of the Russian zone had occurred rather recently, perhaps in the previous month of June. Student riots had been organized and led by people who were not students; one of them was thought to be connected with the Soviet police.

The American diplomatic corps was having its troubles. Dr. Dulles complained about the time lag in diplomacy, and she also referred to the security problem. Many of the official documents were so confidential that they could not be sent to other buildings because so many Austrian employees were involved. Some of the information involved endangered "covers," for it had been secured at great risk by agents working for the Americans. Additionally, there were the irritating delays caused by the need for the Russian officials on the ground to receive sanction from centralized Moscow for even low-level decisions. One of the American officials surmised that the Russians were making themselves unusually difficult because they found compensatory satisfaction in kicking other people around; unable to strike back at their superiors in the Kremlin, they struck at their capitalistic associates.

General Mark W. Clark had left for home on May 5, 1947, the month before I arrived, and his place as High Commissioner in the four-power military Control Council was now occupied by General Geoffrey Keyes. He graciously invited me to dinner at an attractive country estate, presumably expropriated, on the outskirts of Vienna. One course consisted of delicious brook trout, which probably had been caught in one of the numerous fishing streams in the American zone. In any event, most of the food we were eating in this near-starved country had been shipped in from the United States for the support of its occupying forces.

During the course of this pleasant evening, General Keyes remarked that the Russians had two Oriental traits: one was suspicion and the other was infinite patience in achieving their objectives. He should have known, for he sat on the Control Council with the high commissioner of each of the other three zones, and heard the monotonous Soviet vetoes. He further stated that the Russians would deny the validity of an argument if the Americans used it, and then a few days later would be using it themselves. General Keyes's official reports for this particular period were published in 1972, and in reading them one can recognize that he had ample grounds for his critical judgments.

Between appointments I spent considerable time wandering around the streets of Vienna, a metropolis of some two million souls. It reflected little of the fabled glamour of the baroque city or even of the glitter of the Hapsburg Court in the years before the assassination of the Archduke Francis Ferdinand in 1914. A visitor found it difficult to realize that once there had lived here figures as famous as Mozart, Beethoven, Schubert, Brahms, and Johann Strauss, whose lilting waltzes, including the beautiful "Blue Danube," had set countless hearts beating to three-quarter time.

Viennese crowds roughly resembled those of any large eastern

American city, only they were not nearly so well dressed. Quite understandably, the people looked gray and dreary, not gay and cheery. Good clothing was either nonexistent or excessively high priced, owing to the inflation of the schilling. It was then worth two cents on the black market, which was a life-giving evil. I saw few beautiful women, partly because of the scarcity of conventional makeup, including lipstick, although a few of the younger females had managed to secure some, perhaps from the GIs. The Austrian men generally wore drab, soiled, and shabby clothing, including the leather breeches that seemed to have been passed down from father to son and now cost about a thousand schillings. Some of the men sported feathers in their hats, and thus upheld the peacock strain in the male sex. Ironically, one of the brighter spots in the city was the headquarters of the otherwise blighting Soviets. They had decorated the front of their establishment with immense likenesses of Lenin on one side and Stalin on the other, as if to acquaint the luckless Austrians with their future gods.

Some of the Americans interviewed were not averse to speculating about the Austrian national character. The consensus was that these people, in marked contrast with the Germans, were not conspicuously industrious or ambitious; they were more relaxed and more disposed to savor the few simple pleasures of life while they could. When one considers that their basic diet at that time was often less than the theoretical 1550 calories a day, or at about the famine level, their lack of bursting energy should have surprised no one. Though depressed and oppressed, the Viennese still loved good living and beautiful music; in the old days almost every Austrian seemingly could play some kind of musical instrument. Yet, critics said, they tended to lean too heavily on the United States, and with the slightest encouragement would "cry all over you." By the time of my coming they had already received about $200 million in outside aid, most of it under UNRRA.

Shortly after my arrival, an Austrian driver in an Army car took me out to reconnoiter the environs of the city. Rain was falling softly, and the beautiful brown Danube failed to live up to its heralded fascination. We skirted the Vienna Woods, which to a native Californian looked like ordinary stunted trees, and we had an excellent but hardly breathtaking view of the mist-enshrouded city. So far as one could see, the axe had not been put to any part of this forest recently. But in the city proper some of Vienna's oldest trees had been felled during the recent winter to secure some slight relief from the desperate coal shortage.

My talkative chauffeur interested me much more than the rather ordinary scenery. Although an Austrian native in his early twenties, he spoke surprisingly good English, and for this reason was able to hold a job with the Americans as a driver. By working overtime he was able to support not only himself but also his parents and grandfather. Despite his hatred for the Germans, he had been drafted into the army for one and a half years. His contempt for the Austrian girls was unconcealed; their sole ambition, he claimed, was to arrange a rendezvous with an American soldier. For one chocolate bar they would go out into the Vienna Woods all night. They claimed to be "good" girls but he did not believe them; too many of them were giving birth to babies out of wedlock.

Despite such nocturnal activity, the overshadowing cloud in Vienna was the presence of the Russians, for doubts and uncertainties were multiplying about their supposed schemes. On reaching the city the Soviets were disturbed to find that they were not welcomed as liberators but were denounced as pillagers and rapists. Despite their severe electoral setback at the hands of the Socialists, they had not given up propagandizing. They were then publishing a Communist newspaper in Vienna, and I saw what appeared to be a Soviet truck disseminating propaganda leaflets.

Judging from past Russian deeds and misdeeds, the Americans naturally feared some kind of Communist coup. In the eyes of the Soviets, contracts were evidently more binding on the other parties than on themselves. This interpretation seemed to be the most logical explanation for the Russian decision to flout the three-power Moscow agreement of November, 1943, and to treat Austria as a conquered nation not entitled to its prewar boundaries. More than that, in 1945 Stalin had signed the three-power Potsdam Protocol, which categorically stated: "It was agreed that reparations should not be exacted from Austria."

The Russians so interpreted their right to seize "German assets" that these takings became indistinguishable from outright reparations. In their operations the Soviets erased the distinction between Austrian property that had existed before Hitler's takeover, on the one hand, and German property amassed after it, on the other. Contrary to the solemn ban on Austrian reparations at Potsdam, the Russians were not only carting away dismantled factories from Austria, but were resorting to the demoralizing practice of seizing current production from the remaining plants. The Soviets even regarded as German property the oil that had lain in underground pools for centuries before Hitler annexed Austria, and they continued to pump away the petroleum reserves, conspicuously at Zisterdorf.

American officials on the ground could only guess what the Russians were up to, but speculation fluctuated between two extremes. On the one hand, the Soviets might settle for the communization of their own zone, thus forcing a Trizonian spin-off, as had happened in Germany. On the other hand, they might be planning to create a communized Danubian federation of satellites, for the Danube basin, like that of the Mississippi, was a geographical entity. Such a prospect was a nightmare to the American military men in Vienna, for its fruition would cause a Sovietized Austria to link up with communized Yugoslavia, thus flanking southern Germany and threatening bordering Switzerland with a Communist takeover. One American general told me that the Russians would not stop until they bestrode all Europe, and three years later General Mark Clark, formerly High Commissioner in Vienna, concluded on the last page of his memoirs that "there is nothing the Soviets would not do to achieve world domination."

From various American officials in Vienna I learned some intimate details of what had been going on in connection with feeding the Austrians. Major General Desmond D. Balmer said that about three weeks before Molotov disrupted the three-power Marshall Plan conference in Paris, the Soviets started to slack off in their food-relief program in Austria. His view was that the Russians seemed to be following the policy of stopping food shipments on the Danube by means of shipping strikes. At one time, Vienna, in his view, was only two or three days away from starvation.

Russian officials had also voiced bitter complaints about alleged discrimination against them when they received more cornmeal than anticipated in one recent shipment of food. The American explanation was that this kind of mix-up inevitably occurred when grain was taken off a ship without having first been sent to a central warehouse.

Hunger demonstrations, I further learned, had broken out recently in Vienna when the supply of potatoes gave out. The Soviets had large quantities of them in their zone, but provided unconvincing excuses for the delays. Either the tubers had spoiled, they claimed, or shipments had to be held up on account of the winter snows, even though July had arrived.

Interviews with two American officials associated with the agricultural program were also productive. One of them reported that in his many dealings with the Soviets he had formed the opinion that they were really trying to increase production in their zone. Perhaps he felt that they hoped to retain control of the area themselves. He remarked that at best Austria was only 75 percent self-sufficient, and that in better times it had been forced to make up the deficit by exchanging manufactured goods for food from Romania and other nearby countries. But, he suspected, the Soviets might not permit a full reopening of such interchanges because of their desire to secure full control of Austria.

The other United States agricultural official conceded that the Russians were permitting considerable quantities of food to pass over their railway lines, even though they continued to complain bitterly about the American program of distribution. Possibly, he suggested, the Russians wanted to discredit the existing non-Communist government in Vienna, for it had shown "guts" in defying the Soviets.

Whatever their intentions the Russians gave strong indications of planning to make some kind of Communist satellite out of Austria, or at least out of their zone, as they had done in Germany. To this end they seem to have deliberately sought to keep the long-suffering Austrians on a starvation diet, probably on the theory that they might surrender to hunger pangs and become "stomach Communists." Whatever their motives, the Soviets followed procedures that worsened the already desperate famine conditions. Most notorious of all, they were shipping food out of their own breadbasket zone that could more logically and humanely have gone to the three Western zones that urgently needed these calories.

Ever suspicious of foreign agents, the Soviets in their zone had put obstacles in the path of food distributors operating under UNRRA. Moscow had also refused, probably for similar reasons, to permit representatives of the Red Cross to operate freely; fear of capitalistic spies was ever an obsession. In addition, Moscow had exerted heavy pressure, without success, to dissuade the Austrians from accepting the prospective Marshall Plan and enjoying its life-giving benefits.

Continuing friction was inevitable in this four-power cockpit. The Americans were battling for a free and democratic Austria, at a cost of millions of dollars a year, and the Soviets seemed to be scheming, without much enthusiasm, for a communized Austrian satellite. Unpleasantness manifested itself in protracted delays and evasions, some of them probably growing out of what General Clark diagnosed as a "guilt-persecution complex." One difficulty was that the Soviet representative in the Control Council in Vienna, as in Berlin, apparently did not dare to act without consulting the Kremlin, while the Americans were free to act in conformity with their own general instructions.

One major battleground was the four-power Control Council in Vienna. General Clark had found the Soviets adept in lifting phrases out of context and otherwise reading their own twisted meaning into official documents. The "rule of unanimity" prevailed here as in Berlin, with the result that both sides, especially the Russians, routinely attempted to use their veto to attain their ends. But by invoking a technicality, the Allies in Vienna were occasionally able to override the Russians, as they had been unable to do in Berlin.

General Clark tells us in his memoirs that he once said to his Russian counterpart that the latter had made ten demands in the Control Council that could not be met. He then asked what would happen if "I should say, 'All right. We agree to all ten demands.' Then what would you do?" The Russian reply was, "Tomorrow I'd have ten new ones."

Such friction at high official levels was bound to manifest itself also at lower levels. As in Germany, the Western powers were required to fly their airplanes over a narrow corridor through the Soviet zone. On numerous occasions Soviet pilots would zoom alarmingly close, and finally they began to fire their guns perilously near the American aircraft. This harassment stopped only after General Clark informed the Russians that American gunners were under orders to shoot first if they felt that they were in danger.

Soviet obstruction had extended also to railway service through the Russian zone of Austria. In the winter of 1946, Clark also relates in his memoirs, two Soviet officers forced their way onto a train and threatened with their revolvers a sergeant of the U.S. Military Police. In the tradition of Wyatt Earp, he outdrew the Russians, killing one and wounding the other. The Soviets protested bitterly, but Clark held his ground. The American General Balmer himself told me that the presence of the Soviet army was really brought home to him when he could hear Russian artillery firing during maneuvers near his residence.

When General Mark Clark officially left his Austrian command post early in 1947, he estimated that there were still some four hundred thousand displaced persons in that little country, about thirty thousand of them reputedly Jews. Few of these unfortunates wished to return to homelands that were under Soviet jurisdiction, but the Russians insisted that many of them were war criminals or deserters from the Red army. An arrangement was worked out with the Russians under which the refugees could be returned from the American zone if they fell into either of these two categories of suspects. The agreement was violated by Soviet agents, some of whom resorted to forcible measures that amounted to kidnapping. American officials subsequently ended such Russian missions of repatriation altogether.

In summarizing the existing state of Soviet-American relations in

Austria, one American officer in Vienna said that the Russians would occasionally compromise on minor or secondary matters. But they would not back down in four areas: on extorting actual reparations from "liberated" Austria; on seizing Austrian assets that the Russians claimed were German; on the status of displaced persons whom Moscow regarded as returnable; and on the southern-boundary adjustment with Communist Yugoslavia at the expense of Austria. This area, known as Carinthia, the Austrians managed to retain.

In view of all this friction, American officials in Austria were pessimistic about future relations with the Soviet Union. One of them remarked that he had argued some while earlier with a British Tory friend that the Western democracies could deal with the Russians. Now the American would admit that he had been wrong. He regarded the Soviet leaders as constituting the same kind of threat that Hitler had posed, but he believed that they were closer calculators than the impulsive *Führer*. They would not provoke war if they thought the odds were heavily against their winning it.

An American major in Army Intelligence declared that the Soviets had long indoctrinated their men to believe that a war with capitalism was inevitable, but now they were more insistent about it, especially with recruits. Another official, who was involved with Austrian reparations, now believed that the United States was currently involved in both an economic and ideological war, and that the Americans were losing both.

Shortly before leaving Vienna I was flown out to Salzburg and back in one day. The plane was a one-engine, one-passenger LC-5, and I assume that we passed through the authorized air corridor over the Russian zone; no Soviet airplanes "buzzed" us or otherwise interfered with our flight. The personable and intelligent young officer who piloted the craft did a workmanlike job.

Salzburg, near the base of the towering Bavarian Alps, was the second most populous city in the American zone, ranking behind Linz. Brown-roofed, it proved to be a charming town, not badly scarred by the war. But I did observe within a single block two one-legged bicyclists, presumably young soldiers who had survived the recent conflict. The driver at my disposal offered to take me on a twenty-minute drive to scenic Berchtesgaden, made famous as Hitler's spectacular Eagle's Nest, from which he could almost see the border of his native Austria. But since I had come to interview people and not to gawk at the scenery, I declined the invitation, somewhat to my later regret.

Officials at the U.S. Legation in Vienna had warned me that the

American military regime in Salzburg had set up its own show and was running it like a personal dictatorship. I did not sense such an attitude among the people briefly interviewed, other than some military peremptoriness, and I learned little that had not been revealed in Vienna. The Army Intelligence knew of Russian secret agents in the U.S. zone, but since the Americans had nothing to conceal, they were not unduly concerned.

My attention at Salzburg was directed to the problem of displaced persons, who had caused and were causing so much friction with the Russians. This scenic city had more than its share of such uprooted souls, thanks to its location at the small end of a giant funnel. Through it refugees from Central Europe were pouring down to the head of the Adriatic Sea, where most of them planned to board ships for foreign shores, from Palestine to the Americas. The Russians had halted and annoyed many of them, partly because Moscow generally regarded DPs as a menace to their lines of military communications to the west.

My American sources at Salzburg, who may have harbored some anti-Semitic bias, reported that the refugee Jews were the biggest problem among the DPs, partly because they were "scum." Most of these outcasts were not farmers, and they took naturally to black marketeering, at which they were conspicuously successful. They had their own underground railway, and they refused to give their names to the authorities. In this way they could pad their numbers and secure larger rations. As exiles who had been frightfully abused by Hitler, they were receiving favored treatment, including more calories in their diet, for a total of about 2000 daily rather than the theoretical stint of 1550. Understandably clannish, these Jews had become active in politics, and they had recently beaten up a bus driver, perhaps an ex-Nazi, who had been involved in some kind of unpleasant incident.

Upon flying back to Vienna, I continued my probe into the attitudes and status of the American occupiers. An unusual opportunity arose one evening when Captain Plum hosted a party at the small apartment he could call his home away from home. About twenty people were present, including women and men, Austrians and Americans, civilians and military personnel. At one point in the jolly affair, an Austrian civilian uncased his accordion in the Viennese tradition, and the group made merry with familiar songs. I was especially impressed with the facility of those present in communicating with one another in pidgin English and pidgin German.

Between songs, the conversation turned to various topics, including the mistaken but widespread belief that the American civilians and military people in Germany and Austria had "never had it so good."

Much resentment was directed against the article in the *Saturday Evening Post* (February 15, 1947) by the favored captain's wife in Berlin. Specific complaints about life in Austria were numerous. The women were especially disturbed by low pay, which restricted them to only one or two cartons of cigarettes each week. Renters had to lay out ninety dollars a month for hole-in-the-wall apartments, and not enough money was left over to permit proper entertainment. The wives could not save money, and when the families, especially civilians, finally returned to America flat broke, they would have to start life anew at entirely different jobs.

As for the behavior of the American troops, I heard that they were too young, too immature, and too prone to yield to the temptations of the bottle and willing women. There was indubitably considerable fraternizing between Austrians and Yankee soldiers, including a few marriages. One sad tale involved an attractive Austrian schoolteacher who had fallen in love with an American officer. She was forbidden to marry him because she had earlier joined the Nazi party, though allegedly under duress.

American troops and civilian officials were privileged to patronize the Post Exchange (PX), where one could purchase many discounted items, including Swiss watches and German cameras. No doubt there were some abuses, for an amusing story was going the rounds about a Negro soldier who had managed to load himself down with merchandise and who then had gone around boasting, "I'se a walking PX."

The thought crossed my mind that I could use a wristwatch, for I still carried the gold-plated Elgin with a chain given me when I graduated from high school some twenty-seven years earlier. Captain Plum escorted me to the local PX, where he vouched for me and where I picked out an inexpensive Swiss watch priced at about sixteen dollars. On the way out, the guardian of the gate, evidently an Austrian employee on the lookout for black marketeers, asked for the large identification card that he insisted he had given me when I entered. I patted my pockets, looked all around on the floor, but could not find the missing item. Indeed, I could not remember having received it when entering. After further delay and fruitless searching, Captain Plum burst out, "Let's get the hell out of here. It's growing late and they won't hold the plane for you"—or words to that effect. The management finally relented and I left in haste with a souvenir that rendered satisfactory service for many years.

My next stop was Prague, for which I had purchased a ticket with my own money. From here on, the no-cost transportation, so generously provided by the Army, was no longer available. As we sped down the narrow and winding road to the airport, I did not feel completely at ease. Our vehicle was a heavy black limousine, reputed to be one of the ten or so bullet-proof, custom-built cars provided for Hitler or one of the other Nazi bigwigs. The automobile rattled and creaked ominously, and the driver had a disturbing preference for the middle of the road, even in the teeth of oncoming traffic. A breakdown, a flat tire, or a collision of some sort might have left me in the hands of the pathologically suspicious Russian police. Happily we arrived at the airport with little time to spare but all in one piece.

As the farms of the Russian zone receded beneath our Pan American two-motor DC-3, I was hardly optimistic enough to predict a happy future for the luckless Austrians. I could not foresee that Marshall Plan aid would flow to this ex-enemy nation from 1948 to 1952 in the sum of $677.8 million. Perhaps it did something to shake up the Russian occupiers. In 1955, eight long years after my visit, the Soviets suddenly reversed course and concluded the long-delayed Austrian State Treaty, which bound the occupied country and the four occupying powers. The long-suffering little republic regained both its full sovereignty and its pre-Hitler boundaries. Pursuant to a separate agreement with the Soviets, Austria proclaimed its permanent neutrality the following November, although it was permitted a small army for internal purposes.

But the Russians, frustrated with what appeared to be their prolonged efforts to take over all or part of the cow, demanded continuing milk in the form of economic and financial reparations. The Austrians formally obligated themselves to buy back, in money or goods, the properties that the Russians had seized. The extortionate price was $150 million, although these assets had been valued at only $40 million. In addition, Austria was to send to the Russians from its restored resources one million tons of crude oil annually over a period of ten years. Finally, the last Austrian prisoners of war and civilian internees in the USSR were to be released—a sad reminder that many thousands of these unfortunates had been held for about ten years to put the squeeze on luckless Austria.

Depressing though this self-ransom was, Vienna erupted in ecstatic rejoicing over being rid of at least the physical presence of its oppressor. Church bells rang, flags waved, music burst forth, and masses of people danced in the streets. Austria at long last was free from the heavy heel of the Russian boot, and in ten long years it would finish doing penance for having been taken over by Hitler.

In 1957, ten years after my first hurried visit to Austria, I returned to

Vienna as a tourist, this time accompanied by my wife. We stayed at a fine modern hotel that was not far from a new or rebuilt opera house. The city was no longer the drab and cheerless place of 1947. At the last stop of our tourist bus, before one of the palatial showplaces of Vienna, the middle-aged Austrian woman who was our guide delivered a short speech, for she recognized that our party consisted largely of Americans. With a near-choking voice she said that she wanted us to go home and tell everybody how everlastingly grateful the Austrian people were for what the United States had done. The Americans had fed them, resurrected their economy (with Marshall dollars), and rescued them from the Russians. Probably better than any of the other tourists present I realized that the words of our guide came from her heart. (Or perhaps she was thinking primarily of tips from the rich Americans.)

11

Czechoslovakia Between East and West

The Czechoslovak reversal on the [Marshall Plan]
Paris Conference, on Soviet orders, is nothing less
than a declaration of war by the Soviet Union on
the immediate issue of the control of Europe.

Walter Bidell Smith
U.S. Ambassador to Russia
Telegram to Secretary of State, July 11, 1947

As our airplane neared the end of its 150-mile flight from Vienna to Prague, my feelings of anticipation were dampened by forebodings. As an historian, I knew a little about the background of Czechoslovakia and its peculiarly intimate relationship with my own country, to which it had contributed hundreds of thousands of immigrants. Events of recent weeks relating to the Marshall Proposal had heightened the sense of tragedy that had come to be associated with the relatively brief history of this ill-starred, patchwork, polyglot little democracy.

In a sense President Woodrow Wilson was the godfather of Czechoslovakia. His potent Fourteen Points of 1918, with their clarion call for self-determination of minority peoples, held a special attraction for those minorities, such as the Czechs and Slovaks, who had long groaned under the yoke of Austria and Hungary. In May, 1918, Tomáš Masaryk, the George Washington and Abraham Lincoln of the Czechs, signed "The Treaty of Pittsburgh" with representatives of the Slovaks, thousands of whom were employed in the great steel-producing area of Pennsylvania. Masaryk thus gave Slovakia formal assurances of autonomy and the retention of its own language.

When the ramshackle Austro-Hungarian Empire finally fell apart late in 1918 under the stress of World War I, the synthetic state of

Czechoslovakia arose from the ruins. The new babel of tongues consisted of Czechs, Slovaks, Sudeten Germans, Hungarians, Ruthenians, Poles, and others. Many of these peoples resented the new irritations resulting from the wondrous workings of self-determination.

To the surprise of pessimists, this bizarre experiment in statehood worked. The mixing bowl of nationalities took surprisingly well to democracy, and thus became a shining example for central Europe. Despite much ethnic friction, Czechoslovakia was the only democratic nation east of the Rhine and the Alps that lasted continuously from 1918 to 1939, before Hitler unleashed his mechanized fury. The people were industrious and ingenious, for their artisans operated the famed Škoda manufacturing complex. Czech-Slovak culture was higher than that of the Slavs to the east, and phrasemakers were wont to say that Czechoslovakia was the easternmost of the western nations and the westernmost of the eastern. The tiny democracy was also referred to as "the bridge between East and West." Yet cynics could reply, "A bridge is something that men and horses walk over."

Favored though Czechoslovakia seemed to be by fortune, it suffered from a fatal handicap. It was located at the physical and strategic crossroads of Europe, and at crossroads, as on bridges, one is liable to be run down or trampled underfoot. The German Iron Chancellor Bismarck (1815–1898) was often quoted as saying that whoever ruled Bohemia, the heart of the Czech homeland, controlled Europe.

Czechoslovakia suffered from the additional misfortune of adjoining Germany on the west, and Hitler naturally coveted this small neighbor in his inexorable drive eastward toward the Soviet Union and hegemony over Europe. A convenient wedge near at hand was the group of some three million Sudeten Germans who, as fate had decreed, lived in the area of Czechoslovakia adjoining Germany. Many of them evidently preferred merger with the Reich to citizenship in a democracy. Hitler stridently raised the cry of union and self-determination for these Germans, while demanding the Sudetenland and threatening war if he could not get this prize peacefully. We know that the Czechs supposedly had a strong and well-equipped army, stationed strategically in the Bohemian mountain passes that were reputed to be the best defensive line in Central Europe. We also know that the German army, on the testimony of some of its own generals, was not yet fully ready to march. Yet an impatient Hitler was determined to attack if he could not get his own way.

Prospects of a disastrous war begot a conference of the powers at Munich in September, 1938, and Hitler overbore his adversaries. France, though bound by a treaty to protect Czechoslovakia, caved in; the British, themselves not formally obligated, did likewise. The resulting Munich accord on paper was a lopsided, blackmailed compromise. On the one hand, Hitler would annex the Sudetenland and nearby Germanic areas to Germany, and on the other hand, he promised that this was his last territorial demand in Europe. In March, 1939, some five months later, he flouted this pledge and erased the rest of mutilated Czechoslovakia from the map.

This searing betrayal and mutiliation left an indelible mark on the people of Czechoslovakia, especially their desertion and betrayal by the Western powers. Premier Stalin of the Soviet Union was not invited to the Munich conference, and he professed to be grievously affronted by this deliberate snub. He was quoted as saying, though many disbelieved him, that he had been prepared to come to the aid of the Czechs against Hitler. Yet because the USSR did not adjoin Czechoslovakia, he had a good excuse for standing aloof.

Compared with some other nations that were overrun by the Nazis, notably Poland and Russia, ill-fated little Czechoslovakia did not suffer wholesale physical destruction. But the Germans did make a determined effort to wipe out Czech culture, especially among those groups that had continued their opposition to Naziism. Czechoslovakia did not maintain a conspicuously active resistance movement, although it lost a reputed 200,000 citizens in fighting for or beside the Russians. Many others quietly disappeared. All told, 169,000 Czechs and Slovaks were reportedly executed, including Jews. Possibly the most effective contribution of the Czechs to Allied victory was in work slowdowns and unobtrusive sabotage, such as producing wrong-sized parts for weapons and vehicles.

The most spectacular Czech feat was the assassination in 1942 of Reinhard Heydrich, the sadistic Nazi official known as "The Hangman of Europe." In reprisal the Germans utterly destroyed the village of Lidice, which had a population of about 450, killing all 200 men, deporting the women, and scattering the children.

Hitler's invasion of the Soviet Union, launched in June, 1941, opened the door to Czechoslovakia for a possible escape from Nazi tyranny while opening yet another door on the east to the Trojan horse of Communist tyranny. In December, 1943, the Czech government-in-exile signed a twenty-year treaty of alliance with Moscow, to which the Czechs still attached great value as a safeguard against a resurrected and vengeful Germany. The pact bound each side to respect the independence and sovereignty of the other, including noninterference in internal affairs. In effect, the foreign policy of Prague was to be aligned with that of Moscow; internal affairs would be left to the Czechoslovakians—that is, on paper.

Advancing Soviet armies, crunching in from the east in 1945, had liberated Slovakia. The Slovaks assisted the Russians in the fierce fighting, but were ill requited when their deliverers engaged in wholesale pillage and rape. In Prague the expectant Czechs rose against their German oppressors, and in so doing suffered considerable loss of life, followed, I later heard, by widespread Russian indecencies. American forces, advancing speedily under General Patton, could easily have taken the capital. But they were ordered to halt, in deference to a Soviet desire to appear as liberators. As the war jolted to a halt, the battle in Czechoslovakia for freedom from Hitler and Naziism ended, but the struggle for freedom from Stalin and Communism was just beginning.

In February, 1945, a provisional government was devised for Czechoslovakia in Moscow, including a formidable minority of Czech Communists in such key ministries as interior (police), education, and information. The new Czech army was to be trained, organized, and armed by the Russians. In the first general election, that of May, 1946, the Communists received 38 percent of the popular vote, with the result that the new government was a coalition of the several major parties. The Prime Minister, Klement Gottwald, was a Communist who had lived in Moscow, and important ministries fell into the hands of the Czechoslovak Communists. They were evidently being inspired or even directed by the Kremlin. In October, 1945, the new government issued decrees formally nationalizing natural resources and industries, thus making the tiny country highly socialistic. The meddling hand of Moscow was increasingly to be felt in this little country, where the people wished to retain their democratic liberties while being faithful to the alliance with their deliverers in Moscow.

Despite the disturbing presence of Moscow-trained Communists, by the end of 1946 Czechoslovakia had made excellent progress in economic reconstruction. More than $200 million had come from UNRRA and other American-sponsored relief agencies. When the Marshall Proposal was unveiled in June, 1947, the Prague government promptly accepted an invitation to attend the Paris conference, where further details of the aid program were to be worked out. On July 10, 1947, about two weeks before my visit to Prague, Jan Masaryk, the pro-Western foreign minister, together with the Communist Prime Minister Gottwald, flew to Moscow at the request of the Soviet government. They there suffered the spectacular humiliation of having to withdraw their acceptance of the Paris invitation. As partial recompense for this sacrifice, they returned with a five-year trade pact with the Soviet Union. The other expectant nations within the Soviet sphere, whatever their desires, were forced to spurn the Marshall overture.

Some revisionist critics of American foreign policy since 1945 have made much of the charge that the United States provoked the Cold War with the Soviet Union largely because Washington wanted to divert from the Moscow orbit the valuable trade of eastern Europe. The truth is that this commerce had been negligible when compared with the overall volume of American exports and imports. Besides, in normal times much of the trade of the new Soviet sphere would have continued to flow westward in response to the attractions of a free-market economy. The renewal of commerce between the Czechs and the democratic West alarmed the Soviets, who wanted a reorientation of Czechoslovakia's foreign commerce in the direction of the USSR and its satellites. In short, the Russians undertook to reverse the normal channels of international trade in their favor, and in this sense they seized the economic offensive by imposing artificial controls. The commerce of eastern Europe was highly important to the shattered nations of western Europe, who in turn were valued customers of a United States that wanted to avoid another great depression.

As in the Munich crisis of 1938, the Czechs were forced to yield to the threat of armed force, in this case Russian rather than German. I subsequently learned from the American Ambassador in Czechoslovakia, Laurence Steinhardt, what some of these pressures were in July, 1947. They included the presence of the Red army, which then virtually encircled the country and was believed to be needed for the protection of Czechoslovakia against a revived Germany. With regard to international trade, the Czechs were becoming increasingly dependent on Russia and Russian satellites as a result of a network of bilateral agreements. In addition, the Soviets controlled two of the chief seaports needed for overseas trade, for Czechoslovakia had and still has no frontage on the sea. Finally, the Moscow-directed Communists were strong and growing stronger. They had gained complete or substantial control of the key ministries of the restored government; they controlled about half the ten daily newspapers in Prague; and they were in a position to engineer protest strikes through the Communist-dominated trade unions.

In the teeth of such converging pressures, Foreign Minister Masaryk and his colleagues had no choice but to cave in to Moscow's demands. The prospect of a successful resistance against the Communists was even worse than it had been against Hitler at the time of Munich. Masaryk's humiliation was all the greater because he had been preening himself on having maintained Czech independence; now he was forced to sing a different tune after the new Munich at Moscow.

My main purpose in visiting Prague was to form some kind of

assessment of the role that Czechoslovakia was to play in these opening skirmishes of the Cold War between East and West. The Iron
Curtain had already been lowered substantially during the two weeks
before my visit, and the overriding question was when or whether it
was going to clang down all the way to the floor.

On reaching Prague for my five-day stay, I registered at the Alcron
Hotel, one of the more respectable establishments of the city. A card
with the name and address of the hotel printed on it proved useful, for
whenever I became lost during my wandering in the city I would
produce it and have one of the local Czechs direct me by sign language to my quarters. On one occasion a streetcar conductor was so
obliging as to leave his post, take me out into the street, and point out
the right direction. A stranger must not generalize from this one instance, but in various other contacts I received the impression that the
Czechs were a friendly people, perhaps because they could tell from
my garb that I was an American.

One evening shortly after my arrival I joined the spectators who
were watching a large and noisy parade coming down the main street.
This demonstration, if memory serves, was being staged by a small
army of young Communists who were attending some kind of rally in
Prague. In any event, I remember that they were waving red Communist banners and shouting slogans. Yet the parade-loving spectators
lining the streets did not seem to be carried away by the call to combat
capitalism. While I was standing there watching, I happened to put to
my lips a loose cigarette from a packet that I was carrying for purposes
of tipping. This gesture was a mistake. Not being a smoker, I had to
decline invitations from several friendly male Czechs who wanted to
light my cigarette and who must have been offended by my refusal to
accept their gesture of goodwill. At least this trifling incident provided
further evidence of Czech friendliness to one who was obviously a
foreign visitor.

During these observations I concluded that Prague could boast the
largest number of overweight women I had thus far seen on my travels. Officials at the American Embassy later told me that the Czechs
then had no serious food problem, although there was still some rationing, and that the fat females were walking testimony to the heavy
intake of potatoes and other starchy foods. The American Ambassador
even assured me that the women of Prague had the "largest fannies in
Europe." The Czech people were then on a standard diet of calories,
plus available beer. The shops displayed plenty of food, and even the
candy stores seemed well supplied. The Czechs, for all their hardships, were evidently better nourished than any of the people I had
seen thus far in continental Europe.

Food for the mind was also conspicuously on display. The extraordinary number of bookstores spoke well for the literacy level and the reading tastes of this cultured people. One of my sources told me that eating and reading ranked high among Czechs on their list of pleasures, and this observation one could believe.

My most helpful guide to Prague turned out to be a young woman Ph.D. in history, Dr. Dorothy Thompson, whom I had known slightly several years earlier during her graduate study at Stanford. She was then engaged in research on some phase of Czech history, and by happenstance she was also staying at the Alcron Hotel. She remarked that the United States Ambassador, Laurence A. Steinhardt, was a fairly able man but she did not agree with his rather naive view that Czechoslovakia was a free country. Her personal acquaintances among the Czechs, she said, were not free to talk. As evidence of encroaching Soviet influence she reported that the Russian language was now being required in the elementary schools, to the confusion of the children, who were somewhat handicapped by the similarities between the two Slavic languages.

Dr. Thompson graciously took me in hand and briefed me on places to see and people to interview. On one occasion she invited me to dinner at the hotel with a charming middle-aged Czech couple, who spoke fluent French with my hostess. They were evidently of the intelligentsia, for the husband was involved in university work. Yet they did not seem to be much alarmed about the prospect of a Communist takeover in their country, and I have often wondered what became of them during the following February when the shattering coup finally occurred.

With historian Dr. Thompson as my well-informed guide, we visited the Old City of Prague, with its medieval walls, and rode out to the Masaryk home on the outskirts of Prague in beautiful wooded country. There we viewed the grave of Tomáš Masaryk, the founding father revered by his people. In response to what were probably his wishes, no name then appeared on the tablet marking the site.

Most of my inside information came from a dozen or so persons, chiefly at the American Embassy, but several of them were Czech citizens. The Embassy was a palatial building, hardly in the American low-cost tradition, and it was a white elephant to maintain. The coal bill alone for the recent savage winter of 1946–1947 had mounted to $5,000. The staff of the Embassy, secretarial and otherwise, was unusually large, as befitted the most important listening post midway between East and West. Prague was also referred to as the western window of the Soviet bloc—a kind of one-way window.

Ambassador Steinhardt generously granted me an interview at the

Embassy, and his wife called me at the hotel to invite me to dinner. To my regret, and despite her insistence, I was obliged to decline because of a previous engagement. The Ambassador himself was a prominent lawyer-economist who had served as a member of President Franklin Roosevelt's preconvention campaign committee in 1932, and evidently had received the post of Minister to Sweden as a traditional political plum. He had subsequently served as Ambassador to Peru, to the Soviet Union (1939–1941), to Turkey, and to Czechoslovakia (1945–1948).

My friend and guide, Dr. Thompson, gave Steinhardt good marks as an ambassador, not only for his intellectual qualities but also for his experience in or near the Soviet Union at a time when the militant spread of Communism was of mounting concern. He had been stationed in Moscow at the time of the peace-shattering Hitler-Stalin pact of 1939, and the professionals in the foreign service, with a natural antipathy to political appointees, were inclined to look down their noses at him. In 1950, three years after we met, he died in a tragic airplane crash near Ottawa, and the Foreign Service lost one of its most experienced men. His revealing dispatches to Washington for these months in 1947 were published in 1972, and they confirm much of what he had told me personally. He was alert to the smaller danger signals but, like many of his colleagues in the foreign service, he was not as concerned as he should have been about the imminent Communist takeover.

Ambassador Steinhardt believed that whatever leanings Czechoslovakia had toward the Soviet Union were due largely to a common Slav blood, a shared fear of a revived Germany, the nearness of Russia on the eastern border, and the strong home-grown Communist party in Czechoslovakia. Somewhat naively, Steinhardt was surprised that the Communists, though lodged in key ministerial positions in the Prague government, had made so little progress in expanding their power during the past year. The explanation, he felt, was that this was a free country. He probably meant that there was a relatively free press and a large degree of freedom in determining internal affairs but not foreign policy.

Steinhardt emphasized his belief that the Czechs were ardent nationalists, and that this zeal probably would stop the spread of Communism in Czechoslovakia, if it could ever be stopped. The irony was that nationalism, often deplored as the greatest menace to peace in the nineteenth century, might, he suggested, save the United States from the triumph of Communism in Europe. He believed that except for the relatively few Moscow-oriented Communists in Czechoslovakia, the overwhelming majority of the people were still nationalists at heart.

My ambassadorial source explained that there were three kinds of pro-Russians in Czechoslovakia: Communists, ideologists, and those opportunists who believed that it was to the economic advantage of themselves or of Czechoslovakia to tie in with the Soviet Union. Yet, he pointed out, some important Russian raw materials were inferior, conspicuously ore and cotton. Furthermore, the Czechs would have to maintain and increase their export trade with the West if they expected to raise their economy to a satisfactory level. But more to be feared than economic distress, he held, was the unawareness of the Czech Communists that increasing intimacy with the Kremlin might bring on the embrace of death.

In taking the long view Steinhardt was not unduly concerned about a rumored Communist coup at any time in the "near future." On the contrary, he was rather optimistic about the ability of the Czechs to hold the line in the teeth of the overwhelming odds that he was listing in his dispatches to the State Department. He had reported to Washington in June, 1947, six weeks before this interview, that his task was being complicated by loose talk in America about a sheeplike Czechoslovakia following Hungary into the Soviet Communist camp. He might have added that all this speculation could not be stopped, that there were valid reasons for it, and that the situation in Czechoslovakia probably would have deteriorated with or without it. After all, so cynics could remark, America was far away; Soviet tanks were close at hand; and God was high in the heavens.

As for the abortive Czech acceptance of the Paris invitation to cooperate in discussing the Marshall Proposal, Steinhardt expressed surprise that Masaryk, as Foreign Minister, had dared to go this far. The power and presence of Moscow-trained Communists in Czechoslovakia was notorious, and Klement Gottwald, a Communist, was Prime Minister in the coalition government. In confidential dispatches to Washington, Steinhardt had written some ten weeks earlier that Masaryk was trying to carry water on both shoulders. He was attempting to be friendly with the Communist camp and the non-Communist camp at the same time without antagonizing either and without taking a strong position in current disputes. He was trying to make "the best of two worlds," but his fence-straddling course had delivered his influence to his Communist undersecretary or deputy. Some of Steinhardt's strictures were not altogether fair. Like the Calvinists, Masaryk was damned if he did and damned if he did not. If he went too far toward either camp, the Communists would take over. The tight-rope act was the only one that offered the slightest hope of limited independence for his ill-fated and ill-located little country.

Of considerable interest were the Ambassador's observations to me about the Czechs as a people. Europeans, he said, were notoriously inclined to climb onto the bandwagon; everybody knew how everyone else was going to vote. The Czechs were great snoopers and deducers; the gossips were sure, for example, that he was going to be replaced because he had not yet laid in a supply of coal for the coming winter. Yet on the whole the Czechs thought well of the United States, and this conclusion seemed to be supported by the continuing presence of the [Woodrow] Wilson Station in Prague, which was named after the president whose dedication to self-determination had found fruition in the creation of patchwork Czechoslovakia. There was also a Hoover Street. As for Czech leanings toward Russia, the dilemma was not that these people loved the Americans less, but that they feared the Germans more. They had all the more reason to turn toward Russia after expelling the Sudeten Germans with considerable brutality.

Somewhat similar views were voiced by several subordinate officials at the Embassy. One of them told the familiar story of how the Czechs were free to conduct their domestic policy but not their foreign policy. Big Brother Stalin in the Kremlin called the tune. Yet the Communists in Czechoslovakia were not able to bore from within with complete success. They had a secret police force, yet it was not unduly active, and citizens were free to come and go as they pleased. Freedom of the press was considerable, and the people showed commendable courage in speaking out as they did. One American official believed that the Soviets wanted to keep Czechoslovakia as window dressing so that all the world could see how happily a country could flourish where the Moscow Communists had only indirect and partial control.

In another interview at the American Embassy, the conversation turned to the colorful and personable Foreign Minister, Jan Masaryk. Urbanely witty, he is said to have remarked, "I am the small son of a great father." Even though there was a large element of truth in this little joke, the younger man was widely regarded as the most popular person in Czechoslovakia. Yet I learned that he was only a nonparty front man; his deputy, a Moscow-oriented Communist, had the upper hand. My informant added, with obvious exaggeration, that Masaryk had no more control over foreign affairs than I had. The glamorous Foreign Minister was allegedly putting on a big act about his independence of the United States, especially after the humiliating reversal of his acceptance of the Paris invitation. Negotiations for a large loan from America had just been dropped, according to the Embassy official, and some sour-grapes Czechs were explaining that this failure was all to the good.

Highlighting my week in Prague was an interview with Foreign Minister Masaryk himself, arranged by the American Embassy. He must have thought that I was a far more important emissary from the United States than was the case, because his office was concerned enough to telephone me a time or two to make sure that there was no misunderstanding about when and where the meeting would occur.

Masaryk greeted me warmly, despite his severe head cold. He turned out to be handsome, affable, outgoing, charming, and articulate. I was much impressed by his cultivated English accent, and assumed that he spoke Czech just as fluently. During the war he had broadcast to his Czech people from London many messages of encouragement and inspiration; he was widely regarded as the most effective radio broadcaster in Europe during the war, with the exception of Winston Churchill.

The personable Foreign Minister obviously had not fully recovered from the shock of his mortifying backdown in Moscow only two weeks earlier. He blamed Poland for reneging on a commitment to accept the Paris invitation and thus destroying a common front. His own acceptance, he insisted, was not a hasty act but the result of prolonged study. He felt that the American press, notably the Hearst newspaper chain and the Scripps-Howard newspapers, had put him in a difficult position prior to his enforced backdown. They were saying, "At last Czechoslovakia is showing some courage. Masaryk has ceased to be a rabbit and is kicking Russia in the teeth." All this, he complained bitterly, did not sit well with the USSR, with which his country was allied and with which it was obligated to work. "A rabbit," he declared in picturesque phrase, "does not try to rape an elephant."

The personable Masaryk next turned the conversation to the German Ruhr, that great industrial complex which the British wanted to nationalize and which the Russians and the French wanted to control. He said that the Krupps and the other cartel moguls wanted to revive the old industrial Ruhr, and that he could have a position with them that would command $50,000 a year. After the last war, he recalled, American bankers had come over and forced loans on the Europeans. One of them said to him, "Wouldn't you like to have a $50,000,000 loan?" When Masaryk replied in the negative, the response was that he was the first European who had ever turned down such a proposition.

Masaryk finally predicted that there would be no world war for

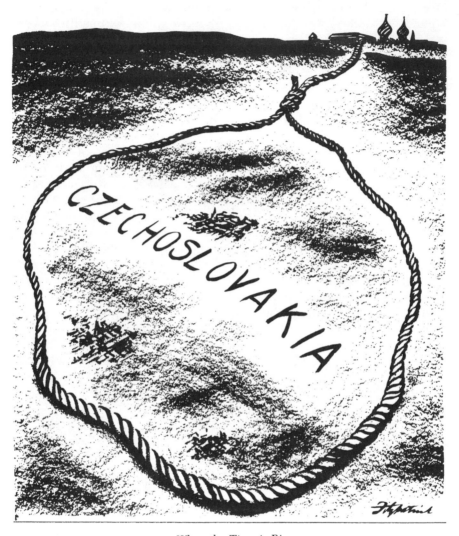

When the Time is Ripe

(Fitzpatrick in the St. Louis *Post-Dispatch*, November 1947.)

many years. If the United States made itself so strong that the Russians could not be confident of winning such a conflict, there was some hope of an ideological compromise. He proved to be a prescient prophet. The United States did make itself strong, and over a period of more than thirty years the East and the West maintained peaceful coexistence—or at least a troubled coexistence, punctuated by relatively small localized wars.

Several months later, in October, 1947, Masaryk was in Washington talking to Secretary of State Marshall at the State Department. The official American records reveal his thinking at that time. He said that many Czech Communists were "sincere patriots," and that the Czechs had proved "indigestible" to any power. They were admittedly sympathetic to their ally, Russia, but they had a more advanced culture than Russia and cherished their independence. In another conference Secretary Marshall asked Masaryk why during the postwar period the Russians had deliberately destroyed the goodwill they had built up in America during the war. His answer was that these actions "sprang from suspicion of the outside world and from the Soviet obsession that the U.S. is bound to suffer an economic collapse. . . ." Moscow believed that after this happened, the United States would withdraw from world affairs "and leave the fate of Europe to Soviet decision"— that is, Communist domination.

Masaryk's observations throw a floodlight on the origins of the Cold War, for among its mainsprings one must include the dread of a depression in America and the expectation of one on the part of the Russians. The Americans themselves clearly feared another economic tailspin, especially if Europe collapsed, as seemed quite likely. This economic motivation undoubtedly ranks high among the reasons why Washington first broached and then implemented the Marshall Proposal.

Returning to the American Embassy, I gathered pertinent information from another official and his Czech assistant, with special attention to the three million or so Sudeten Germans. One should recall that Hitler had used annexation pressure from this minority group, plus much of his own, as a pretext for his initial steps in the complete dismemberment of Czechoslovakia. When the war ended in 1945 and the Czech government was restored, the Sudeten Germans were understandably treated with great brutality and much injustice by vengeful countrymen. Their expulsion was authorized by the powers in the Potsdam Protocol, and about 2,500,000 of them suddenly became displaced persons who greatly complicated the confused process of rehabilitating food-short Germany. Perhaps as many as 10 percent of the Sudeten Germans were allowed to remain, but only after proving their loyalty and their nonadherence to the Nazi cause.

Expelling the Sudeten Germans—one of the great expulsions of history—was directly related to the complete takeover of Czechoslovakia by the Communists in 1948, seven months after my departure. The confiscated land was seized and parcelled out by a Communist minister who saw to it, so one learned at the American Embassy, that those of his own Marxist persuasion or leanings received special favors. As happened in the expulsion of the Protestant Huguenots from Catholic France in the seventeenth century, the exiling of the Sudeten Germans deprived Czechoslovakia of many of its most highly skilled artisans. This deficiency was conspicuous in the fabrication of glass products, many of which reportedly were thereafter inferior and overpriced. For this reason a few of the most highly skilled Sudetens were persuaded to come back.

Rehabilitation of Czech heavy industry—notably the famed Škoda armament works—was naturally being encouraged by the Soviets, who presumably were interested in tanks as well as agricultural machinery. The Czechs were developing a market for weapons in Latin America, and were also seeking a large arms contract with Turkey, on which Moscow probably would put a damper. The stubborn and hated Turks, who controlled the outlet from Russia's Black Sea at the Dardanelles, were obviously not rotating in the Soviet orbit.

Two other officials at the Embassy rather gullibly confirmed the common judgment that the great majority of Czech Communists were nationalists first and pro-Soviet Communists second. They had shown commendable courage in resisting Kremlin pressures, and they were much depressed by the recent forced rejection of the Marshall overture. Many more people claimed to be Communist than actually voted Communist, for they had their eyes primarily on the rewards of collaboration. If the Russians should suffer a severe setback in the diplomatic arena, there would be a tremendous falling-off of adherents from the Communist bandwagon.

Additional comments at the Embassy on the Czech character proved revealing. Warped by some three centuries of oppression and racial friction, these people had become secretive and had learned to "work the angles." Any further loans to them should be based on sound security, not on sympathy. Both the Czechs and the Poles liked the United States in a general way, but they had no real appreciation of the magnitude and importance of America's contribution to the war effort. Nor, for that matter, had the Russian people.

The press attaché at the U.S. Embassy supplied information that laid bare the blueprint used by the Communists to infiltrate a country. One of their first steps was to secure jurisdiction over the press, including newspapers, magazines, and textbooks. From the early postwar reconstruction of the Prague government, the Minister of Information, as I mentioned earlier, had been a Communist. There was no formalized censorship of the press when I was there, but the Communists were making excellent progress toward it. They had managed to obtain control of half of Prague's big newspapers and to secure the lion's share of the newsprint for themselves. This in itself was an effective type of indirect censorship. The leading Communist newspaper even delayed publication of the news so that it could more slavishly follow the lead of Foreign Minister Molotov and also *Pravda,* the official Moscow newspaper.

The American press attaché was tired of hearing the cliché that the Czech Communists were Czechs first and Communists second; if they were real Communists, they were Communists first and Czechs second. He also said that many turncoat Czechs who had collaborated with the Germans were clever enough to turn Communist when the Russian army came. Many of them beat their fellow collaborators to the punch by denouncing them and subjecting them to the fury of the newly liberated.

The Czech Communists began to propagandize early and never ceased their agitation. Communist infiltration extended even to movies, many of them direct from Russia and barefaced propaganda. I witnessed an American film at a Prague theater that aroused my curiosity. The sound track was in American English and the printed translation in Czech appeared at the bottom of the film, but all references or credits to the American source had been carefully removed. Perhaps the Communist censors believed that it would pass for a British or even a Russian production. Soviet films were generally less popular in Prague than the Hollywood variety.

The labor attaché at the Embassy likewise proved most helpful. He observed that there was no real shortage of workmen in this country, partly because a considerable number of the most skilled Sudeten Germans had been allowed to remain or return. Productivity was not at a high level for various reasons. One was that during the seven bitter years from 1938 to 1945 the Czech laborers had learned that it was patriotic to malinger, loaf, or deliberately bungle the job. They could hardly be expected to shake off these ingrained habits overnight.

Throughout the recent war the Soviets had been suspicious allies of the capitalistic Americans, whose Embassy in Moscow was reportedly "bugged" with electronic devices. It undoubtedly was later. The Russians were distrustful ex-allies, and Czechoslovakia was one of the early battlegrounds of the Cold War. Through financial aid and material assistance, the United States was trying to thwart what appeared to it to be aggressive Soviet designs. From various Embassy officials in Prague I heard that the official headquarters were under constant surveillance by the Soviets; the Americans working there strongly suspected that their telephone wires were being tapped.

Ambassador Steinhardt was fully aware that some of his Czech employees, secretarial and otherwise, were on the Russian payroll. The Embassy, with commendable ingenuity, was putting out documents deliberately designed to mislead the Communist agents who were copying them. One American official spent much of his time spying on the Communists who were spying on his colleagues. The strategy was not to dismiss known Communist spies, for they could be watched more effectively and be misled more convincingly if they were kept inside the tent rather than outside it.

Indicative of the mildness of censorship at this time was the presence in bookstores of the bitter exposé of the Soviet system by a defecting Russian official, Victor A. Kravchenko. The author professed to be a Soviet industrial engineer and a former captain in the Red army. Sent to Washington with the Soviet Purchasing Commission, he defected to the West in 1944 and wrote in the Russian language his best-selling book. Translated into English and published in the United States under the title *I Chose Freedom*, its impact was so great that it ranks as one of the major literary guns of the early Cold War.

One American foreign-service officer was certain that his automobile was being "tailed." Another was inconvenienced when a spike was driven into an official tire and water was poured into the gasoline tank. These incidents were not proof of Moscow-directed sabotage; they may have been juvenile pranks or simple vandalism by Czechs who did not like Americans. But all of these annoyances contributed to a thickening atmosphere of uneasiness and suspicion.

Also rewarding was an interview with a Dr. P., a Czech who worked for the Ministry of the Interior. This office had jurisdiction over the police, who were among the first objectives of Communist infiltrators. He said, rather unconvincingly, that he was not aware of any Russian pressure on him. More than that, he insisted that the Communist party was really the democratic party in this country because it had polled a 38 percent plurality of the vote in the election of 1946. If democracy meant people, he declared, here were the people. One could hardly believe that he was so naive as not to know that there was an intimate connection between the Communist party of Czechoslovakia and that of the Soviet Union, ideologically if not physically.

Dr. P. then asked how conditions were in Germany, where he understood that many factories had come through the war virtually intact. Without contradicting him on this point, I only said, "But they are hungry." He replied, "We were hungry for six years; they do not know what hunger is." Then he added that to the people of Czechoslovakia the animalistic Germans were not people, and that the naive Americans should not be misled by humanitarian sentiments.

What this obviously biased Czech citizen reported confirmed an observation of Dr. Dorothy Thompson. The schools of this troubled little country, she said, did not teach history so much as nationalism, as Communist-dominated countries habitually do, even more than most of their democratic rivals. She also spoke of four friars who had arrived at the dining room of the Alcron Hotel. They made the mistake of speaking in German, whereupon the Czech head waiter informed them that all the tables were reserved. The management, after some heated discussion, finally overruled him. A Czech national told me that to the Germans all Slavs were animals, and that the United States was not so popular in Prague then as a year ago because it was allegedly striving to restore Hitler's "Thousand Year Empire." Hatred and fear of Germany, especially after the Czechs had burned their bridges by expelling the Sudeten Germans, were stronger than distrust of Soviet Communism.

Such was the information I had gathered when our airplane zoomed out of Prague late in July, 1947. Czechoslovakia was forced to back away from the Marshall Plan, and no dollars would flow to it over the so-called bridge between East and West. Despite the overtrustful assurances at the Embassy, I had forebodings of an impending Soviet takeover, but was hardly prepared for the speed of its coming. In February of 1948, some seven months later, the Czech Communists, presumably inspired and certainly directed in part by Moscow, staged a bloodless coup d'etat by seizing complete control of the government. They were aided by the lethargy and stupidity of the bourgeois politicians. As at the time of Munich, the Western powers wrung their hands, unable or unwilling to intervene effectively.

A month later, on March 9, 1948, the National Assembly adopted a new constitution that was patterned after the Soviet constitution of 1936. The next day the broken body of Foreign Minister Masaryk was found on the pavement below an open bathroom window. The Communists announced a suicide, and they had considerable support for their interpretation. On the other hand, new evidence has come to light of a faked suicide and a forced ejection.* One theory is that the Communists, fearing that their victim might flee the country and keep up the struggle against Moscow by radio, instructed their agents to hurl him out of the window. Communist sources gave out the story

*See Claire Sterling, *The Masaryk Case* (New York, 1969).

that he had taken his life because of despondency over criticism in the West of his collaboration with the Kremlin. Whether his death was by suicide or murder, I can personally testify that Masaryk had been much distressed and depressed. Whether Communist thugs or Communist pressures did the job, he was clearly done to death by the Communists.

A distinguished journalist, Howard K. Smith, interviewed Masaryk during the same summer that I did. He quotes the harried Czech as having said: "We do not have a free choice. Czechoslovakia does not lie between East and West. It lies between Russia and Germany. I would have no choice. I would go East. But it would kill me!" Whether or not the Communists physically killed him, they certainly killed democracy as the West defines it.

During the ensuing two decades the Czechoslovak government began to edge daringly toward the heady wine of democracy and freedom. This potential defection from Moscow threatened to undermine the loyalty of the Kremlin's six satellite states and also of the defensive Bohemian bastion of the Soviet Union itself. Late in August, 1968, the Soviet tanks rumbled into the little country in a massive display of force, spearheading several hundred thousand troops. Only a few dozen Czech patriots vainly sacrificed their lives. To keep up appearances the Russians had brought in supporting troops from four other Warsaw Pact countries: The German Democratic Republic [East Germany] and the People's Republics of Poland, Hungary, and Bulgaria. The Prague government, under the gun, was forced to reverse its democratization program and sign a treaty sanctioning the presence of Soviet armed forces. Again the Western powers suffered a paralysis of power and will.

When confronted with hopeless odds, tragedy-cursed Czechoslovakia had bowed to Hitler in 1938–1939, then to the Moscow-oriented Communists in 1948, and then to Moscow itself in 1968. The Soviet Union would not allow coveted freedoms and the Czechs could not fight alone with even the faintest hope of success. In all three crises they took the sensible course and the one that was true to their nonsuicidal character. They could vividly remember what had happened when the Finns fought the Soviets in the Winter War of 1940–1941 and when the Hungarians had barehandedly fought Russian tanks with stones in 1956. A Czech who yields and backs away may live to fight some other day—or perhaps his grandchildren will.

— 12 —

Scarred and Scared Scandinavia

Others, particularly the Scandinavians, are pathologically timorous about the Russians.

George Kennan
September 4, 1947

My next stopping place was Stockholm, the clean and well-watered capital of Sweden. In journeying this far north I was forced to make a painful decision in finally bypassing Poland. Airplane connections with Warsaw were uncertain; hotel reservations were only promissory notes; the city was one of the most brutally battered of the recent war; and not much new could be learned there about secret Soviet designs. At Stalin's insistence, and despite the hollow assurances of the Yalta agreements, Poland was now securely imprisoned behind the Iron Curtain.

In thumbing back now through my cancelled passport, I am reminded that in addition to dispensable Poland I had secured visas to visit Spain, Portugal, Switzerland, Eire, Finland, and Greece, all of which were finally excluded from my tour. A visitor could hardly have hoped to pay a meaningful call on all of these countries in one short summer, but there was method in my apparent madness. The location of the consulates in San Francisco had forced me to go there for most of the visas many weeks before departing for Europe. My plan was to make final choices when actually on the ground, and to be governed by the time factor, transportation, and possible accommodations. The final conclusion was that I could glean little new about the need for a Marshall Plan in Spain, Portugal, Switzerland, Eire, and Finland. The Finns, after having lost their second war with the Soviets in four years, had already undergone unexpectedly lenient "Finlandization"—that is, autonomy in domestic affairs but Soviet approval of foreign policy. Incidentally, my application for a Russian visa was denied with the standard explanation that Inturist, the Soviet travel agency, had become inoperative during the war.

My chief regret was in having to bypass Greece. I had majored in Greek during my undergraduate years, and consequently had something of a feel for this cradle of Western civilization. Fears that war-torn Greece would slip down the Communist drain had triggered the turning-point Truman Doctrine of March, 1947, several months earlier. The battle to keep this little nation in the Western orbit was still being waged with no real assurance of success. Not until Yugoslavia's Tito broke away from the domination of Moscow the next year and ceased supporting the Communists in Greece was the West able to score a convincing victory. The outcome of the Greek struggle was of intense interest to the architects of American foreign policy in Washington, but my crowded itinerary, combined with the uncertainties of travel schedules and hotel accommodations, influenced my final decision to head on north. I had been informed in London that big things were brewing in Stockholm; yet before I left Sweden, the information officer at the U.S. Embassy told me that foreign correspondents were hard pressed to find news worth sending home.

My Swedish DC-3 took off promptly from the Prague airport on a flight north that was exceptionally smooth, first over Poland and then the Baltic Sea. Although part of the time the sky was overcast, I could glimpse three or four steamers below. From the air one was reminded anew that Sweden was primarily a land of forests and lakes, with relatively little arable land and with its best agricultural acreage in the south. The checkerboard farms and the red roofs of the houses, many of them generously spaced among the woods, reminded me strongly of the German landscape.

As an American historian, I knew only a little about the history of Sweden, but was to learn somewhat more. The Swedes have been blessed among people, for the hand of providence placed their wooded country on the periphery of central Europe, where the armies of the great powers had surged back and forth. In accounting for Sweden's unusual prosperity and high standards of living, the critic must remember that the last armed conflict in which the Swedes were involved dated back to 1813—134 years earlier.

Such immunity from the horrors of war exacted a high price, as in Switzerland. The Swedes had adopted a policy of armed neutrality, which meant compulsory military service for able-bodied adult males. The Swedish army, though untested in battle, seemed formidable enough in 1914 and in 1939 to have a relatively high deterrent effect in averting German invasions.

Throughout the World War of 1914–1918, Sweden had remained on the sidelines, to the envy of her less fortunate neighbors to the south, though she did lose an appalling number of merchant ships and lives to German submarines. As a result of bloodlines and commercial ties, the Swedes had considerable sympathy for the German cause, and they did not go overboard in swallowing the Wilsonian dogma that this was a war to make the world safe for democracy. Sweden was blessed with some of the finest deposits of iron ore in the world, and large shipments to Germany in return for German coal helped significantly in keeping the Kaiser's war machine functioning.

In World War II the Swedes were much less sympathetic to Hitler's regime than they had been to the Kaiser's Germany, especially after the Nazis suddenly overwhelmed and enchained neighboring Norway in 1940. This attack, one should remember, was prompted largely by the desire of the Germans to forestall the Allies and to continue receiving Swedish iron ore through the Norwegian port of Narvik. In February, 1942, the Germans planned an invasion of Sweden, but the Swedes learned of the scheme and immediately began to mobilize their army. Hitler's generals advised the *Führer* that the task of crushing Sweden would divert too many troops that were urgently needed for the Russian front.

Fearful of antagonizing Hitler, the Swedes, as in World War I, continued to ship their iron ore, ball bearings, and other materials to Nazi Germany in return for urgently needed coal. In so doing, they endured much criticism from the envious but desperate Western democracies. As the war lengthened, Hitler became increasingly bogged down in Russia; and when the United States and its allies launched their great D-Day invasion in June, 1944, the Swedes grew bolder. They gradually throttled down or stopped their profitable exchange of iron ore for coal, and, in response to Allied pressures, ended completely the shipment of steel ball bearings.

A revealing incident involving Sweden was related to me some weeks later at the War College by Edward Page, Jr., a foreign-service officer who had been stationed in Moscow during the war. At one point, U.S. agents had the good fortune to buy up a supply of Swedish ball bearings that the Russians desperately needed. The Americans offered to fly the shipment into the Soviet Union as a gift in their own B-25 bombers, but the NKVD, the Russian secret police, returned a blunt negative. Their suspicions aroused, they evidently feared that these obliging "capitalists," using ball bearings as a cover, might be looking for something of military advantage to them in a future war. Mr. Page reasoned that the undiplomatic Americans had probably mishandled the affair. If they had only hinted to the Russians that such a shipment might possibly be forthcoming, then Moscow would have been encouraged to do the asking.

As if to do penance for their good fortune, the Swedes aided their less fortunate neighbors and also the embattled Allies. They dispatched so much assistance of various kinds to the Finns, during the Winter War with the Russians and after, that they weakened their own defenses against possible Russian or German assaults. Even though they were incurring the wrath of the Nazis, the Swedes rescued and sheltered British and American aviators who were shot down in their attacks on the German Reich. Sweden also welcomed and succored refugees from the countries of northwestern Europe, especially the Dutch, and even including some Poles. The Swedes smuggled materials of war into German-occupied Norway for the tenacious underground resistance. They even continued wartime rationing of food so that they could export supplies for the relief of Western Europe. All these sacrifices add up to a commendable total that was little acclaimed at the time, and it speaks volumes for the humanitarian instincts of the fortune-blessed Swedes.

At the time of my arrival in Stockholm, the people looked gaunt and hungry, dour and sour. The beautiful blonde Swedish women, about whom one hears so much, were conspicuously scarce. Those that I observed did not look healthy; certainly there was no resemblance to the overweight females of Czechoslovakia. The people in general seemed somber and utterly lacking in gaiety. The claim was being made that the reduced Swedish bread ration was the lowest in the world, although there was a good deal of other kinds of food. I made this discovery at a cafeteria near my hotel and had some trouble ordering a meal of strange dishes without knowing the Swedish language. At length I was rescued when the attendants extracted an English-speaking woman from the kitchen. The shelves of the stores in Stockholm were even piled high with California canned fruit, which particularly interested me because I had worked in the California fruit industry for about eight summers while a student in high school and college. Purchases of this kind from the United States were depleting the already shrinking Swedish gold reserves.

Of special concern to me was the relation of Sweden to the so-called menace of Moscow. The brutal attack on next-door Finland by the Russians in the Winter War of 1939–1940 had greatly alarmed the Swedes. For some years there had been an indigenous but negligible Communist party in Sweden, but the brutal Soviet invasion of a neigh-

bor and the aggressiveness of the Kremlin following Hitler's demise
had dampened the Communist cause.

As for the political lineup in Sweden, the nation was committed to
the middle way, somewhere between capitalism and communism.
The Social Democrats were by far the most popular party; the Communists, who had come out a poor fifth in the parliamentary elections
of 1944, held only 15 seats out of a total of 230. In 1948, presumably as
a result of anti-Soviet antipathy generated by the Cold War, the 15
seats faded to only 8 in the election of that year. There could be no
doubt that Sweden was nowhere near being a Communist or even a
pro-Communist country. But because it had walked the tightrope of
neutrality during the recent conflict, the victorious Allies were reluctant at the outset to welcome this fortunate country as a member of
the United Nations, launched in June, 1945. Admission was deferred
until November, 1946.

As was my practice, I registered at one of the attractive hotels in
Stockholm, found the American Embassy, and presented my credentials. I then sought from about a half-dozen officials there information that would give me a clearer picture of the status of Sweden in the
international community.

The First Secretary, L. Randolph Higgs, proved to be most helpful.
He believed that most of the Swedish Communists were of the grass-
roots variety, not Moscow-spawned. They openly took part in the political process by attacking the Social Democrats, and their strategy
was to soft-pedal political issues and focus on the economic problems.
Mr. Higgs confirmed my impression that the Communists had lost
ground heavily at the time of the Russo-Finnish war because of
Sweden's pro-Finnish sympathies. The Social Democratic newspapers, voicing the views of the dominant party, were refraining from
attacking the Soviets. At the same time, they were criticizing the
shortcomings of the United States without meaning to be unduly
bitter.

Mr. Higgs concluded that the Swedes were on something of a hot
seat. They realized that they could be high on the Soviet grab list, but
reasoned that the Russians would focus first on the Mediterranean and
the warm-water Bosporus Strait. The cautious Swedes evidently
hoped to defer the evil day by hunkering down and not attracting
attention to themselves. They had also negotiated a trade agreement
with Moscow in November, 1946, which they hoped would promote
political as well as economic harmony. By its terms Stockholm extended credit in the sum of $2.785 billion for the purchase of Swe-
dish goods over a period of fifteen years.

My informant did not tell me that the United States had formally protested against a large loan by Sweden to Russia in October, 1946. The Swedes had politely told the United States to mind its own business, for they were a sovereign nation. But Mr. Higgs did predict that the Soviets would probably overrun all Europe eventually; if that happened, he concluded, the United States had better retire to an Atlantic Wall.

Swedish socialism, as all the world knew, had produced a welfare state that was elevating the standard of living to one of the highest in the world. (Ironically, the well-sheltered Swedes had and still have one of the world's highest suicide rates.) The Swedish laborers, Mr. Higgs observed, did not look much beyond the next paycheck; the great attractions to them were "high wages and low prices." The labor leaders in Sweden, unlike those in many pro-Communist countries, were conservative. Obviously corporate management preferred right-wing labor leadership to that of Communists.

The Second Secretary at the Embassy, Francis L. Spalding, confirmed the view that the Swedes had driven a hard bargain with Germany during the recent war. They had exchanged the product of their mines for German manufactured goods, and in this way had soaked up German manpower and materials. Additionally, they had fortunately wound up owing the bankrupt Germans money for these goods, rather than the other way around. Sweden's stance was such that Hitler managed to get what he wanted up to a point without having to use soldiers to police his source of supplies.

After Germany collapsed, Mr. Spalding further observed, the Swedes contrived to cause some criticism in both the Soviet Union and the United States. Swedish defensive measures, like those of Finland in 1939, were obviously directed at the USSR, and these precautions ("provocations") evoked resentment from the Soviet press, if not from the foreign office. At the same time, many Americans were applauding Sweden's prudence. Yet the United States had protested against the trade agreement of 1946 between Moscow and Stockholm as too cozy an arrangement. The filling of orders for the Soviets, Mr. Spalding observed, was not a popular task in the Swedish factories. As for Communism in the labor movement, the Communist leaders had engineered a six-month strike in the metal works and had finally lost out.

A Mr. Garrison, also at the Embassy, believed that the Swedish Communists were not disciples of Moscow but were Communists by way of protest, not knowing what they were letting themselves in for. Referring to the invasion of Norway by Hitler in 1940, he said that the Swedes had been afraid to mobilize immediately after this thrust lest they provoke an attack on themselves. In addition, they were suffering from weakness because they had sent too much of their own artillery to Finland for use against the Russian invaders in 1939 and later. He further noted that the neighboring Norwegians were saying that they would never be caught napping again, yet they were doing little to strengthen themselves against another incursion.

A public-affairs officer at the Embassy, James J. Robbins, observed that the Swedes were isolated, selfish, and reserved. He was disturbed that some Swedish firms, conspicuously those recently on the American black list as pro-German, were now receiving unaccountable favors from the United States. He believed that the Swedes were suffering from a guilt complex because they had not entered the war with their fellow Scandinavians. There probably was some truth in this observation. A joke then going the rounds told of an Irish nationalist who reportedly boasted: "Two great nations had the foresight to stay out of the recent war: the peace-loving Irish and the cowardly Swedes."

Academicians were highly regarded in Sweden, and an interview was arranged for me with Professor Herbert Tingsten, a distinguished scholar. He remarked that his country was ingrown and increasingly absorbed with domestic problems. The people of the United States, he felt, knew more about Russia than the Swedes themselves did. Most of the books that Sweden was receiving about the Soviet Union were coming from America. He mentioned specifically the exposé by the alleged Russian defector, Victor Kravchenko (*I Chose Freedom*) and the revelation of the behind-the-scenes friction between the U.S. military and the Soviet Union in General John R. Deane's *The Strange Alliance*, first published in New York in January of that year, 1947.

Professor Tingsten was opposed to the so-called conspiracy of silence about Russia, as well as to the tendency of the Social Democratic press to play up the lynchings and other shortcomings of the United States. He felt that Sweden's good luck in avoiding war for more than a century had created the misleading conviction that the nation could never become involved in one again. A few weeks earlier, a group of Swedish journalists had gone to Russia and could write only about the flowing champagne, the heaped-up caviar, and similar trivia. He was firmly of the opinion that whether the West opposed the Soviet Union or not, the Moscow Marxists would pursue their predetermined objectives of Communist world domination.

A final interview was scheduled with a Dr. Linblom, a prominent Social Democrat who, if memory serves, greeted me in the office of the prominent Stockholm newspaper with which he was connected in an editorial capacity. In explaining the relative indifference of the

Swedes to possible peril from Moscow, he said that the Americans had stationed a considerable number of people in Russia during the war (including General Deane), and that the Swedes had not witnessed the disturbing friction at first hand.

Still suffering from the economic dislocations of the war, Sweden ultimately received Marshall Plan aid from the Americans amounting to $107.3 million between 1948 and 1952. But, true to her traditional neutrality, she shunned the twelve-power North Atlantic Treaty Organization (NATO), formally launched in Washington in 1949 to "contain" the USSR. Another deterrent to Sweden was the menacing presence of the Russians. Finland, a next-door neighbor, was being held as a hostage, and for Sweden to have joined NATO might well have provoked the Soviets into intensifying their Finlandization or resorting to more disagreeable precautions.

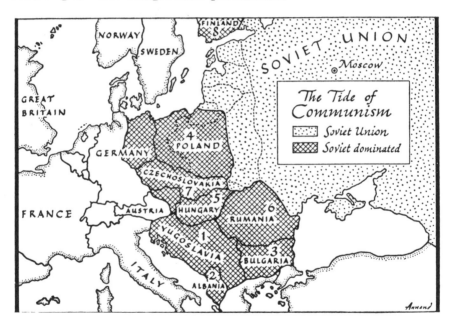

The Order of Soviet Domination, 1944–1948

(Thomas A. Bailey, *A Diplomatic History Of The American People*, 9th edition, © 1974, p. 791. Reprinted by permission of Prentice-Hall, Inc., Englewood Cliffs, New Jersey.)

In leaving Sweden, I took off by commercial airplane for Denmark, although ideally I should have included Norway in this northern swing. But this opportunity was bypassed, partly because time was growing short, but more importantly because little of significance could be learned that was not already common knowledge.

In a lightning stroke, the Germans had invaded Norway in April of 1940. The Norwegians, despite the Fascist traitor Vidkun Quisling, maintained a stout underground resistance and consequently suffered much destruction and considerable loss of life. After the war ended, elections to the Norwegian parliament (Storthing) were held in October, 1945, and the Communists made a poor showing. Of the 150 seats to be filled, they captured only 11.

Behind the scenes, as I subsequently learned when the official documents were published in 1972, the Soviets had been showing some disquieting interest in Norway's Spitzbergen archipelago. This strategic area was located far to the north in the chill Arctic Ocean and, if fortified, would command the shipping routes to and from the seaports of northern Russia. The USSR had no other direct outlet to the Atlantic Ocean. To the regret of the Allies, the absence of airfields and other bases at Spitzbergen had enabled the Germans in World War II to inflict frightful damage on the convoys of British merchant ships bringing military supplies to the Soviets by the icy northern route.

A fourteen-power treaty, signed at Paris in 1920, had neutralized and demilitarized strategic Spitzbergen; but Moscow, tainted as it then was with Bolshevism, was not invited to join the signers. The geographical position of the Soviet Union was such that the Russians were understandably unhappy over this blackballing. This snub was made the more bitter by the inclusion of Italy and Japan, both of which ultimately became open enemies of the Soviet Union in World War II.

In 1944 the Soviets had asked to become partners with Norway in defense of the main island of Spitzbergen and the sole defender of Bear Island. They also sought an abrogation and renegotiation of the multipower treaty of 1920, the signers of which had cold-shouldered them. Washington was fearful that the Soviets would use a military lodgement at Spitzbergen to jeopardize the naval operations of the United States in a possible future war. As a consequence, in February, 1947, Norway was advised by Washington that acceptance of the Soviet proposals would "seriously impair the overall security interests of the United States" and could be interpreted as "appeasement" of the Russians, at a time when the aggressive Soviets were increasingly in bad odor. Moreover, a threatening Communist foothold in Spitzbergen would have a direct relationship to the ongoing negotiations in Washington for the retention and expansion by the United States of military rights in Denmark's Greenland. Iceland was also involved, for it had declared its independence of Denmark in 1944. Both of these outposts would be menaced in some degree by the proposed Soviet move.

The strongly worded opposition of Washington to the proposed Russian presence in Spitzbergen evidently had some effect. After the Norwegian government had pursued a temporizing policy of partly yielding and partly evading, the Norwegian parliament met in secret session (February, 1947) and voted 101 to 11 to deny the Soviet request for bases. The 11 negative votes all came from the entire bloc of Communists. A detective would want no better evidence that the Norwegian Communists were more favorably disposed to the interests of the USSR than to those of the United States.

War-blighted Norway became a deserving beneficiary of the United States under the European Recovery Program (Marshall Plan), from 1948 to 1952, in the amount of $255 million. Despite disapproving frowns from the USSR, which menacingly adjoined Norwegian territory on the extreme northeast, Norway pluckily became a charter member of the North Atlantic Treaty Organization (NATO) in 1949.

In bypassing Norway and flying from Stockholm to Copenhagen, I had occasion to pick up a British newspaper on the airplane. It published the story of a woman in the United States who had recently murdered her husband by drenching him with petrol and throwing a lighted match on him. Her explanation was that she was tired of arguing with the father of her ten children. Such overemphasis on bizarre cases was undoubtedly giving Europeans a false picture of daily life in America. Journalists on the European side of the Atlantic were well aware of the elementary truism: Harmony never made a headline.

My brief stop in Copenhagen did not involve a call at the American Embassy, where I doubtless could have picked up some useful information if it had been open. These two days happened to be Saturday and Sunday, August 2 and 3, 1947, and the officers were presumably away from their posts. I partially remedied this deficiency by later examining the confidential documents for 1947 that were then being exchanged between Copenhagen and Washington.

Weakly defended, Denmark had collapsed when Hitler struck with devastating speed in April, 1940. The feebleness of armed resistance accounted largely for the absence of wholesale destruction. But as the war dragged on, the passive resistance of the Danes increased, to the accompaniment of serious riots, especially after shortages of foods required rationing. I could see a number of abandoned bunkers in Copenhagen in which carefree children were now playing, and from our airplane as we glided in we could observe a red cross painted on the roof of a hospital—a grim reminder that even the angels of mercy had not been immune from aerial attack.

After Hitler's short-lived empire collapsed, the royal government of

Denmark was restored to power, and the first parliamentary elections were held in October, 1945. The Social Democrats emerged with the most seats, while the Communists ran a poor fourth, having won only 18 of 130 seats. Two years later, in October, 1947, some three months after my arrival, new parliamentary elections reduced the Communist seats to 9 from the former 18, thus leaving this leftist group in a hopeless minority. We may reasonably conclude that the obviously aggressive behavior of the Soviets had dampened even the slight Danish tolerance for Moscow's brand of Communism.

Behind the scenes the Russians were showing a disquieting interest in Denmark's Greenland, primarily, we may assume, for strategic reasons. In April, 1941, about a year after the German takeover of Denmark, the stranded Danish minister in Washington signed a highly significant agreement. It made motherless Greenland a temporary protectorate of the United States, with full recognition of Danish sovereignty. This pact was condemned by Hitlerite Germany and later by the Danish Communists as invalid, because it had been negotiated by an unauthorized and orphaned envoy. One of the first acts of the restored Danish parliament in 1945 was to confirm this agreement unanimously. Whatever the legalities, the United States continued to find Greenland extremely useful for airfields, radio installations, and weather stations, as it had during the recent war.

In October, 1947, some weeks after my brief stay in Copenhagen, the Russian minister there inquired if Greenland was for sale, possibly because the Soviet press had been critical of America's retaining bases there. Communist elements in Denmark were conspicuously desirous of excluding the United States from Greenland. But the doughty Danes stood firm, backed as they were by Washington. Four years later, in April, 1951, an agreement was signed between Denmark and the United States for the joint defense of Greenland within the framework of the North Atlantic Treaty Organization.

Copenhagen impressed me as one of the most attractive cities I had ever seen. The wide streets, the neat brick apartments, and the pervasive cleanliness were impressive. Beauty parlors were numerous, and so-called pornographic magazines were on seductive display. As in Stockholm, the streets were filled with bicycles, and the ladies, young and old, permitted their skirts to fly about with careless abandon. When one considered what these people had endured under the recent German occupation, they seemed unusually prosperous and happy, at least superficially. I spent several hours on a Saturday night at the famous amusement park known as the Tivoli Gardens, where the visitors were laughing happily at or near the various stands, stalls, games, and mechanical wheels. These people reminded me of a light-hearted crowd of American farmers and their families at a country fair in Indiana.

An American tourist in Stockholm had told me that the rather grim and glum Swedes were quite unlike their Danish brothers, who were fun-loving, outgoing, and obliging. I received somewhat the same impression from my limited observations. In Copenhagen a taxi driver actually returned my tip; I thought it was an act of goodwill, but perhaps he had added his gratuity to the bill and was simply being honest.

At all events, real deprivation and need lay behind these seemingly happy faces, largely because many of Denmark's export markets had shriveled up in the poverty-stricken European countries. The Danes gladly accepted the benefactions spawned by the Marshall Plan, totaling $273 million from 1948 to 1952, and managed to scramble back onto their economic feet. More than that, Denmark expressed its fear of Communist aggression by abandoning a long tradition of neutrality and becoming a charter member of the twelve-power North Atlantic Treaty Organization in 1949.

The Beginnings of Benelux

When the Hun [German] is poor and down
He's the humblest man in town;
But once he climbs and holds the rod
He smites his fellow man–and God.

Jakob Cats
Dutch poet, *c.* 1600

The airplane trip on August 3, 1947, from Copenhagen to Amsterdam, a distance of some four hundred miles, went off without a hitch. As we approached our destination we seemed to be flying much of the time over the islands and shoals of the North Sea. At the airport the Dutch officials viewed my passport with the greatest suspicion that I encountered during my entire trip, and I learned later that they were unusually vigilant with regard to currency control. After their experience with the occupying Nazis, they evidently had developed a deep distrust of foreigners.

Official neutrality had served the Dutch well in the World War of 1914–1918, although they were next-door neighbors of the Germans, to whom they were bound by ties of race and religion. During this war Holland had suffered heavy losses of merchant shipping to the German submarines, as had its Scandinavian neighbors. But that was one price that this tiny nation had to pay for its precarious neutrality.

In World War II the Dutch tried to play the same neutral role again, but succeeded for only eight months and ten days. The neighboring Nazi virus had infected a considerable number of Dutch, some of whom volunteered for Hitler's armies. The impatient *Führer*, alleging that he was beating the British and French to the punch, launched a lightning invasion of the Netherlands on May 10, 1940. The futile but determined resistance of the Dutch, hopelessly overmatched, was quickly crushed. The city of Rotterdam, the second largest in the country, capitulated, but several hours later German aerial bombers brutally destroyed the entire center of the city. Most of the older houses were demolished, including the birthplace of Erasmus (c. 1466–1536), the great scholar and humanist. This act of wholesale barbarism may have been perpetrated to shock the Dutch people into complete submission and also to intimidate the British. If so, it failed on both counts. German sources have claimed that the bombers were only trying to destroy the areas at the bridges, but Hitler had already brutally bombed civilian centers in Poland.

Nazi terrorism at Rotterdam was only a foretaste of future horrors, for the proud little country suffered a terrible ordeal during the war. Thousands of men were deported as slave laborers; the Jews were persecuted so mercilessly that only about one-tenth survived "the final solution." The shocking conditions under which they lived were revealed nakedly to the world in 1952 through the published diary of Anne Frank, a German-Jewish adolescent who died in 1945 after hiding in a warehouse for two years. Meanwhile a strongly supported resistance movement developed, with the result that countless Dutch patriots lost their lives.

Worst of all was the nightmare of the last eight months of the war, during which the country was desperately fought over by the defending Germans and the invading Allies. From the end of 1944 to the liberation in the spring of 1945, famine conditions prevailed. In the final weeks, people in the western provinces were subsisting on an estimated three hundred to four hundred calories a day, provided largely by sugar beets and tulip bulbs. Some vital relief was supplied by ships from Sweden and by air drops engineered by the Allies. The withdrawing Germans, vindictive in both defeat and retreat, flooded anew a considerable area of reclaimed farmland, thus further worsening the food crisis.

Bypassing Rotterdam, I confined most of my on-site inspection to the first and third largest cities: Amsterdam, the key seaport, and The Hague, the capital. Amsterdam, located at the mouth of a surprisingly wide Rhine River, had suffered little visible damage, but The Hague was about one-third destroyed. A number of abandoned bunkers were plainly visible. In the entire country, only about 60 percent of the houses had come through unscathed. Yet the industrious Dutch, with their famous stubborn determination, were pitching in and repairing what damage they could. Their food intake had risen to about twenty-five hundred calories a day, and this level was a tolerably high standard for these difficult times. The people had sufficient energy to make tens of thousands of battered houses habitable and to drain some of the recently flooded acreage. Much of the reconstruction was actually new construction, especially in the building trades.

Not all the damage done to the economy was visible. In addition to what the Germans had stolen or carted away as booty, the once lucrative two-way trade between the Netherlands and a prostrate Germany had largely dried up. The Germans had little to sell and perhaps even less purchasing power. The shipping industry of Holland was partially crippled, and besides, the Dutch were losing their once profitable commerce with their rebellious East Indian empire. At the same time, they were having to spend immense sums of money in an effort to crush the rebels who had proclaimed an independent Indonesian Republic in 1945, shortly after the surrender of the invading Japanese. After four years of futile and expensive fighting, the Dutch finally recognized the independence of Indonesia late in 1949, but only after pressure from the United Nations, including the United States. No longer would nine million Dutch control seventy million Asians. The arm-twisting, anti-imperialistic posture of the United States did not increase the popularity of Americans in the Netherlands.

Two American military attachés at the Embassy in The Hague told me that the Dutch had a good case for their attempt to suppress the Indonesian rebellion. But they were inept in presenting their side to the public, and consequently were surprised to find world opinion arrayed against them as imperialist-colonialists. This role they had played for more than four centuries, but the wave of the future was engulfing them.

The green countryside in Holland looked prosperous enough. I saw my first Dutch windmills, although they were not nearly so numerous as armchair travelers were led to expect. As a reminder that this reclaimed little country was a foremost producer of dairy products, one could see hundreds of black-and-white cows grazing, some of them being milked out in the pastures by hand instead of by the mechanical contraptions so widely used in America. There was an impressive amount of farmland in production, although I was surprised to find that so much acreage should be devoted to the incomparable Dutch tulips rather than to products that had a higher food value, especially at a time when so much of Europe was still desperately hungry.

Transportation was likewise causing headaches. A considerable amount of rolling stock on the railroads had been destroyed or damaged by the war, as a visitor could note in the widespread tangled wreckage. Repairs and replacements were under way, but still there was a shortage of streetcars for the cities and passenger cars for the railroads. The crowds on the public conveyances resembled somewhat those of New York during the rush hours, and such aggravating conditions did not improve dispositions. I well remember my difficulties in forcing my way onto one of the electric interurban cars with a couple of bulky suitcases. One middle-aged Dutchman, probably a business or professional man, growled some kind of complaint when my baggage came too close to his feet for comfort.

As in Copenhagen, a visitor to Holland was impressed with the swarm of bicycles and bicyclists, some of them carrying babies. Old and young alike were pumping away, and in one instance a whole family rolled merrily by on a tandem affair. Some of these conveyances were sturdy three-wheeled contraptions, so equipped that they could carry a substantial load. The ingenious Dutch had evidently discovered the secret of cheap and nonpolluting transportation that paid an additional bonus in wholesome exercise. Another silent form of transportation was furnished by the network of canals, of which Amsterdam boasted far more than fabled Venice. On or near these waterways one could see boats, barges, and a few optimistic fishermen who seemed never to be pulling any fish out of the water.

As was my habitual strategy, I soon located the American Embassy at The Hague and established my contacts. These headquarters were not difficult to find, for they were located on the second floor of the Shell Oil Building (Shell Oil was presumably an outlet of the powerful Royal Dutch Petroleum Company). Most of my information regarding current conditions came from the military attachés and from Cutler D. Huyler, Jr., information officer. He had a good deal to say about the operation of the United States Information Service, including its public library.

One of Huyler's complaints was that at first the personnel sent over from the States had not measured up to the highest standards. He mentioned further that the government in Washington was cutting back on the staffing; it had recently lopped off three men. The next day, Mr. Huyler related, the financially pinched British hired them. More than that, London had provided three professors of English who could be used to build up better relations with the Dutch and offset Soviet propaganda in Holland. I gathered from these comments that the battered British, located closer than the Americans to the borders of Russia, were more concerned about holding their own in the war of words than was Uncle Sam.

The tiny USIS library at The Hague offered only thirty-two hundred volumes, and because of a tightened budget it could remain open only from two o'clock to six o'clock in the afternoon. Mr. Huyler felt that

the United States was not living up to its responsibilities in the propaganda battle against the Moscow-oriented Communists. The British
were evidently doing a much better job. Yet they were misled by
press representatives who wrote about the United States without ever
having crossed the Atlantic. The kind of stuff that the British newspapers published was not doing the cause of the West much good. A
notorious offender, he added, was a "wretched tabloid," the London
Daily Mirror.

At the American Embassy I learned that the Communists in Holland were few in number, comprising about 7 percent of the electorate. They were also in financial straits, presumably because of the
neglect or poverty of Moscow. One basic reason for this weakness was
that the Catholics were strong in Holland, and "good" Catholics both
distrusted and feared the atheistic dogma of the Moscow Marxists. In
the parliamentary elections of May, 1946, the Catholic party had
emerged as the strongest, while the Communists trailed as a poor fifth.
In one chamber they had won only four seats out of fifty; in the second, only ten out of ninety-three.

Despite this feeble showing at the polls, the Dutch Communists
were attracting the watchful eye of the Soviets. Through the Moscow
newspaper *Pravda* the Russians had protested against the prospect of
the Netherlands joining Benelux—the customs union then being fash-
ioned by Belgium, the Netherlands, and Luxembourg, and formally
launched the next year (January 1, 1948). Yet in one area the Dutch
Communists were able to show some strength; that was in the labor
movement in Amsterdam. The Communists had seriously threatened
to tie up the shipping involved in supporting the war in Indonesia
against the rebels, but such efforts had not proved crippling.

An amusing commentary on the weakness of Communist propaganda in Holland was provided by my informant at the USIS. The local
Communists had come to him asking for the loan of American films,
even those that had an obvious pro-American slant. The Soviet Embassy did not have any available, and the Dutch Communists did not
like those being put out by the British. They preferred capitalist propaganda from the most powerful of the capitalistic nations to poor movies or none at all.

Before leaving Holland, I took a short side trip by interurban trolley
to Haarlem, a substantial city about ten miles due west from Amsterdam. Some months earlier, at Stanford University, I had met a
pretty young Dutch girl from this area who was then visiting California in the hope of recovering her health. The ordeal of the Nazi occupation, with its scarce food and unrelieved tension, had evidently
caused her to develop a serious case of stomach ulcers. She had given

me her address, together with an invitation to visit her if I ever reached her country. When I arrived in Holland, I seized this opportunity to see more of the country and its people, and possibly the inside of a private dwelling.

On reaching Haarlem, I had to walk for a considerable distance among the picturesque red-brick Dutch houses, but finally located the desired residence. No one seemed to be at home, and I inquired of the neighbors in my American English if this was the correct address. They seemed somewhat suspicious, perhaps remembering the inquiries that had been made during the war by Nazi agents, but they finally assured me that I had come to the right place. When no one responded to my persistent knocking, I slipped a note under the door so that the young lady would know I had called. She ultimately received my message, for I found a letter of regret in my home mail many weeks later.

While waiting for the return transportation from Haarlem, I discovered near the station an ice-cream stand that was selling for a modest sum a generous serving of delicious white ice cream. The August evening was hot and I was thirsty, with the result that I must have come back for at least a half-dozen refills of this unrationed delicacy. I could personally testify to the excellence of the Dutch dairy industry, supported as it was by all those black-and-white cows.

At the Embassy Mr. Huyler had remarked that the Dutch were more like Americans than any other Europeans. Judging from my limited contacts, they seemed hard-bitten, rather like the Germans, and this trait was understandable in the light of the prolonged ordeal they had undergone. They were also stubborn individualists and strong traditionalists. They showed little inclination to embrace a Marxist ideology under the dictatorial direction of Moscow. The constitutional monarchy under which these people lived had sunk deep roots into the past. One day I was reminded of the ruling Queen Wilhelmina and the ancient monarchy when I unexpectedly found a Dutch flag on display in my hotel room in The Hague. Upon inquiry among the servants, I learned that the banner was there to honor the birthday of the little princess.

The sturdy Dutch were prime candidates for American help under the Marshall Proposal, and especially deserving because of their plucky resistance struggle against the common Nazi foe and their crying need for rehabilitation. Among various handicaps, their dollar credits had melted away. The Dutch grasped America's offer of assistance with gratitude and ultimately received official benefactions amounting to $991.6 million—a major boost on the rugged road to recovery.

Next on my itinerary in Belgium was Brussels, the clean and attractive capital city, which was about 120 miles from Amsterdam. On the train ride of several hours, during which the well-tilled farms flitted by, I had ample time to reflect on the background of what I was about to learn during my two days in Belgium, August 6 and 7.

An American could be reasonably certain of moving into a friendly atmosphere in Belgium and this proved to be the case. In 1914 the Germans, in the first days of World War I, had burst into Belgium in an effort to outflank Paris, win the war in the west, and then turn to meet the Russians invading from their rear. The lunge into Belgium came in violation of a neutrality pact signed by the European powers in 1839, including Germany (then Prussia). Britain and France, as co-guarantors of Belgian neutrality, were sucked into the conflict, while the Belgians themselves put up a heroic but largely futile defense.

Even discounting lurid propaganda tales, Germany's occupation of Belgium was brutal, and the resulting shortage of food produced famine conditions. A young millionaire mining engineer, then in Britain, was called upon to organize an agency for feeding the Belgians. Herbert Clark Hoover thus became a folk hero in Belgium and a household name in America as a result of his successful and highly publicized endeavors. I was confident that a mere mention of his name and of my connection with Stanford University as a fellow alumnus would open hospitable doors.

"Poor little Belgium," a prime exhibit in the anti-German propaganda campaigns of World War I, was again victimized by the invading Germans in World War II. In 1937 Hitler formally guaranteed the neutrality of Belgium in another of his famous scraps of paper. Relying on this hollow pledge, the Belgians readied their defenses in the hope that any blow from Germany against Europe would fall somewhere else. In May of 1940 Hitler struck, charging that France and Britain were about to violate Belgian neutrality and attack him. He burst into Belgium, speedily overran the defending forts, outflanked the "impregnable" and unfinished French Maginot Line, and knocked France out of the war.

King Leopold III, hopelessly entrapped, surrendered speedily and unconditionally to the enemy, despite the opposition of his cabinet. As a well-treated prisoner of war, he refused to rule, and when he was freed by the victorious Allies in 1945, his people would not permit his return. Many of them felt that he should renounce all claim to the throne. So bitter and widespread were the charges of treason and collaboration, some of which I encountered, that he was not permitted to come back until 1949. The continuing unrest was so persistent that the next year he turned over the throne to his son.

Luckless little Belgium was thus devastated twice, caught as she was between two coalitions of the great powers in two successive world wars. Ironically, Hitler's last-gasp offensive on the western front again burst into Belgium, this time through the thinly defended Ardennes Forest, and this onslaught resulted in the Battle of the (Belgian) Bulge. During this desperate drive, Hitler unleashed a flurry of V2 rocket bombs on the great Belgian seaport of Antwerp, a supply base for the Allies and a prime objective of the final German thrust.

As usual, I promptly made contact with several officials in the American Embassy, which, as in The Hague, was located in the Shell Oil Building. Once these American representatives had seen my credentials, they were frank in giving their assessment of conditions in Belgium, with special reference to the need for the proposed Marshall Plan and to the dangers posed by the activities of the Communists.

As for physical damage, I was pleasantly surprised to learn that the Belgians were not so badly off as rumored. For one thing, only a relatively small part of the country had been fought over for any length of time. The Germans had entered too fast in 1940 and had left too rapidly in the closing stages of the war, except notably in the southeast area in or near the so-called Bulge. Nor had the invading Germans stripped Belgium as they had France. One American official at the Embassy believed that Hitler had intended to make the French permanent vassals, but that he had expected to incorporate Belgium— a contented and prosperous Belgium—into the Reich.

In accounting for the surprising prosperity of the Belgians, my informant noted that these people, many of them skilled craftsmen, traditionally loved to work. In addition, their special breed of draft horses reportedly could do the work of two ordinary horses. I even saw a large dog harnessed to a traditional dog cart. But the Belgian men would not go down into old coal mines that were deep and unsafe; they much preferred to import Baltic immigrants and other expendables for this purpose. The industrial plant of Belgium, especially the steel factories had come through the war in fairly good shape, for most of the fighting had occurred in the agricultural areas. Moreover, the resource-rich Belgian Congo had continued to pile up a gold surplus, during the war, and this reserve had come in handy during the reconstruction months. To top it all, inhabitants of much-invaded Belgium were shrewd traders who had over the centuries learned to live with occupiers and profit at their expense, whether they were Austrians, Spaniards, French, or Germans.

Belgium had temporarily lost most of its lucrative prewar trade with the German hinterland, for conquered Germany was too hungry and unproductive to buy much from abroad. But the thrifty Belgians had been able during the last weeks of the war to capitalize on their key port of Antwerp, which was of critical importance in supplying the Allied armies invading Germany. The wages of the stevedores had risen so high and the harbor fees were so costly that the shrewd Belgians were able to make money from their deliverers.

In recent months Antwerp had been tied up by strikes so frequently that foreign importers, including Argentinians, were threatening to take their business elsewhere. Some of the stoppages were evidently inspired and led by Communists, and partly for this reason General Clay in Berlin was happy to use the German seaport of Bremen rather than Antwerp. Bremen was completely under the control of the American Military Government; strikes were forbidden; and the coolie wages of thirty-five cents a day came out of the near-empty pockets of the defeated and occupied German taxpayers. In due time, my informants believed, Belgian trade with the interior of Germany would be revived, partly because the German ports of Hamburg and Bremen would not be able to handle all the mounting traffic.

Soviet agents, I also learned at the Embassy, had evidently shifted their main emphasis from Paris to Brussels, at least temporarily. In any event, one could notice a marked increase in the size and caliber of the Soviet Embassy, which, as usual, was much too heavily staffed for any conventional diplomatic business. The leading Communist newspaper in Brussels had only one-third of its subscriptions paid up; the deficit was presumably supplied by the Kremlin. My sources believed, despite this evidence of increased activity, that Moscow had lost considerable interest in the Belgian Communists, who were notoriously unresponsive to party discipline from Moscow. The Kremlin may even have written off the whole operation in disgust. The educated guess in Brussels was that the Soviets were planning to pluck off Belgium when the ominously large French Communist party won control of France.

Belgian Communists, I additionally gathered, were losing ground, although they had played a prominent role in the strong resistance movement in the later stages of the war. They comprised only about 10 percent of the voting population, and the circulation of their main newspaper had dropped off greatly. The explanations offered for this decline seemed reasonable enough. The Belgians had full stomachs, and Communism usually thrives on malnutrition and misery. The local Communists, with few Moscow-trained people, had poorer leadership than the Socialists, and astute leadership was essential for a revolutionary movement. The Belgian population was predominantly

Catholic, and to good Catholics the godlessness of the Kremlin was anathema. Finally, the Belgians were strong individualists; most of them dreamed of owning their own few acres of ground, not a tiny garden on a large collectivized farm.

Beyond doubt, the Belgians had a special attachment to the United States that dated back to 1914, when white-knight Herbert Hoover had rushed to the rescue with shiploads of food. The people of this pint-sized country admired the gigantic achievements of the go-getting Yankees, and after the war many young men wrote to the American Embassy in the hope of emigrating to this promised land, even as enlistees in the United States Army. The Belgians recognized in America a kindred melting-pot country, for they were themselves a mixture of various races and nationalities. Whether Catholics or Protestants, they spoke two languages, French and Flemish. A visitor could note here and there, as in French-speaking Canada, bilingual public signs and advertisements.

Considerable British blood also bubbled in the racial cauldron. Belgium was strategically located across from the British Isles, and was often referred to as a pistol pointed at the heart of England; that is, if it were in the hands of a powerful enemy. Belgium could claim many historical ties with the British, and more than a sprinkling of upper-class Belgians had been educated in England. All these links helped to account for the unexpected amount of English one heard spoken in Brussels.

Not surprisingly, the American GIs had hit it off reasonably well with the Belgians, at least so I heard. There was, of course, some rowdy behavior, as there always is among combat soldiers on leave who are far from home and who drink too much. The better-disciplined British troops on the whole seem to have behaved better, perhaps because they did not have as much money to spend on liquor and women.

Some of the liking of American soldiers for Belgium grew out of the dislike they had developed for the haughty and disdainful French, whose dirty pictures they had bought in Paris. One Embassy official explained that his job in France during the war was to try to persuade the American GIs to like their Gallic hosts better. The visiting soldiers had preferred to spend their leaves in friendlier Brussels or Liège, where there was also some quiet gouging but where the plumbing was better and where good beer, rather than wine, was plentiful and cheap. The Belgians seemed more tolerant than the people of France of the inability of the American soldiers to speak French, even bad French. For generations the French-speaking Belgians had been accustomed to hearing the French of their own countrymen uttered with a Flemish accent.

From the military attachés at the American Embassy came word that France, not Germany, was then the key to the major strategic problem of Belgium. The Belgian army then fielded only about two divisions, both of which were supplied with British uniforms and tanks. The people of Belgium had no desire to play the role of a neutralized doormat again; they had twice tried, in 1914 and 1940, and had twice been ravaged. They felt that war was coming again, as it had always come and they regarded Germany as a kind of necessary evil—a sort of latent volcano that would one day erupt again. Belgium had no defense in depth, and hence could not hope to fight a winning war on its own ground. The painful alternative was to retreat to French soil and there take a stand.

This prognosis fortunately did not work out at all as feared. On January 1, 1948, came the formal launching of the seminal customs union known as Benelux, which embraced Belgium, the Netherlands, and Luxembourg. All three countries qualified for assistance under the Marshall Plan, and Belgium-Luxembourg eventually received from Washington a total of $559 million. In March, 1948, the epochal Brussels Treaty was signed. It bound the three Benelux countries to Britain and France in a mutual-aid pact involving support against possible attack. Only prostrate Germany was specifically mentioned, but the Soviet Union was clearly the unnamed potential aggressor. The Brussels Pact, reflecting European suspicions and fear, thus became the nucleus of the North Atlantic Treaty Organization (NATO) of 1949, which was bound together by a mutual-assistance treaty that included the United States and eleven other nations. Those critics who now argue that only the nervous Americans feared the Russians should take special note of these earlier initiatives by others.

Nor did France become the fall-back zone of Belgium, as predicted. In 1966, President De Gaulle of France, the lone-wolf nationalist, announced the withdrawal of all French troops and installations from NATO control and the removal of NATO headquarters from French soil. The NATO headquarters were thus moved from the spacious fields of France to the cramped confines of little Belgium, with great reluctance on the part of Washington and at heavy cost to the long-suffering American taxpayer.

My interviews in Brussels completed, I departed by train for Ostend, the North Sea port from which the small packet boats left for England. From the car windows the green countryside resembled that of much of the rest of Europe already visited. After about an hour, the train pulled into the picturesque but substantial city of Ghent, which had figured prominently in early American history. Here, on Christmas Eve in 1814, the three American peace commissioners and their three British counterparts signed the treaty that brought the miserable little War of 1812 with Great Britain to an end. Probably none of the six signers really believed that this would be the last peace treaty ever to be concluded with Britain, but so it turned out to be.

At length we reached Ostend, a major commercial and fishing port whose history was rooted in the centuries. In 1604 it had been captured by the Spaniards in a three-year siege in which the city was almost completely destroyed. In World War II the Allied forces had subjected it to a heavy bombardment, with considerable destruction of buildings. Still visible were the remains of the dreaded submarine pens and the Nazi forts. By peaceful contrast, the summer-resort beaches were well populated.

Following a crowd of passengers to the dock, I boarded a cross-Channel packet boat, whose operators had prominently posted a plaque detailing its war record. This memorial resembled one that had been displayed on the craft bringing me from England to France. The sea was smooth but not so calm as on the earlier crossing; I saw only two spots on the decks where a person or two had been actively affected by *mal de mer.*

The passengers were a varied lot, including a swarm of schoolchildren who were returning from the Continent after some kind of Cook's tour. My notebook entry at this point reads: "Go by air next time." A poignant reminder of the continuing shortages of the recent war came when a British mother hungrily gulped down some leftover luncheon meat that her children did not want. "Cahn't stand to see good food go to waste," she explained apologetically. Also conspicuous were the sweet-toothed English tourists who were returning with large supplies of chocolate bars, most of them presumably purchased in Switzerland.

As we approached Dover and its white cliffs, I observed the tank traps of World War II near the beaches, as well as the barbed-wire entanglements that were still strung out. In contrast with the lush farming land of Europe, the soil of England, with its extensive grazing land, seemed to be markedly inferior, at least in this area. But I was glad to stand on it again among a people who spoke a common language, who charged fair prices, and who had reasonably bright hopes for the future.

— 14 —

Britain on the Brink

Britain's position today is tragic to a point that challenges description. . . . As a body politic Britain is seriously sick. She is incapable of viewing her own situation realistically and dealing with it effectively.

George F. Kennan,
Washington, D.C., September 4, 1947.

At the railroad terminal in London, I hailed an ancient black cab and rode in style to my old quarters at the seedy Princes Court Hotel. The accommodations could not have improved, but they were inexpensive, conveniently located, and familiar. Rather than go to the trouble of looking up a "better 'ole," I followed this path of least resistance.

Early the next morning, August 11, 1947, I appeared at the U.S. Embassy for a briefing by the cultural officer, Joseph E. Charles. Several of the officials there asked me how the American public was reacting to the Communist menace, which seemed to be creeping insidiously from central Europe toward the English Channel. When I replied that the great mass of our people at home were not giving much thought to the Communist threat abroad, the response was one of surprise and disbelief. All of this suggests the truism that those nearest the firing line are the most conscious of who is doing the firing.

Referring to the proposed suggestion by Secretary Marshall for European recovery, Mr. Charles pointed out that there was still no Marshall Plan, only a "Marshall Hint." Most Britons still felt that the Yankees owed them a great debt for having held the fort for so long against the furious assaults of Adolf Hitler. The British were displeased by the prospect of having to line up with the other nations with begging bowl in hand, to solicit alms. They were already fed up at home with the wartime admonition, "Take your place in the queue," and they felt that the United States should not only bail them out but give them top priority in doing so. Yet Mr. Charles seriously doubted that Congress would authorize $5 billion a year over a five-year stretch for a really effective rehabilitation plan. He turned out to be right, for the total Marshall bill for Europe eventually came to $12.4 billion.

Developments in Britain, Mr. Charles feared, were providing ammunition for American isolationists. They undoubtedly would put heat on Congress to vote down any appropriations under a Marshall Plan. For one thing, Britain had gone socialist when British Labour triumphed in 1945, and American taxpayers were not keen about subsidizing socialism. "Too damned much Communism, too damned much socialism" was a common criticism by conservatives. At almost this same time, George Kennan, Director in Washington of the Policy Planning Staff, was writing confidentially (September 4, 1947): "The tragedy of the Labour Government lies in the fact that after waiting several decades for a chance to put certain principles into effect, it has finally come into power at precisely the moment when those principles became essentially inapplicable."

Irresponsible members of Parliament had recently aroused American isolationists by needlessly raising the issue of nationalizing British steel production. Winston Churchill, now a part of His Majesty's loyal opposition, had provided ammunition for American critics by charging that Britain had largely "frittered away" the American loan of $3.75 billion on unworthy projects. Actually, on the day I returned to England, August 8, 1947, Washington was officially informed by an adviser in Paris that Britain's dollar reserves were melting away at the rate of $100 million a week. Yet Mr. Charles believed that Churchill had become unpardonably demagogic; the British Conservatives had nothing to offer that would have remedied the situation in the slightest, for a grave crisis was at hand and something had to give. The recent confiscatory tax on foreign movies, mostly American, had been imposed too rudely, Mr. Charles felt.

American isolationists were also critical of the alleged laziness of British workers. Why should American miners, who put in five and one-half days a week, help the British miners who worked only five? Actually there was a critical problem in England of providing enough cars to haul away the coal once it was piled up outside the mine shafts.

Nothing was to be gained by working more hours to dig more coal when that already mined could not be moved.

In certain industries, Mr. Charles further observed, the union ban on overtime hours, designed in part to reduce unemployment, was creating difficulties. An excellent example was the British equivalent of *Time* magazine; it was coming out three days late because the printers would not work on Saturdays and Sundays, even for overtime pay. In some industries, production exceeded prewar levels, with a demand for more workers; in other places, unemployment prevailed. The shortage of purchasable consumers' goods was leading to less compulsion to work for money, and this lack of incentive in turn was resulting in even fewer consumers' goods—a classic case of a vicious circle. The white-collar class, which condemned the laziness of labor, was setting a horrible example. Mr. Charles reported that many commuters boarded the 9:00 or 9:30 train for their offices, arrived at 10:30, ate lunch from 1:00 to 3:00, drank tea at 4:00, and then caught the 4:30 train for home.

These dreary observations were reinforced during a luncheon meeting at the House of Commons that was arranged by the Embassy. Our guest was a Conservative member of Parliament, John Cyril Maude, the forty-six-year-old lawyer son of the distinguished British actor, Cyril Maude. Schooled at Eton and Oxford, he believed that the workers would not pitch in until they had to suffer; he expected two million unemployed by the end of the year. A first secretary at the Embassy had told me that the British had become "shiftless nigger" types because their nerves had been stretched taut for so long during the war. But Maude believed that because the Industrial Revolution had first blossomed in England with headstart advantages, the British had not had to work so hard as their counterparts on the Continent, notably in Belgium, France, and Germany.

Incentives were lacking, Maude suggested, because the workers could not buy merchandise with their money; either desirable wares did not exist or they required ration coupons. Income taxes took most of the overtime pay; in one case, he said, a workman put in an extra day of overtime, but his union fined him by taking away his pay. Some laborers cut back on their hours as soon as they neared an undesirable income tax bracket; others worked their union-established stint and then took off for the dog races. Tickets for sporting events were one kind of consumers' goods in abundant supply.

Tens of thousands of houses had been destroyed or damaged in the recent war by German bombers, Maude reminded us, and housing was desperately needed. In some cases, husbands and wives were forced to live apart. One reason why many men would not go into the coal mines was that if they had a house to live in, even bad quarters, they would not move to a mining town where no quarters were available. Maude spoke of a town in his constituency of fifty-six thousand inhabitants where some five thousand people were on the waiting list for housing. The coal problem, which had resulted in part from a transportation bottleneck, simply could not be solved by laboring a half-day more. The way this industry was then geared, the miners could dishonestly register an extra hour or two and not do any extra work.

The Embassy also arranged an interesting interview for me with Brendan Bracken. A longtime Conservative member of Parliament, he had been a close associate of Churchill in 1941 as Parliamentary Private Secretary, and successively Minister of Information (1941–1945) and First Lord of the Admiralty (1945). He proved to be unusually frank and outgoing.

Bracken exuded both optimism and pessimism, mostly the latter. He expressed the belief that conditions in Britain would have to get worse before they got better. Yet these remarkable people, who had shed blood, sweat, and tears in beating Hitler, would not fail. They should accept no more loans from the United States, but should learn to stand on their own feet. He further observed that one of the ominous problems for British industry was that former markets had become competitors; daughter Canada was now one of the major industrial nations of the world.

The socialist Labour party, Bracken felt, meant well. The country really needed to go to work, despite organized labor, but it would not do so until it had experienced genuine privation. Fortunately the Labourites were in power; otherwise the country would have been paralyzed by several general strikes. The "rule of stint" was now an unwritten union law; no bricklayer could lay more than 320 bricks in a day. Bracken concluded with some bitterness that "We now have a new ruling class—the miners." Thirty years later the same complaint could be heard, perhaps with better reason.

Another official at the American Embassy confirmed what I had already learned from John Maude and Brendan Bracken about labor and production, but with a somewhat different emphasis. He pointed out that since the Industrial Revolution had come to England first, the pioneering British were now saddled with ancient or obsolescent equipment, while their foreign competitors were building new and more productive factories. "The first is always the worst," he declared. The British had made serious mistakes with regard to slums and overcrowding, and other nations could observe these and try to avoid duplicating them

A British pollster, my American informant said, was reporting that Britons had tried everything in the current crisis except hard work. When the coal shortage developed and the current postwar slump came, all under the Labour party, the confidence of the workers was shaken, and England was now engaged in a gigantic slowdown. A feeling was current that even if the lower classes suffered, the upper classes would have to suffer along with them, although not to the same degree.

One modern factory, my source continued, had provided the best conditions of employment, yet it had suffered a heavy turnover of labor. A poll-taker quickly discovered that this particular plant had a reputation for being a "sweater." The labor problem was complicated by young people, many of whom resented the bother and burden of having to care for old relatives. One poll reported that on three separate occasions younger people had run after the pollster to ask how they could go about committing their old folks to a tax-supported institution.

After listening attentively to the Conservative point of view, I found an antidote by subjecting myself to an overwhelming dose of comment from the radical left. Unquestionably, my most memorable interview in England was with Harold Laski, a brilliant figure in the Labour party, whose pleasant home lay on the outskirts of London. Arrangements for the visit were made by the American Embassy, and Mr. Charles accompanied me on a drive of about a half-hour among the picturesque cottages strewn about the countryside.

Laski, a small man with a small mustache and horn-rimmed spectacles, was one of the most scintillating personalities I have ever encountered. He spoke rapidly and crisply with great precision, without welcoming any interruption or contrary opinion. I found it almost impossible to get in a few words edgewise, even when he was egregiously in error. My notebook reminds me that he sounded like a professional lecturer on a phonograph record speaking with great speed to about three hundred people. He liked to strengthen the impact of his remarks by using the preface, "Now this is in absolute confidence."

The career of this phenomenon had thus far been spectacular. A precocious graduate of Oxford with first-class honors in history, he had early joined the socialist Fabian Society and then the British Labour movement. He knew something of Canada, where he had taught from 1914 to 1916 at Montreal's McGill University; he had also lectured at Harvard University from 1916 to 1920. There Laski had formed a lifelong friendship with Professor Felix Frankfurter, of the Harvard Law School and later of the Supreme Court. As a teacher at Harvard Laski had attracted some attention, not all favorable, by his active opposition to the anti-Red drives of the dying Wilson administration. He seemed to me somewhat naive about American public opinion, despite his four years of residence in the United States. He deprecated American capitalism and sneered at the delusion of the great American dream—that is, a potential millionaire's checkbook in every dinner pail.

In 1920 Laski had returned to England to join the faculty of the London School of Economics, where he rose to the rank of Professor of Political Science, a position that he held until his death in 1950. In London he became a foremost academic theorist and a highly influential lecturer. A prodigious "producer," he published some thirty books on economics and political science, to say nothing of hundreds of articles and pamphlets. During these years he campaigned actively and effectively for Labour members of Parliament and, with his outspoken socialist bias, he had involved himself verbally in the Spanish Civil War (1936–1939). As one would have expected, he had supported the pro-Communist, anti-Fascist popularfront movement in devastated Spain.

Laski loomed large in the Labour party as an eloquent and lucid expounder of socialist doctrines. For this reason I attached special significance to his comments about the stewardship of Prime Minister Clement Attlee, whose Labour party had supplanted Churchill in 1945, and also about the burly Foreign Secretary, Ernest Bevin. Laski himself had served for many years as a member of the Executive Committee of the Labour party, and a year earlier had held the post of Chairman. This group could only discuss problems and make recommendations; hence Laski's influence was not great. Conservatives branded him a "deep-dyed Red" and the "one man brain trust" of his party.

On this occasion, Laski was evidently of the opinion that violence of some kind would inevitably mark the transition from capitalism to socialism. A British weekly newspaper had printed words to that effect purporting to come from him, and in 1946 Laski had sued for libel. He lost his case after several earwitnesses came forward to refute his denials. Loyal followers thereupon raised the equivalent of $52,000 to defray the heavy court costs, or so the contemporary press reported.

Like many men who lecture widely or speak off-the-cuff freely, Laski was inclined to be careless with the facts. My escort from the

Embassy recalled an amusing incident that had occurred at one of the professor's Tuesday evening conferences. Laski had voiced some extravagant statements regarding a picketing case recently before the Supreme Court, on which his friend Felix Frankfurter now served. An American visitor sitting quietly in the audience finally spoke up and expressed strong dissent. To make his point more convincing, he informed Laski that he had himself argued that particular case before the same high court and knew whereof he spoke.

Professor Laski had little to say about his own Labour party, about which he knew much, except to castigate Foreign Secretary Bevin for his anti-Communist policies regarding Greece and for his foot-dragging regarding the Middle East. Palestine was then in the throes of being transformed from a British mandate into the sovereign state of Israel. Himself born a Jew, Laski praised President Truman for having issued a statement the previous October urging the British to admit one hundred thousand Jews to Palestine at once. Two days later, Governor Thomas E. Dewey of New York trumped Truman's card by backing the admission of "several hundreds of thousands" of Jews. Laski blamed Bevin for not accepting the President's humanitarian offer; the Foreign Secretary, he charged, was handicapped by being inordinately ambitious and immensely vain. Our host evidently did not seem to realize that Truman's appeal was an obvious gambit in the upcoming American elections, especially in the Jewish stronghold of New York.

The relatively recent elevation to the premiership of Clement Attlee, a quiet and colorless man, did not evoke enthusiasm from Laski. He thought that the selection of Herbert Morrison, now Deputy Prime Minister, would have been better, although he did refrain from repeating Churchill's alleged barbs that Attlee was "a modest man" with "every reason to be modest," and that he was "a sheep in sheep's clothing." Laski went on to say that Foreign Secretary Bevin, a trade-union man, followed the traditional anti-Bolshevik line of the Foreign Office. As for the overall picture, Laski was firmly of the well-founded opinion that Great Britain would have to pass through exceptionally bad times during the next four years.

Our loquacious host had visited the Soviet Union during the previous summer, and his comments on the subject proved interesting and provocative, if not always credible. He had traveled widely and had interviewed the right people; he had even included, he alleged, two long private sessions with Stalin and two with the Politburo. Perhaps he meant members of that body, for I could hardly believe that this prestigious group of ten men (including Stalin) would meet in two formal sessions with a visiting Labour lecturer. (I later checked with the *New York Times,* which reported only one meeting of Stalin with Laski, who had been accompanied by three Labour delegates.)

Contrary to conventional wisdom, Laski believed that Stalin was not a dictator, for he had to secure the approval of the Politburo. (One is reminded of President Truman's naive remark after Potsdam that poor old Uncle Joe Stalin was not a bad sort; he was just "a prisoner of the Politburo.") Foreign Minister V. M. Molotov, Laski believed, was less pro-West than Stalin.

As for the Soviet satellites or near-satellites, Laski concluded that Czechoslovakia was more liberal than any one of America's Southern states. (He probably was thinking of the then-voteless black population.) To my amazement, and contrary to most of the information I had been able to gather, Laski remarked that Poland was really slanted toward the West and was not so much under the domination of Moscow as generally supposed.

Laski was convinced that the Soviet leaders did not want war and that all of them agreed that the nation could not sustain a major conflict for at least fifteen years. Exceptions were the militant younger generals who had won their spurs in the last war and who were thoroughgoing chauvinists. Yet Laski had seen some of the terrible destruction and was persuaded that their views would not prevail; he was sure that the Russians contemplated no military aggression.

Two major problems, Laski felt, were of pressing importance in the USSR. One was to delouse ideologically those three million or so Russian soldiers who had seen the wealthier capitalistic West and its superior living standards, including inside plumbing. Another task was to key the people up for the sacrifices needed to support rigorous programs of planned economy. But to rally the masses behind the Soviet leaders, the Kremlin had to play up the bogey of "capitalistic encirclement," portraying Uncle Sam as the chief encircler. Yet in so doing the Kremlin had created a Frankenstein's monster, for the American people were so imperceptive as to take seriously the alarming words and actions of the Soviet leaders. At this point Laski probably put his finger on an illuminating truth.

Professor Laski granted that the Soviet leaders were secretive, cruel, and dilatory; they thought nothing of coming two hours late to an appointment without an apology. But, though the Russian people were in bad shape, they were better off now than they had been under the tsars. If I could have interrupted the torrent of words, I might have interjected that it was pointless to compare present conditions with those that had existed thirty years earlier. Even under the tsars, conditions would probably have changed somewhat for the better.

In speaking to Russian students, Laski had noted their great reverence for President Franklin Roosevelt and for what he had done for the Soviet Union in the form of military assistance and other aid. Stalin fully realized, so Laski believed, that the Russians would not have won the war if they had not received massive lend-lease shipments from the United States, although the sphinx of the Politburo was not shouting this self-abasing view from the Kremlin walls. Laski frankly deplored much that was dictatorial in the Soviet Union, but he credited himself with having persuaded Stalin in a long private interview to adopt the privilege of the writ of *habeas corpus*. This seemed incredible in view of Stalin's barbaric purge trials, the ruthless liquidation of several million land-owning peasants (*kulaks*), and the additional millions deported to die in Siberian prison camps (the Gulag archipelago). *Corpus delicti* or *habeas cadaver*, rather than *habeas corpus*, could more appropriately be associated with Stalin's name.

Laski also related an interesting story about the origins of the deep distrust harbored by Foreign Minister Molotov for Secretary of State James Byrnes. It allegedly dated back to one of the earlier fruitless conferences of foreign ministers. While waiting for the interpreter to translate their English into Russian, Secretary Bevin and Secretary Byrnes exchanged brief witticisms. A suspicious Molotov assumed that they were laughing at him, and consequently took great offense.

In leaving the subject of Russia and the Communists, Laski declared that both he and Stalin had nothing but contempt for the tiny and ineffective British Communist party. (He might have added that the Kremlin had little love for the deviationist Labour party in Britain.) Laski further defended the Soviet regime by insisting that Moscow had consistently honored its foreign debts, except for those inherited from the tsars in 1917. He was certain that if President Roosevelt had only championed a big loan to Russia at the end of the war, American public opinion would have supported it 100 percent. But nothing happened because the Russian regime was too proud to ask for money.

If I had been able to make myself heard, I would have said that American public opinion is never 100 percent favorable on any issue, but that there had been considerable support for a loan to Russia in the closing months of the war and even for a brief period after it. But such generous impulses had been chilled by the obviously aggressive actions or attempted actions of the Russians, ranging all the way from Finland and Poland to Iran and the Far East. The declassified American documents now show that the Soviets had not been too proud to ask for a loan, but that they had asked for one with the conviction that the United States simply had to extend huge credits in order to fore-stall another great depression. In these circumstances they demanded unrealistically favorable terms, and these Washington understandably rejected.

Laski further asserted that the United States was opposed to Tito and his Communist regime in Yugoslavia because the Americans were capitalists and resented the expropriation there of estates and other private property. He ignored the fact that probably not one American in ten thousand was aware that such expropriations had taken place. But millions knew that Tito's air force, in the previous summer, had taken five lives by shooting or forcing down two U.S. airplanes. They had allegedly been encroaching on Yugoslavian air space.

Some of Laski's final shots related more directly to economic prob-lems. He believed that the United States would have to accelerate its program of economic imperialism, and that this course would lead to war, just as British imperialism had done in 1914. Such oversim-plification was open to question, but by this time I had given up trying to register my dissent.

Laski went on to remark that the British army could be radically reduced and that the displaced soldiers could be put into useful pro-duction (at a time when there was widespread unemployment). Cer-tainly the government had to come to grips with the problem of per-suading Britain's labor force to work at full capacity. As readers of the daily newspapers well knew, a strike against increasing the hours of labor had been called in an important (nationalized) colliery, and stor-ies were frequently appearing about unions that were fining or sus-pending members for working overtime. Mr. Charles subsequently explained that despite such disruptions, the lower one-third of the population was now better fed than ever before.

Speaking further as an economist, Laski complained about the large amount of unproductive labor in Britain engaged in unimportant tasks. On the other side of the scales, he complained about the huge profits (18 percent) that the British manufacturers felt they had to make, and about the scandalous evasion of the income tax to which they resorted. The picture that he painted was somber, but Mr. Charles reassured me shortly after we left that Britain had started on its economic decline several years before the outbreak of the Great War in 1914.

In addition to the unforgettable visit with Laski, the American Em-bassy was kind enough to arrange a luncheon session with Kingsley Martin, who had already served as the left-leaning editor of the influential *New Statesman and Nation* for some seventeen years. A

Cambridge man and the author of about seven books, he was listed in the British *Who's Who* as an Assistant Lecturer in Political Science at the London School of Economics. He quickly made known his pro-Communist views, although my notebook records that he seemed "very sane beside Laski."

Martin had recently returned from a two-week inspection of Poland. To my astonishment, he stated flatly that the Poles ran their own country; they were 95 percent Catholic and hence would not go Communist for fifty years. Yet information current in the Western world was that Poland had fallen under the domination of Moscow, through the medium of Polish puppets, at least two years earlier. Martin went on to say that the Poles resented the recent withdrawal of proposed American relief from Poland, and that such action had increased pro-Russian sentiment in this luckless country. The people there, he felt, would have a rugged time achieving economic recovery without a helping hand from the United States.

Yet the Poles, as all the world knew, had recently declined to join in the Marshall program, in response to arm-twisting from Moscow. But Martin did not emphasize the dictatorial hand of the Kremlin. Poland, he believed had shied away because it assumed that the grandiose American scheme would fail. The story he had picked up was that the Soviets, reluctantly attending the Paris conference, had yielded to their pride and backed away from the Marshall proposal. Rather than risk being blamed for obstruction, they preferred to have Uncle Sam alone bear the onus of the predicted and hoped-for failure. I found it difficult to believe that a man in Martin's responsible editorial position could swallow so readily this made-in-Moscow line.

After belittling the Marshall overture, Martin threw a few barbs at its predecessor, the Truman Doctrine, for attempting to save Greece and Turkey from the heavy hand of Communism. He was certain that this bold pronouncement had increased the number of Communists. The great blunder of the British in Greece, he held, was in failing to set up a middle-of-the-road government. Truman's intervention may or may not have swollen the ranks of Greek Communists temporarily, but most objective observers would agree that the infusion of American aid was an important factor in helping to save Greece for the West

As for Britain's troublesome Palestine mandate and its Jews, Martin accused Foreign Secretary Bevin of blatant anti-Semitism. His prejudice was reported to have developed from some earlier unfortunate experiences with Jews. This antipathy was all the more formidable, his critic charged, because he was an intelligent and immensely able

The Way Back

(Fitzpatrick in the St. Louis *Post Dispatch*, July 1947.)

man—a smooth liar and a formidable debater, yet withal too emotional. According to the untrustworthy Martin, Bevin feared that if the British withdrew from their Palestine mandate, the Russians would soon move in.

Martin believed that the United States was playing a double game in the Middle East in response to two pressure groups: the oil companies and the American Jews. Yielding to the Jews, Washington was preaching a liberal policy. But quietly, and in deference to the oil companies, the Americans were backing the British to stay. Martin further expressed extreme distaste for the Egyptians, whom he accused of being racketeers. The real oppression in Egypt had not been British but the Egyptian misrule of Egyptians. Why, he asked, should the London government turn the unoffending Sudanese over to the jurisdiction of these racketeers?

Kingsley Martin, as befitted his evident preference for the Labour government, flatly declared that the British lower classes had never known so little real poverty. My Embassy escort, Mr. Edwin Kenworthy, confirmed this judgment when he observed that British children appeared to be exceptionally healthy up to about age seven, when the milk ration was cut back. Laski and Martin had both commented with some distaste on the statistic that the United States then enjoyed about one-half the productive capacity of the world. Martin in particular was somewhat scandalized by newspaper reports about the surplus apples then being dumped in America. He offered the interesting view that American capitalism might be saved by dumping the nation's surplus abroad indefinitely.

As we left the luncheon table and parted company with Martin, Mr. Kenworthy remarked that the acid-penned editor was a strange man indeed. In social contacts he seemed friendly, agreeable, and well disposed toward the United States. Then he would return to his editorial desk and renew his inky blasts at the envied capitalistic colossus.

During this return visit to London, I again spent considerable time walking the streets and observing the natives in their own urban habitat. Of special interest was the number of black men accompanied by white women; this sight was still quite unusual in the United States. The ladies of purchasable virtue continued to be out in force, and the favorite approach of these "Marble Arch Rangers" or "Hyde Park Rangers" seemed to be "Darling, want to have a good time?"

My wanderings took me to many of the sites inspected by ordinary tourists, including Charles Dickens' Old Curiosity Shop and the British Museum, where I stood in awe before an original copy of the Magna Carta. But my favorite spot was the famed Hyde Park, citadel of free speech, where I heard various speakers, from crackpots to concerned Britons, vent their views with absolute freedom. To me this was the best show in town, but few passersby paid any attention to the speakers, and certainly the police left them strictly alone to denounce the government and advocate its overthrow by means ranging from votes to violence.

Some Hyde Park malcontents blew off steam against Uncle Sam as they touched on such themes as America's corruption of the English language and the misdeeds of American trusts. Orators with a socialist or Communist bent were crying "To hell with the Yankees" and blaming Britain's woes on capitalistic enslavement by the United States. Ironically, Americans of a century or so earlier were themselves decrying their bondage to the "bloated British bondholders."

Among the other complaints heard at Hyde Park were those relating to the shortcomings of the American movie industry. In the breakfast room of my hotel I heard similar criticism; the critics there may have raised their voices for my benefit when they observed that I was dressed like a fortune-favored American. One self-appointed reviewer remarked in disgust that he had seen an American film the previous night, "The Hucksters," and that the stupid British official ought to be beheaded who had wasted scarce dollar exchange on such garbage. Such a man was denounced as a traitor to his country. Another Englishman grumbled that he was absolutely delighted that the London government had recently cut the importation of American movies by 75 percent. He was absolutely "sick of them."

My hotel was definitely third-rate, but I did have tea and cakes at one of London's finest, I believe Claridge's. My hostess was a recent student at Stanford, and she was accompanied by her mother, both of whom were most gracious. Taking pity on an American who had to endure the culinary hardships of not-so-merry England for a few days, they presented me with a small box of fresh farm produce, including some tiny pats of butter. I felt guilty about having this kind of fare to consume surreptitiously and turned the whole thing over to the British secretarial staff of a building that I had occasion to visit. These young ladies received the delicacies with almost pathetic gratitude, for the authorities had not completely lifted wartime austerity. In fact, ten days after I departed, the Labour government ordered a "siege economy," which imposed severe rationing on food, travel, and motoring.

The crotchety woman called the "manageress" of my hotel was less grateful when, in addition to an earlier pack of American cigarettes, I gave her a chocolate candy bar on the eve of my leaving. Why she seemed miffed remains a mystery; perhaps she felt that the British were tired of accepting charity from their opulent American cousins.

On the staff of this same hotel was an attractive middle-aged English woman who expressed great interest in emigrating to America rather than having to face up to the years of deprivation that obviously loomed ahead in England. She had tried to find employment as a housekeeper for elderly bachelors or widowers, but gave up this search when she found that the prospective employer usually wanted his female employee to share his bed with him occasionally. "After all!" she exclaimed in disgust. I promised to make some inquiry about jobs in the United States, but before I could tackle the problem she sent me a letter thanking me for my interest, and stating that she had decided to stick it out in her homeland in the "stiff upper-lip" tradition.

I had brought with me to Europe a small quantity of chewing gum, some of which remained as the time approached for my leaving England. Putting a few loose sticks in my pocket, I strolled over to a nearby park where children were playing, and offered one piece to each of several little girls. They all accepted without hesitation and with bashful thanks. One of them said she was not going to chew her precious present at once but save it for her birthday, which was not far off. As we were chatting, the mother came up and joined our little group. I explained to her my desire to rid myself of excess baggage before leaving London. It occurred to me that otherwise she might develop suspicions about the motives of a middle-aged stranger who was handing out free sticks of gum to innocent little children. I had forgotten that the visiting GIs had freely dispensed this delicacy in response to the childish query "Any gum, chum?" When I spoke of returning to America the next day, the mother took her little girl's hand and remarked cheerily over her shoulder as they left, "Lucky you."

As we lifted off for home in a crowded DC-4 on August 17, 1947, I could feel much sympathy for the war-strained and war-drained British people. The burden of two devastating conflicts with Germany had dropped the British empire from its commanding position as a great world power to one of second-rate status. As if to give point to this transformation, two days before I left London the independence of India was proclaimed, with appropriate comment in the British press on the epochal event.

Initial Marshall Plan appropriations for Britain were not voted by Congress until April, 1948, eight months after I left London. British feelings of resentment spawned by America's alleged ingratitude were largely soothed by the generosity of the four-year grant-gift to Britain under the Marshall Plan—$3,198,800,000. This sum substantially exceeded the amount granted to second-place France. With such a helping hand the British struggled back onto their economic feet, only to face recurrent economic crises in subsequent decades. At times Britain was thought to be in a permanent state of collapse but on every occasion there seemed to be a surprising amount of life left in the old lion. One could almost believe the words of the consoling song of World War II, "There'll Always Be An England."

Cold Warriors at the War College

... The greatest error of the war on our side was the failure to distinguish clearly the personality of our Russian allies and to recognize and to explain frankly to our peoples the real nature of our wartime association with them

George F. Kennan,
Lecture, National War College, June 18, 1947

Winging our way westward, we finally touched down in New York on August 18, 1947, without noteworthy incident. After the visit to Europe, what struck me most forcibly on arriving in the metropolis were the towering clumps of skyscrapers, nonexistent in the Old World. I was also impressed anew by the bright lights, the many black faces, the numerous radios, and the superior sanitary facilities. A thirsty traveler could not only get ice water, but he could count on its being safe to drink. At a drinking stand in London, near the British Museum, there was still a metal cup secured by a chain that was possibly of Victorian vintage.

In preliminary social gatherings at the War College in Washington, the five civilian instructors, including myself, became informally acquainted, and everyone was soon on a first-name basis. Three of us were fresh from the university world, and two were men of academic background who had been drawn from positions in the government. I had already come to know and admire Dr. Wallace Sterling when he was a graduate student in history at Stanford University. He had gone on to become a prominent member of the faculty of the California Institute of Technology, where, among other distinctions, he was widely known to the radio world as a high-quality news analyst for the Columbia Broadcasting System. Friendly, personable, and a superb raconteur, he was especially well liked by the officer-students. Two years later he became President of Stanford University, and he served in that capacity for almost two decades with outstanding success.

Officers of distinction, drawn from the several armed services manned the top posts. Brigadier General Truman H. Landon continued as Deputy Commandant (Air Force), and Major General Lyman L. Lemnitzer had succeeded General Alfred M. Gruenther as Deputy Commandant (Army). Vice Admiral Harry W. Hill, the Commandant of the College, represented the Navy. All of these officers continued their distinguished careers after their service at the National War College ended. Admiral Hill was appointed superintendent of the Naval Academy at Annapolis; Generals Gruenther and Lemnitzer rose to command the NATO forces; and General Landon became Commander in Chief of the U.S. Air Force in Europe.

The first semester at the War College ran from early September to mid-December, 1947. Instruction was aimed at developing a broad background of information about the major nations of the world, especially in history, economics, government, and foreign policy. The second semester was to be devoted to problems that were basically military and designed to enable the officers to grapple with global strategy.

Most of the officers appeared to be in their forties, and they were reputed to be the cream of the crop. The National War College was designed to be the most prestigious of the service schools for mid-career training. My recollection is that there was only one student as lowly as a lieutenant colonel in the Army, or its equivalent in other services. The Army was represented by 32 students, the Marine Corps by 6, the Navy by 24, the Coast Guard by 1, the Air Force by 28, the Department of State by 16, Great Britain by 3, and Canada by 3. The total was 113.

No publicity was given to the presence of the six outsiders, partly, one may assume, because there were isolationists and pacifists in America who did not want the national defense so closely tied in with foreign military establishments. In addition, the higher-ups deemed it desirable to conceal this intimate arrangement from the Soviets , who might suspect that three of their nominal allies in the recent war were ganging up on them. On occasion we Americans would refer facetiously to the six foreigners in our midst as "the unmentionables," even though Russian agents had probably discovered their presence at an early date.

A major part of the instruction was a series of hour-long lectures, averaging four or five a week for a total of about seventy-five. They were all presented by well-qualified men, in some cases by the out-standing authority in a particular field. Each lecture was followed by a question period of a half-hour or so, during which the students and staff would direct questions to the speaker. The civilian instructors subsequently met with small groups of about a dozen students com-prising so-called committees, during which we kicked around ideas growing out of the lecture or issues related to it. The task of the instructor was to keep the discussion on the track and to steer it into avenues of fruitful inquiry. The officer-students were richer in worldly experience than in bookish knowledge, and consequently were often able to contribute useful information from their own ob-servations and experiences. On one occasion reference was made to the Union of South Africa, and a British member took issue with one of my observations. I quickly backed water when he informed the group that he had lived there for a number of years.

One valuable feature of the instruction was a research paper that involved at least some exploitation of the printed documentary sources. Although few of the officers had enjoyed any previous experi-ence with historical methodology, many of the papers turned out to be surprisingly good. One presentation by a foreign-service officer on the problems of black Africa stands out in my memory. During the pre-vious year, a prime subject of investigation had been the Katyn massa-cre, which required the student investigators to determine whether the Germans or the Russians had murdered and buried some forty-two hundred uniformed Poles in 1941. General Landon remarked to me that the evidence was not conclusive one way or the other, but sub-sequent evidence has directed suspicion more strongly at the Soviets than was the case in 1947.

My own duties involved relatively little teaching, in the sense of ladling out information from the front of the classroom. As far as real sweat was concerned, we civilians were scandalously overpaid. We sat there on upholstered seats in the beautifully air-conditioned audi-torium and took careful notes on the wisdom emanating from scores of leading experts. We were absorbing a liberal postdoctoral education, and what was more, we were being paid to receive it; all of this was quite the reverse of my previous experience in college or graduate school.

The schedule called for me to present only three lectures. The first was an evening affair, to which the wives of the officers were also invited, and it consisted of a kind of a general report on my recent observations and experiences in Europe. The War College had superb facilities for visual aids, which included not only photographs but also specially drawn maps, charts, and related art work. My talk was illustrated with thirty slides that portrayed either what I had seen or the kind of thing I had witnessed. Not being a shutterbug, I had taken no camera and had to dig up relevant pictures from various official or unofficial publications. One of my colleagues told me afterwards that the two scenes that remained conspicuously on the screen in the background the longest portrayed the corpses of a Hitlerian crematorium and a depressing scene in a camp for displaced persons. Such was the luck of the draw.

In December, 1947, near the end of the semester, I delivered two formal lectures in my capacity as a supposed authority on American diplomatic history. One of them outlined the evolution of basic American foreign policies—such as nonentanglement, nonintervention, the Monroe Doctrine, the Open Door, Pan Americanism, and freedom of the seas (which was of special interest to the Navy men). I illustrated my discourse with lantern-slide charts prepared under my direction by the visual-aids experts. They showed the ups and downs of these policies over the years, somewhat in the nature of a fever chart. My second formal lecture sketched the problems relating to the pressures of public opinion in the formulation and execution of foreign policy.

The reception accorded both of these efforts was not unfriendly though Admiral Hill, at the end of the first presentation, privately criticized me for having set too high a standard for myself. The management of the College thought well enough of my contributions to invite me back to give one or both during the two following years, even though considerable travel was required. Invitations were also forthcoming to speak at various other service institutions, including the Naval Academy at Annapolis. During my last appearance at the War College, reference was made during the question period to General Eisenhower, who was now being "civilianized" as President of Columbia University, a post he had assumed in June, 1948. I remarked that if we could not invite academicians to lead our armies, we could not logically ask army men to head our academies. This still strikes me as an eminently sound doctrine, but my feeling was that this reference to the genial general did not sit well with the top brass.

A wide spectrum of learning was represented by the list of lectures. Much attention was devoted to international economics. There were experts on international law, on Soviet law, on labor, and even on the dispersal of cities to offset atomic bombing. There were authoritative presentations on the state of affairs in areas ranging from Japan, China, and India to Palestine, the Middle East, Turkey, Greece, Yugoslavia, and Latin America. The major countries of Europe—Italy, France,

Great Britain, and especially the Soviet Union—all received due attention.

The foreign service was well represented in the list of lecturers. George Kennan (Mr. X), borrowed for the occasions from the State Department, delivered five or so brilliant analyses relating to the Soviet Union, particularly its foreign policy and government. W. Averell Harriman, United States Ambassador in Moscow during the war years (1943–1946), gave us his impressions of what the Soviets were striving to achieve. Dean G. Acheson, who served from 1945–1947 as Under Secretary of State and who looked like a cultured Englishman, made a suave presentation. Ambassador Laurence A. Steinhardt, whom I had interviewed in Prague a few weeks earlier, favored us with a lecture on Czechoslovakia that confirmed much of what he had told me in private.

A single lecture came from Maynard Barnes, who had been the chief United States foreign-service officer in Bulgaria when the Communists took over in 1947. He was by now a badly shaken man who had not fully recovered from the shattering episode, which had involved the hanging of the leader of an opposition party. Now that George Kennan had been detached from the War College staff by the State Department, Barnes represented the foreign service in the top hierarchy.

The "party line" at the War College was that the Soviet Union, by its aggressive postwar designs and acts, had forced the Cold War on the Western democracies. I can think of only one among the officers, staff, and visiting lecturers who proclaimed or even held the opposing view. As earlier noted, I myself came to accept it, especially after numerous and extended talks with American officials in Europe who had experienced close contacts with the Russians.

Among the invited lecturers there was one avowed leftist, evidently brought in as a kind of devil's advocate to prove that we could listen respectfully to contrary views. This academician was a political scientist from a New England college, and he was well known for his advocacy of the view that the Cold War had been forced on an unoffending USSR by an imperialistic United States. My recollection is that in 1942 or 1943 he had publicly advocated a premature second front, even at the certain cost of futile and frightful slaughter. Such a disaster would allegedly inspirit the hard-pressed Russians by showing them that the Western Allies meant well.

This left-leaning visitor partially disarmed potential critics by stating at the outset that he had recently been involved in an automobile accident during which his head had crashed through the windshield.

He was therefore not sure that he could be held completely responsible for what he was about to say. He then went on to observe that the Soviet Union and the United States had never been allies. If he meant in spirit, he had a case; if he meant in actuality, he was wrong. The Declaration of the United Nations, dated January 1, 1942, was a military alliance signed by the twenty-six countries then at war with the Axis, including the USSR. This document bound the signatories to the principles of the Atlantic Charter, which forbade territorial or other aggrandizement, and which upheld the Wilsonian principles of self-determination. These Churchill-Roosevelt ideals were evidently aimed primarily at the designs of the Soviet Union, and they are usually overlooked in the semantic dispute over whether Stalin or the West violated the alleged understanding later reached at the Yalta Conference of 1945.

Our pro-Soviet lecturer claimed that Stalin had made a good-faith bargain at Yalta that guaranteed him hegemony over all eastern Europe, and that the West had broken the pact, thereby releasing him from its trammels. The truth is that the Yalta agreements, on two successive printed pages dealing with liberated Europe and Poland, used the words "free elections" twice and "democratic" nine times. The speaker's surprising conclusion could only be reached by accepting the Soviet definition of "democracy," which means something quite different from the concept in English. It is possible that Roosevelt at Yalta did not fully understand the Soviet connotation, but it seems reasonably clear that Stalin knew what Roosevelt had in mind when the President fought for "democratic" regimes in Poland and other liberated countries.*

I took full notes on all these lectures, and in reviewing them now am amazed by the amount of information scribbled down. In addition, I preserved a record of the wartime experiences related informally by the officers at the College and others, and later would flesh them out by talking into a dictaphone. The secretarial staff at the College graciously typed them up for me.

One group of lectures dealt at length with the atomic bomb as a new and terrible factor in the so-called art of warfare. Among the speakers

---

*Prime Minister Churchill had flown to Moscow in October, 1944. There he and Stalin agreed that Russia and Great Britain would have 50-50 influence in Yugoslavia and Hungary; Russia was to have 90 percent influence in Rumania and 75 percent in Bulgaria, while Britain was to have 90 percent influence in Greece; Poland was not listed. It will be noted that the United States was not a party to these divisions, which were apportioned with absurd precision. Winston Churchill, *The Second World War*, vol. VI: *Triumph and Tragedy* (Boston, 1953), p. 227.

were Admiral William S. Parsons, who had flown the first atomic bomb over Hiroshima; President James B. Conant of Harvard, who had been a member of President Truman's Interim Committee that recommended the dropping of the atomic bomb on Japan; General Leslie R. Groves, the officer in charge of the atomic-bomb project; David E. Lilienthal, the chairman of the U.S. Atomic Energy Commission; and Dr. J. Robert Oppenheimer, the former director of the atomic-energy research team at Los Alamos, New Mexico. The last named was a quiet man who impressed us as a towering intellect. At the time we little knew that he would oppose making the hydrogen bomb on technical and moral grounds, and that the McCarthyites would so blacken him that he was stripped of his clearance in 1954 by the U.S. Atomic Energy Commission. He was ultimately exonerated.

All these lectures, especially those relating to the atomic bomb, were highly classified. Indeed, the administration of the College was much concerned with security, and Admiral Hill ran a tight ship. He once remarked with great emphasis that he did not know how many atomic bombs the United States then had in its stockpile, and he did not want to know. Such knowledge, he felt, was a terrible responsibility. We later learned that Soviet agents, beginning at least as early as 1943 with the scientist Klaus Fuchs, had been funneling top-secret atomic information to Moscow.

Experts at the War College correctly assumed that Russia was working on the A-bomb, and their guesses were that success would crown these efforts somewhere between three and ten years hence. The time involved proved to be about two years, and this mistaken estimate was probably in part the result of Soviet espionage in the United States and also in Canada. There the exposure in 1945 of a spy plot involving the Soviet Embassy in Ottawa resulted in a major scandal. As nearly as one can ascertain at present, in the autumn of 1947 the Americans had a stockpile of several score of bombs that were operational or were ready to be made operational.

Many laymen on the outside probably feared that the War College was cooking up ways and means of blasting the Soviets into less aggressive behavior. Russian spokesmen were quoted in the contemporary press as complaining that American negotiators had the "atomic bomb in their pocket" or that they were "rattling the atomic bomb." There was in fact a negligible amount of loose talk among a few irresponsible Americans about using this ultimate weapon in a preventive war. But as an insider I can testify that there was no serious advocacy of such a heavy-handed alternative, at least not during the first semester. Those who discussed the subject at the War College made it clear that America had no aggressive intentions regarding the Soviet Union; that the United States did not have a large stockpile of atomic bombs; that it had only a skeleton army in Europe; that the Soviets were the only potential aggressors worth worrying about; and that the A-bomb would never be used against the Russians except to halt an armed drive toward the West. Winston Churchill stated in 1949 that the monopoly of the A-bomb by the United States was all that had kept Stalin's military might from overrunning western Europe. Finally, the doctrine at the War College was that a preemptive strike was unthinkable. There was a general agreement with Bismarck that a preventive war was equivalent to cutting one's throat for fear that one would die.

In all honesty, one exception must be noted. On the staff of the War College there were about twenty officers of the regular armed forces, who were not to be confused with the students. They sat in on the committee deliberations, but seldom had anything to say. During one session we were discussing ways and means of getting along less belligerently with the Russians. Suddenly one of these men—perhaps a hard-bitten Army major—burst out with words to this effect: "Why in the hell are we wasting time discussing ways of getting along with the Russians? Now that we have the atomic bomb, let's blast hell out of them before they can get it. Then the problem will be solved."

There was a moment of awkward silence. Then the officer-students hushed him up by telling him that preventive war was out of the question; it was not the American way of doing things. That was the first and last time that I recall having heard the slightest suggestion at the War College that the bomb would ever be used for purposes other than defensive ones.

One of the lecturers was associated with the Atomic Energy Commission of the United Nations. He conceded that through inadvertence the American proposal for sharing atomic energy had been leaked prematurely and thus had hardened Soviet opposition in advance. As all the world knows, during the subsequent debate at the UN, the Russians insisted that the United States first destroy its stockpiles of bombs—the only viable deterrent it had against a Russian drive westward. The final proposal for atom-sharing could not get past a veto by the Russians in the Security Council of the United Nations; they knew that they would be producing A-bombs in a few years. Besides, the American scheme involved unpalatable on-site inspection by UN observers. The pathologically suspicious Russians were opposed to having foreign inspectors on their soil in a meaningful capacity, and this was to be the immovable obstacle to various attempts at the reduction of nuclear weapons during the ensuing three decades. One should note that the American proposal for sharing atomic power was approved by the United Nations Atomic Energy Commission by a vote of ten to zero, with Russia and Poland abstaining.

Revisionist critics have blamed the United States for not passing on the "secret" of the atomic bomb to its faithful Russian allies during the war. The failure to do so merely deepened Soviet suspicions, the argument runs, especially since the Americans shared their scientific findings with the British, but not with the French. A partial explanation is that the British were partners with the United States in making the bomb; the Russians were only nominal allies, involved in a temporary and uneasy marriage of convenience. They had fully demonstrated that they could not be completely trusted. During the war the United States had given them military secrets, with scant or no reciprocation. If the tables had been reversed, and the suspicious Soviets had created the bomb first, would they have shared their earth-shaking secret with the United States, their capitalistic enemy? Merely to ask the question is to answer it.

Little attention was paid at the War College to the ongoing negotiations behind closed doors in Paris over Marshall Plan shopping lists for a sickly and sinking Europe. One imported lecturer referred to the proposed scheme as a "calculated risk," and one resident colonel asked why the United States should fatten up these future victims of the Russian bear. A general feeling prevailed that the ball was in the court of the sixteen prospective beneficiaries, and that something would be worked out by the recipients. We now know that Washington rejected as wholly unrealistic the preliminary estimates of the expectant nations, which amounted to a staggering $29.2 billion. The conferees in Paris then went back to the drawing board, and with considerable "friendly aid" (arm twisting) from the United States, recommended in their "first report" the appropriation of $19.31 billion over a period of four years.

The gift list of the sixteen-nation Committee of European Economic Cooperation, which was dated September 22, 1947, was formally presented to the government in Washington about three weeks after the War College had opened for the fall semester. The colossal figure of $19.31 billion did not include interim aid for France, Italy, and China; these countries were to receive collectively stopgap appropriations from Congress totaling $540 million. This sum was in addition to the more than $10 billion already disbursed by Washington since the war in the form of loans, grants, and UNRRA shipments. In the weeks that followed the "first report" recommendations from Paris, further refinements took place in secret sessions with the Europeans, again with friendly persuasion from American representatives.

The consolidated request of the sixteen war-blighted nations continued to be part of a chain reaction. On October 5, nearly two weeks after the presentation of this gift list, a Communist conclave of nine nations in Warsaw announced the formation of the Cominform (Communist Information Bureau) to coordinate the activities of the European Communist parties. This may have been the immediate answer of the Kremlin to the "dollar imperialism" of the Marshall Plan blueprint from Paris. On January 1, 1948, fearful little Belgium, the Netherlands, and Luxembourg officially launched a revised version of their Benelux customs union, started during the war. It led by logical steps to the Brussels Pact of March, 1948, which included France and Britain, and then to the defensive twelve-nation North Atlantic Treaty Organization of April, 1949, which was joined by the United States. In neither treaty was the Soviet Union named as the potential foe, but no one was fooled. The New York *Daily Worker*, a Communist sheet, branded the NATO alliance "International Murder Incorporated."

Alert to such marching events, President Truman urged Congress on December 19, 1947, to appropriate $17 billion in Marshall aid over a four-year period, 1948–1951, with an initial outlay of $6.8 billion. He thus planned to halt what he termed "selfish totalitarian aggression." A heated debate ensued in Congress that lasted more than three months. Among the most active supporters of the new giveaway program were the farmers, who needed to ship their surpluses, and organized laborers, who wanted to avoid the feared depression. Many businessmen concluded that neither the nation's interests nor their own would be well served by Europe's bankruptcy. Their concern for markets was intermingled with a fear of what might happen to their personal fortunes if Communism continued to spread westward—a fact often overlooked by revisionist historians. Internationalists also perceived that America and Europe were in the same leaky boat, and they were joined by humanitarians who felt that dollar-bloated Uncle Sam owed something to these prostrate people. Conspicuous among such sympathizers were millions of Italian-Americans and other immigrants who feared for their hungry relatives, especially if the Soviets were to win control. Finally, there were many conservatives who were frightened by the prospect of seeing the Communists, or even the socialists, take over western Europe.

Opponents of the European Recovery Program (ERP) were numerous and noisy. They included the isolationists, who were not convinced that disaster in Europe would spell depression in rich and productive America. Thrifty elements, including an economy-minded

Congress, also believed that Uncle Sam had played Uncle Santa Claus long enough for these ungrateful "furriners." (Away with this new "Share the American Wealth Plan.") The chorus of complaints was joined by short-sighted conservatives, who argued that it was folly to subsidize socialist governments like the one in Great Britain. These right-wingers were brothers to the anti-Communists, who proclaimed that this new "operation rat hole" would merely provide handouts that would ultimately reach Communist Russia and its satellites, thus adding to their fearsome strength and war potential. This ill-assorted group of protestors even included the Communists and other leftists in America; they were slavishly following the party line from head-quarters in Moscow, while denouncing the "Martial Plan."

Ironically, the Moscow-connected Communists in Prague them-selves gave the languishing Marshall aid appropriation a critically needed boost through Congress. On February 25, 1948, came the spectacular but bloodless Communist coup in Czechoslovakia, with Moscow agents present, and one more sovereign state slipped down the Soviet drain. On March 10 occurred the violent and mysterious death of Foreign Minister Masaryk. Three weeks later a jolted Con-gress passed the initial appropriation of $5.3 billion for the first twelve months of a four-year European Relief Program. The next day the Soviets began serious interruptions of the ground traffic to and from four-power Berlin—the beginning of the strangling Berlin blockade.

Opposition to the Marshall Plan appropriation in the Senate had been so strong that if the Communist menace had not loomed when and as it did, the European Recovery Program could hardly have passed Congress, at least in the form it took. A furious battle was waged by a group of some twenty conservative Senators, led by Re-publican Robert A. Taft of Ohio. He assured the Senate that "the program is completely without economic justification," and he had some support in this opinion from reputable economists, whom Cold War revisionists have generally ignored. He doubted that giving away money to make money would be effective, and he argued that the size of the appropriation should be reduced—and thus made even less effective. But he wavered when he concluded that he favored Ameri-can aid to Europe "to the extent which appears to be absolutely neces-sary" in "the world battle against communism." The final vote in Congress was determined not solely by altruism or materialism, but by what was conceived to be enlightened self-interest. Ironically, the victorious Allies and the United States had collected some reparations from Germany after World War I; after World War II the United States in effect paid Germany reparations in Marshall Plan aid amounting to $1,390,600,000.

All this outlay was baffling to the ever-suspicious Soviets. They could hardly be blamed for concluding that the capitalistic Americans were up to no good when they proposed to pour out untold billions of dollars to prime a European pump that might never again attain pre-war production levels. Nor could the Russians fail to perceive that Uncle Sam was taking over the role of the defunct Hitler as the chief foe of Soviet Communism—perhaps the greatest irony of the postwar years. One could almost hear the mocking laughter of *Der Führer's* ghost.

In the midst of all this nationwide debate over Marshall aid, millions of naive Americans still failed to understand that the Soviet Union and the United States were each pursuing objectives that their leaders conceived to be in their respective national interests, just as they had done before, during, and after the war. Soviet-American conflict began with the Bolshevik Revolution in 1917, not with the Hitler-Stalin pact of 1939. Neither nation could fully appreciate that its rival had its own rational reasons for the course it was taking, given the clashing ideologies. One system was based on totalitarianism; the other on democratic freedoms, including capitalistic free enterprise. In Soviet eyes, legitimate defensive requirements demanded the creation of subservient satellite states, including Germany, on Russia's western flank. Then there had to be friendly states bordering these friendly states, in an ever-widening and never-ending circle. In American eyes, such encroachments by the Russians would delay the economic recovery of Europe, ruin export markets, and pose a dangerous military threat to the Western democracies. What Communist Russia regarded as a defensive move appeared to capitalistic America to be an offensive one; much depended on whether one was looking west through Kremlin windows or east from Washington windows.

Many of the historical revisionists of latter years began their research with a pro-Marxist bias. They often took their stance in Moscow, where the secret documents were unavailable, although the researcher now has access to the once-classified American papers of the war and postwar years. (If one is going to discuss intelligently the intentions of two men playing poker, one would be well advised to see both hands at the same time.) Revisionists espoused the line that American involvement in the Cold War was not only unnecessary but unreasoning. Their view was that an exhausted Russia had no intention of fighting anyone. Moreover, the USSR was quite incapable of sweeping to the English Channel, especially since the West had the atomic bomb.

The top military experts, whose business it was to know such things, believed that the Soviets were fully capable of a successful attack and in fact might well be contemplating it. The Russian leaders may not have had any such intentions, but by word and deed they implanted fear of such a blow. The feeling in Western circles was that they probably were being restrained by the small atomic arsenal of the United States, but the Soviets seemed rather indifferent to the efficacy of atomic warfare against a country as vast as theirs. At times the Americans seemed more afraid of the A-bomb than did their ideological foes, who appeared to be more fearful of the "dollar imperialism" of the Marshall Plan.

Nor were the Americans alone in their fears about the intentions of the Kremlin; everywhere I went in Europe I encountered similar reactions. The Conservatives of England, with ex-Prime Minister Churchill their chief spokesman, had raised the cry early in the game. In a speech at Fulton, Missouri on March 5, 1946, a year before President Truman was to respond with his Truman Doctrine before the Congress, Churchill solemnly declared that "an iron curtain has descended across the Continent." He called upon the United States to join in a fraternal association with Britain to halt this westward thrust. An outburst of condemnation arose from an America that was still naive, for many people believed that Churchill was unalterably biased. It is true that he had denounced the "foul baboonery of Bolshevism" from an early date, yet it is also true that he was the most conspicuous of the few in England who had sounded the alarm against the rising menace of Hitlerism in the 1930s.

Americans had no desire to impose their ideology on the Soviet Union. A victorious United States had created an immense power vacuum by hastily withdrawing its fresh and mighty armed force from Europe at the end of the war. The Russians, for their part, had kept an overwhelmingly powerful army in being and had even strengthened it in certain categories. The masters of the Kremlin were not dedicated to the principle of live and let live. When the Bolsheviks seized power in 1917, they had loudly proclaimed their intention of imposing their Marxist-Leninist doctrine upon the rest of the world, by force if necessary. In the intervening forty years the leopard had not changed its spots.

Ex-Ambassador to Russia W. Averell Harriman challenged the argument that all would have been well if the United States had only treated the Russians right. He told the War College group that during the recent conflict the United States had gone overboard with generous policies and practices, with the result that the Americans had merely deepened Soviet suspicions regarding what the capitalistic world was plotting against them. In Harriman's view from Washington, the Moscow regime had broken with the United States, rather than the reverse. Yet from the vantage point of the Kremlin, the Americans had first parted company with the Russians by trying to thwart them in what they regarded as their legitimate goals, including security against another German onslaught.

Serious mistakes were made by both superpowers in their dealings with each other—that is, if the critic assumes that the two nations had common ideological aims, which they definitely did not. One of the many ironies of these postwar years is that the Soviets were basing their policies on the confident expectation that a new and crippling depression would prostrate the United States. Yet by their aggressive behavior they forced the Americans to implement the Marshall Plan, which may have done more than anything else to avert the predicted economic collapse.

Given these clashing ideologies and their built-in friction, it is pointless—almost childish—to try to determine which side was more to blame for the onset of the Cold War. The Iron Curtain descended as naturally as a thunderstorm in July. Lenin designed it; Stalin built it; Churchill spectacularly named it. Virtually every important move that the United States made in the Cold War and its preliminaries, especially the Marshall Plan, came in a vicious-circle response to what America perceived, whether correctly or not, to be a made-in-Moscow menace. All those truths became increasingly clear during the critical Marshall Plan summer of 1947.

Epilogue

In looking back over my yellowing notes, which are now thirty years old, I am repeatedly reminded of the French proverb, "The more it changes the more it remains the same." In 1947 the overshadowing problem was how to get along with the Russians. In 1977 it still is. In 1947 the so-called free world was complaining about the alleged failure of the Soviets to live up to their agreements at Yalta and Potsdam; today we are complaining about the alleged failure of Moscow to live up to the agreement signed by thirty-five nations at Helsinki in 1975— a pact that presumably guaranteed certain human rights and the free flow of information.

Recently I consulted several Russian historians at Stanford University, including some who are specializing in the tsarist era. When I remarked that certain revisionists were placing the major blame for the coming of the Cold War on the United States, the response was "rubbish." I was further reminded that no researcher can yet consult the secret Soviet archives and that some of the so-called revisionists are not well-grounded in Russian internal history or even the Russian language. My informants had in mind particularly the long tsarist era of despotism, which included pathological distrust of foreigners, secret police, terrorist bomb plots, Siberian exile, contempt for human life, and naked imperialism. Then after 1917 came Bolshevism, followed by long years of ostracism by the fearful non-Communist world. The paranoia that developed on both sides should not be surprising.

Present-day revisionists, my sources observed, assume that the authoritarian Moscow government from the beginning has had somewhat the same outlook on the outside world as the constitutional monarchies of Western Europe, including Great Britain. Such writers have thus made the mistake of concluding that the suspicious Russians could be dealt with on the normal basis of give-and-take—the kind of exchange that results in a precise meeting of minds and firm commitments to mutually understood written agreements. This somewhat naive concept has spawned a vast amount of error and mis-understanding. One is reminded of the legend of the two English fishwives who were shouting at each other from houses separated by an alley. They could not agree, it was judged, because they were arguing "from different premises."

Those Russian specialists whom I have consulted agree that the Cold War really began in 1917 when the Bolsheviks took over and declared ideological warfare on the "capitalistic" world. Until 1956 they openly proclaimed that they would use all means, presumably including force, to attain world revolution. But in February 1956 Premier Khrushchev declared before the Twentieth Party Congress that, in conformity with peaceful coexistence, "we renounce any policy that might lead [to] millions of people being plunged into war. . . ." One could read too much into this pledge, for Khrushchev was the man who engineered the crisis of 1962 by emplacing nuclear missiles in Cuba.

The simple truth is that the Communists have been dedicated from the outset to at least Cold War ideology. For obvious reasons, they soft-pedaled this commitment after the United States entered World War II on their side. When Hitler's defeat was achieved, their ideal of world revolution emerged afresh. After Truman belatedly reacted to the outward thrustings of revived Communism, he was unfairly blamed for having started the Cold War.

In 1947 the Soviets were claiming, with some plausibility, that they had no aggressive intentions but merely wanted to add several layers of friendly states to protect their strategic western borders. Ever since 1945 the USSR has consistently avoided hot wars of its own but has waged them by proxy with Soviet weapons through clients or sur-rogates, notably in Korea and North Vietnam. Into both of these conflicts a Communist-fearing United States was sucked, thus wasting its strength and playing into Moscow's hands. The topdog Soviet bu-reaucrats have never "had it so good," and hence presumably are not eager to jeopardize their privileged status with a global holocaust.

Nuclear technology has introduced a new level of anxiety on both sides, and by the 1960s a policy of mutual coexistence was finally acknowledged. By this time the two superpowers could plainly see that the alternatives were coexistence or no existence. Still the costly and frightening race in nuclear weapons escalated, as lesser nations gradually forced their way into the terrifying nuclear club—terrifying because of the increasing possibility that even an accidental explosion would trigger a global doomsday.

The Nixon-Kissinger regime inaugurated a more relaxed policy of détente with the USSR in the 1970s, and it resulted in give-and-take concessions on both sides. Yet conservatives in America complained bitterly of this one-sided arrangement that had Uncle Sam doing most of the giving and the Russians doing most of the taking. While the United States was exporting enormous shipments of grain and sophisticated technology to the Soviet Union, criticisms were heard that stupid "Uncle Sucker" was generously providing the shovel with which to be buried.

Another American complaint was that the Soviets evidently regarded détente as valid only in limited parts of the globe. Despite this new era of supposed amicability, Soviet weapons continued to pour into North Vietnam, Syria, Egypt, and Angola for use against American weapons, whether in the hands of Americans or of peoples whom the United States was supporting.

In the mid-1970s concern was increasingly expressed in the Western world over what seemed to be the efforts of the Russians to build up superior strength in all main warlike categories. In 1976 Janes's *Fighting Ships*, an authoritative British publication, made it clear that the existing and projected strength of the USSR went far beyond that required by any recognizable defensive needs. Secretary of State Kissinger later remarked that it was pointless to talk about Soviet superiority in weapons when each side presumably possessed enough nuclear missiles to wipe out its adversary's population many times over. Yet one could not be completely sure. Alarmist reports were circulating by 1976 that the Soviet government was building enormous bombproof underground shelters to accommodate much of the urban civilian population. The implication was that most Russians could survive an initial American salvo while Soviet nuclear missiles were meanwhile wiping out an unprotected United States.

On the other hand, this rumored underground construction, if it is a fact, may be yet another attempt by the Soviet dictatorship, as in 1947, to direct further attention to the American bogeyman. In this way the masses could better endure the interminable shortages of ordinary consumer goods that have plagued the Bolshevik experiment from the beginning. At all events, the Soviets professed to be about as fearful of American intentions in 1977 as they had been in 1947. Such fears, whether groundless or not, were reciprocated in the United States, which was widely regarded as the last great bastion of democracy.

At its birth in 1776, the American republic became an oasis of freedom in a world of despotism. In 1976, when the nation celebrated its bicentennial, the wheel was coming full circle. A map of the world published in *Freedom at Issue* (January–February, 1977) depicted in solid black or black hatchings the nations that were unfree or only partially free. This blighted area, on the basis of the map projection used, ominously covered about three-fourths of the land area of the globe. Of the 159 countries, many of them tiny, only 42 could be labeled free, 49 partly free, and 68 unfree. In the Assembly of the United Nations the United States was being routinely, lopsidedly, and gleefully outvoted by a bloc of Communist and Communist-sympathizing nations of the so-called Third World.

Lenin had thus parlayed his suitcase of 1917 into a vast ideological domain, although not a monolithic one. It threatened to engulf what was left of the democratic world. Only 19.6 percent of all peoples now live in countries that are rated completely free, in some cases questionably so. Yet the nations of western Europe that were free in 1947 have held the line and have since been joined by West Germany, Austria, Portugal, and partly liberated Spain. An observer could well believe that these countries were saved for freedom primarily because of the postwar Allied occupation, which was continued subsequently through the North Atlantic Treaty Organization. Together with the life-saving Marshall Plan, the American military presence has thus far served to check and even roll back the outward thrust of at least Soviet-style Communism in western Europe.

Note on Sources

This book is not a historical monograph on the Marshall Plan, or on the origins of the Cold War, or on the American occupation of Germany and Austria after World War II. Although it touches at some length on all these topics and others, it is essentially a personalized report on what I saw and heard, often from high sources, during an Army-sponsored inspection tour through Europe, especially occupied Germany and Austria, in the summer of 1947. Interspersed is some analysis of my own findings. In short, I am my own principal primary source, and my contemporary observations are recorded in the journals, notebooks, and correspondence that I kept or wrote at the time. These materials have been deposited in the archives of the Hoover Institution at Stanford University, under the designation, "The Thomas A. Bailey Collection on Europe in 1947." It may be consulted there by qualified scholars.

In preparing this account for publication, I have checked and refreshed my memory by consulting many of the official published documents, most of which have been released only in recent years. In a number of instances I have compared my observations and recollections with articles in the contemporary press, including the Army-sponsored *Stars and Stripes*, to insure a higher degree of accuracy.

Relevant official documents for the years of World War II and the postwar years appear in the annual volumes of *Foreign Relations of the United States*. Material of particular relevance is published in *Foreign Relations of the United States, Diplomatic Papers: The Conferences at Malta and Yalta, 1945* (Washington, D.C., 1955) and *Foreign Relations of the United States, Diplomatic Papers: The Conference of Berlin (The Potsdam Conference), 1945* (2 vols., Washington, D.C., 1960). It may be noted that the Potsdam "Protocol of Proceedings," which was signed by Truman, Stalin, and Attlee, is the closest approximation to a treaty of peace for Germany that was ever agreed on. In many respects it was more severe and unworkable than the much-criticized Treaty of Versailles in 1919.

For present purposes I have also used *Foreign Relations of the United States, 1947* (2 vols., Washington, D.C., 1972–1973). Volume II contains 335 pages on the occupation and control of Germany, plus an excellent bibliography of primary sources and secondary works. Not listed are such valuable accounts as John Gimbel, *A German Community under American Occupation: Marburg, 1945–52* (Stanford, Calif., 1961); John Gimbel, *The American Occupation of Germany: Politics and the Military, 1945–1949* (Stanford, Calif., 1968); and Franklin M. Davis, Jr., *Come as a Conqueror: The United States Army's Occupation of Germany, 1945–1949* (New York, 1967).

Official negotiations on the Marshall Plan (European Recovery Program) itself are detailed in *Foreign Relations of the United States, 1947*, vol. 3, pp. 197–484. The most recent and thorough account of the subject is John Gimbel, *The Origins of the Marshall Plan* (Stanford, Calif., 1976), which not only uses an impressive number of manuscript sources but refers to many other accounts relating to the subject.

A revealing record by the American Military Governor in Berlin is Lucius D. Clay, *Decision in Germany* (Garden City, N.Y., 1950). An especially valuable collection is Jean E. Smith, *The Papers of General Lucius D. Clay: Germany, 1945–1949* (2 vols., Bloomington, Ind., 1974). A contemporary and spirited personal memoir that is highly critical of the Russians, is Frank Howley, *Berlin Command* (New York, 1950). General Mark W. Clark has a revealing chapter relating principally to his experiences as high commissioner in Austria in *Calculated Risk* (New York, 1950).

The postwar historical controversy between the so-called revisionists and the traditionalists has centered heavily on who was to blame for the onset of the Cold War. The best balanced recent account is John L. Gaddis, *The United States and the Origins of the Cold War, 1941–1947* (New York, 1972), which has an excellent bibliography. My own views, which generally support those of the traditionalists, were set forth at length in Thomas A. Bailey, *America Faces Russia* (Ithaca, N.Y., 1950). It will be noted that this book was written shortly after my Army-sponsored trip to Europe in 1947.

Practically all of the Americans whom I encountered during the summer of 1947 were gravely disturbed by what appeared on the surface to be the aggressions or aggressive intentions of the Russians. The same is true of those individuals, mostly American officials, who have published or caused to be published their recollections of these years. Among them the most noteworthy are: Dean Acheson, *Present at the Creation: My Years in the State Department* (New York, 1969); Charles E. Bohlen, *Witness to History, 1929–1969* (New York, 1973); James F. Byrnes, *All in One Lifetime* (New York, 1958) and *Speaking Frankly* (New York, 1947); James B. Conant, *My Several Lives: Memoirs of a Social Inventor* (New York, 1970); John R. Deane, *The Strange Alliance: The Story of Our Efforts at Wartime Cooperation with Russia* (New York, 1947); Dwight D. Eisenhower, *Crusade in Europe* (New York, 1948); Leslie R. Groves, *Now It Can Be Told: The Story of the Manhattan Project* (New York, 1962); W. Averell Harriman, *America and Russia in a Changing World: A Half Century of Personal Observation* (Garden City, N.Y., 1971); W. Averell Harriman and Elie Abel, *Special Envoy to Churchill and Stalin, 1941–1946* (New York, 1975); Cordell Hull, *The Memoirs of Cordell Hull* (2 vols., New York, 1948); Joseph M. Jones, *The Fifteen Weeks, February 21–June 5, 1947* (New York, 1955); George F. Kennan, *Memoirs: 1925–1950* (Boston, 1967); William D. Leahy, *I Was There* (New York, 1950); Walter Millis, ed., *The Forrestal Diaries* (New York, 1951); Henry Morgenthau, Jr., *Germany Is Our Problem* (New York, 1945); Robert Murphy, *Diplomat among Warriors* (Garden City, N.Y., 1964); Robert E. Sherwood, *Roosevelt and Hopkins: An Intimate History* (rev. ed., New York, 1950); Walter B. Smith, *My Three Years in Moscow* (Philadelphia, 1950); William H. Standlee and A. A. Ageton, *Admiral Ambassasor to Russia* (Chicago, 1955); Edward R. Stettinius, Jr., *Roosevelt and the Russians: The Yalta Conference* (Garden City, N.Y., 1949); Henry L. Stimson and McGeorge Bundy, *On Active Service in Peace and War* (New York, 1947); C. L. Sulzberger, *A Long Row of Candles: Memoirs and Diaries, 1934–1954* (New York, 1969); Harry S. Truman, *Memoirs: Year of Decisions* (Garden City, N.Y., 1955) and *Memoirs: Years of Trial and Hope, 1946–1952* (Garden City, N.Y., 1956); Arthur H. Vandenberg, Jr., ed., *The Private Papers of Senator Vandenberg* (Boston, 1952); and William L. White, *Report on the Russians* (New York, 1945).

Index